実況中継 **CD-ROM**ブックス
高校英語

二本柳啓文のトークで攻略

早大への英語塾

GOGAKU SHUNJUSHA

はじめに お読みください

音声CD-ROMの使い方

★付属のCD-ROM内の解説音声はMP3形式で保存されていますので，ご利用には**MP3データ**が再生できるパソコン環境が必要です。

★この**CD-ROM**は**CD-ROM**ドライブにセットしただけでは自動的に起動しません。下記の手順を踏んでください。

Windows でご利用の場合

① CD-ROM をパソコンの CD-ROM ドライブにセットします。

② コンピュータ（もしくはマイコンピュータ）を表示し，**[NIHON_SODAI]** という表示の CD-ROM のアイコンを，まず右クリックして，次に **[開く]** を選択します。

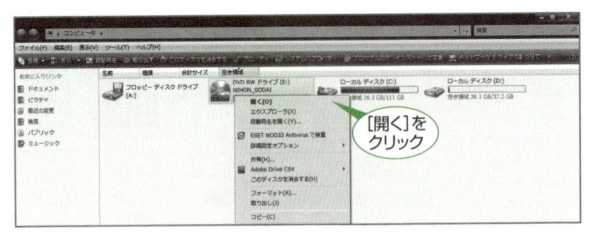

③ Lesson01 ～ Lesson06 と「学部別対策」の各フォルダが表示されますので，その中からお聞きになりたい回のフォルダを開いてください。

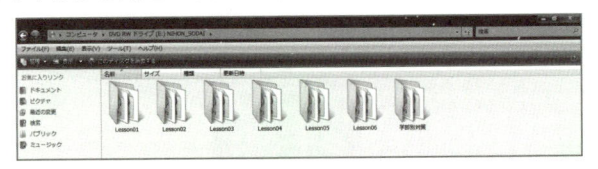

④ ③で選択された回の設問ごとの音声ファイルが表示されます。その中からお聞きになりたいファイルを開いてご利用ください。

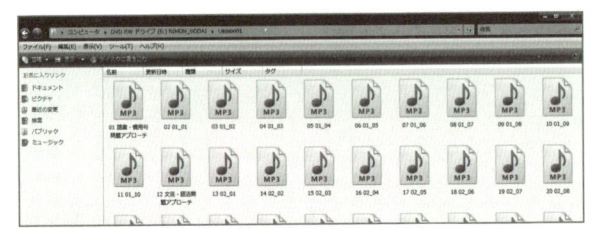

※上記のサンプル画像は一例です。お使いのパソコン環境に応じて，表示画像が多少異なることがございます。あらかじめご了承ください。

Mac でご利用の場合

① CD-ROM をパソコンの CD-ROM ドライブにセットします。
② **[NIHON_SODAI]** という CD-ROM のアイコンが表示されたら，そのアイコンをダブルクリックして内容を表示します。
③ Lesson01 ～ Lesson06 と「学部別対策」の各フォルダが表示されますので，その中からお聞きになりたいフォルダを開いてください。
④ ③で選択された回の設問ごとの音声ファイルが表示されます。その中からお聞きになりたいファイルを開いてご利用ください。

> 本書添付のCD-ROMはWindows仕様のため，Macでご使用の場合，お使いのパソコン環境によって，フォルダ名・ファイル名が文字化けして表示されてしまう場合があります。ただし，"iTunes"等で再生いただく際には，正しく表示されますのでご安心ください。

⚠ 注意事項

❶ この CD-ROM はパソコン専用です。**オーディオ用プレーヤーでは絶対に再生しないでください。**大音量によって耳に傷害を負ったり，スピーカーを破損するおそれがあります。

❷ この CD-ROM の一部または全部を，バックアップ以外の目的でいかなる方法においても無断で複製することは法律で禁じられています。

❸ この CD-ROM を使用し，どのようなトラブルが発生しても，当社は一切責任を負いません。ご利用は個人の責任において行ってください。

❹ 携帯音楽プレーヤーに音声データを転送される場合は，必ずプレーヤーの取扱説明書をお読みになった上でご使用ください。また，その際の転送ソフトの動作環境は，ソフトウェアによって異なりますので，ご不明の点については，各ソフトウェアの商品サポートにお問い合わせください。

早稲田大学合格のために

■ 本書の構成

Lesson1～Lesson3： **出題形式別**の解説です。読解総合問題が大部分を占める早大入試では，ここはいわば「パート練習」にあたります。あなたの**受験予定学部で出題されていない設問形式にも積極的に取り組む**ことをお勧めします。

Lesson4～Lesson5： **総合問題**です。Lesson4 では標準的な長さの長文総合問題，Lesson5 では超長文問題を扱います。前半の「パート練習」で培った実力を縦横無尽に駆使する，いわば「合奏」にあたるところです。なお，Lesson4 と Lesson5 の英文に関しては，CD-ROM にネイティブ・ナレーターによる音声も収録されています。復習の際にぜひ有効活用してください。

Lesson6 は**ライティング問題とリスニング問題**について扱っています。リスニング問題に関しては，もちろん音声が用意してあります。

■ 本書の活用のしかた

必ず事前に解いてから解説に接すること。

ここは必ず守ってほしいところです。でないと効果が半減します。解かずに解説を読んで（聞いて）しまうと，自分の足りないところが見えなくなり，「実直さ」のどの部分に磨きをかければよいのか把握できなくなってしまうのです。

解答時間の目安としては，
Lesson1～3 は各設問をできるだけ速く。
Lesson4 は1題 20 分。

Lesson5 は 1 題 30 分。
　Lesson6（ライティング）は 1 題 10〜15 分を目安にどうぞ。

■ 講義を聞きながら

　本書は CD-ROM による音声講義と連動しています。本書の文字情報と CD-ROM の音声講義を併用した上で，**各設問の正解の根拠を理解し，かつその正解を導く上で自分の足りなかった要素（語彙の知識や解き方の視点など）は何か**を考えてください。足りなかった要素が見つかったら，1 つの Part 終了後，その足りない部分を改善するためにやるべきこと（単語集等の見直しや同形式の設問の演習など）はないか検討し，必要に応じて実行します。**この作業が得点力に結びついていく**ので，是非とも真剣に検討してください。

■ おすすめの復習

　設問の正解根拠を理解できているか，という視点で全設問にあたります。また，復習段階では，問題文の日本語訳にも取り組んでください（必ずしも書く必要はありません）。さらに，Lesson4 と Lesson5 の英文に関しては，**CD-ROM の収録音声にあわせて英文を目で追いかけながら内容を把握する復習を，最低 10 回は繰り返す**と速読リズムが身につきます。

　では，以上の点に注意して，何が何でも早稲田大学合格を果たしてください。

　　　　2011 年 9 月

　　　　　　　　　　　　　　　　　　　　　　　　　二本柳　啓文

CONTENTS...

※目次に掲載の TRACK は，パソコン上で CD-ROM 内の各フォルダを開いたときに表示される，音声データの内容です。

＊学部別対策 ……………………………………………… xii
- TRACK 1　はじめに
- TRACK 2　学部別対策

Lesson1 短文問題
1. 語彙・慣用句問題 ……………………………………………… 1
- TRACK 1　おすすめアプローチ
- TRACK 2　問題1 語彙
- TRACK 3　問題2 読解問題の中での語彙
- TRACK 4　問題3　　〃
- TRACK 5　問題4　　〃
- TRACK 6　問題5 慣用句
- TRACK 7　問題6　〃
- TRACK 8　問題7 読解問題の中での慣用句
- TRACK 9　問題8　　〃
- TRACK 10　問題9　　〃
- TRACK 11　問題10 整序問題の中での慣用句

2. 文法・語法問題 ……………………………………………… 10
- TRACK 12　おすすめアプローチ
- TRACK 13　問題1 文法・語法
- TRACK 14　問題2　　〃
- TRACK 15　問題3 読解問題の中での文法
- TRACK 16　問題4　　〃
- TRACK 17　問題5 読解問題の中での語法
- TRACK 18　問題6 前置詞・副詞
- TRACK 19　問題7　〃
- TRACK 20　問題8 読解問題の中での前置詞

TRACK 21 問題9 読解問題の中での前置詞

3．正誤問題 ･･･ 21

TRACK 22 おすすめアプローチ
TRACK 23 問題1 文構造
TRACK 24 問題2 〃
TRACK 25 問題3 〃
TRACK 26 問題4 品詞
TRACK 27 問題5 〃
TRACK 28 問題6 〃
TRACK 29 問題7 受動態
TRACK 30 問題8 準動詞
TRACK 31 問題9 〃
TRACK 32 問題10 誤りなし

Lesson2 中文問題

1．空所補充問題 ･････････････････････････････････････ 31

TRACK 1 おすすめアプローチ
TRACK 2 問題(1)
TRACK 3 問題(2)
TRACK 4 問題(3)
TRACK 5 問題(4)
TRACK 6 問題(5)
TRACK 7 問題(6)
TRACK 8 問題(7)

2．英問英答問題 ･････････････････････････････････････ 39

TRACK 9 おすすめアプローチ
TRACK 10 問題1－(1)
TRACK 11 問題1－(2)
TRACK 12 問題2－(1)

TRACK 13 問題2-(2)
TRACK 14 問題2-(3)

3. 会話問題 ……………………………………………… 48

TRACK 15 おすすめアプローチ
TRACK 16 問題1
TRACK 17 問題2-(1)
TRACK 18 問題2-(2)
TRACK 19 問題2-(3)
TRACK 20 問題2-(4)
TRACK 21 問題3-(1)
TRACK 22 問題3-(2)
TRACK 23 問題3-(3)
TRACK 24 問題3-(4)
TRACK 25 問題3-(5)
TRACK 26 問題3-(6)
TRACK 27 問題3-(7)
TRACK 28 問題3-(8)

Lesson3 長文問題：基本編

1. リード部付き内容一致問題 ……………………………… 69

TRACK 1 おすすめアプローチ
TRACK 2 問題1
TRACK 3 問題2

2. 内容一致問題 ………………………………………… 75

TRACK 4 おすすめアプローチ
TRACK 5 問題1
TRACK 6 問題2

3. 同意語句選択問題 …………………………………… 91

TRACK 7 おすすめアプローチ

- TRACK 8　問題1
- TRACK 9　問題2
- TRACK 10　問題3
- TRACK 11　問題4

4．文整序問題 ……………………………………… 98
- TRACK 12　おすすめアプローチ
- TRACK 13　問題1
- TRACK 14　問題2
- TRACK 15　問題3

5．文補充問題 ……………………………………… 111
- TRACK 16　おすすめアプローチ
- TRACK 17　問題

6．タイトル選択問題 ……………………………… 123
- TRACK 18　おすすめアプローチ
- TRACK 19　問題1
- TRACK 20　問題2

Lesson4　長文問題：実践編

長文問題1. ……………………………………… 136
- TRACK 1　問題(1)
- TRACK 2　問題(2)
- TRACK 3　問題(3)−1
- TRACK 4　問題(3)−2
- TRACK 5　問題(3)−3
- TRACK 6　問題(3)−4
- TRACK 7　ネイティブ音声

※問題文がナチュラルスピードで朗読されています。音声にあわせて，英文を目で追いかけながら，内容を把握する練習をしましょう。速読リズムが身につきます（以下同）。

長文問題 2. ··· 148

- **TRACK 8** 問題 (1)
- **TRACK 9** 問題 (2)
- **TRACK 10** 問題 (3)
- **TRACK 11** 問題 (4)
- **TRACK 12** 問題 (5)
- **TRACK 13** ネイティブ音声

長文問題 3. ··· 164

- **TRACK 14** 問題 (1)
- **TRACK 15** 問題 (2)
- **TRACK 16** 問題 (3)
- **TRACK 17** 問題 (4)
- **TRACK 18** 問題 (5)
- **TRACK 19** 問題 (6)
- **TRACK 20** 問題 (7)
- **TRACK 21** 問題 (8)
- **TRACK 22** 問題 (9)
- **TRACK 23** ネイティブ音声

Lesson5 超長文問題

超長文問題 1. ·· 180

- **TRACK 1** 問題 (1) − 1
- **TRACK 2** 問題 (1) − 2
- **TRACK 3** 問題 (1) − 3
- **TRACK 4** 問題 (1) − 4
- **TRACK 5** 問題 (1) − 5
- **TRACK 6** 問題 (1) − 6
- **TRACK 7** 問題 (2)
- **TRACK 8** ネイティブ音声

超長文問題2. 201

- **TRACK 9** 問題(1)
- **TRACK 10** 正解とはならないその他の選択肢
- **TRACK 11** 問題(2) − 1
- **TRACK 12** 問題(2) − 2
- **TRACK 13** 問題(2) − 3
- **TRACK 14** 問題(3) − 1
- **TRACK 15** 問題(3) − 2
- **TRACK 16** 問題(4)
- **TRACK 17** ネイティブ音声

Lesson6 ライティング問題・リスニング問題

1．一文要約型ライティング問題 233

- **TRACK 1** おすすめアプローチ
- **TRACK 2** 問題1
- **TRACK 3** 問題2

2．意見論述型ライティング問題 238

- **TRACK 4** おすすめアプローチ
- **TRACK 5** 問題1
- **TRACK 6** 問題2

3．講義型リスニング問題 242

- **TRACK 7** おすすめアプローチ
- **TRACK 8** リスニング問題音声　※ネイティブ音声
- **TRACK 9** 問題解説

4．会話型リスニング問題 254

- **TRACK 10** おすすめアプローチ
- **TRACK 11** リスニング問題音声　※ネイティブ音声
- **TRACK 12** 問題解説

学部別対策

文学部・文化構想学部

形式：200点中英語の配点は75点。中文・長文6，会話文1，英語要約1で，長文は全問マーク。文学部と文化構想学部の形式は全く同一。難易度は文学部のほうが上。

必出設問
空所補充問題（p.31）
リード部付き内容一致問題（p.69）
英問英答問題（p.39）
文整序問題（p.98）
会話問題（p.48）
一文要約ライティング問題（p.233）

合否の決め手　Ⅲの文補充とⅤの一文要約が勝負！正答率は70%を上回りたい。

ひとこと対策　各文章題の設問は1種類しかないので，本書の設問別アプローチがそのまま対策として有効。

教育学部

形式：150点中英語の配点は50点（英語英文学科のみ英語の得点が標準化後1.5倍される）。長文4，会話文1で，全問マーク。

学部別対策

必出設問
語彙問題（p.1）
文法問題（p.10）
リード部付き内容一致問題（p.69）
英問英答問題（p.39）
空所補充問題（p.31）
内容一致問題（p.75）
会話問題（p.48）など

合否の決め手　時間配分は，読解1題20分×4で会話文は10分！しかも，ゆっくり急いで丁寧に読まなければならない。合格最低点は学科によって異なる。

ひとこと対策　文系ジャンルだろうが理系ジャンルだろうが，えり好みせずにどん欲に精読する姿勢を堅持すること。会話文は難度が高いが，あまり時間をかけすぎないこと。

社会科学部

形式：130点中英語の配点は50点。長文3，会話文1，正誤判定10で，全問マーク。

必出設問
正誤問題（p.21）
会話問題（p.48）
英問英答問題（p.39）
語彙問題（p.1）
同意語句選択問題（p.91）
内容一致問題（p.75）など

合否の決め手　会話文や正誤判定に難問が多いので，長文問題が勝負だが，設問形式が様々。70%の正答率を目標にしたい。

ひとこと対策 設問形式や英文の内容から考えて，教育学部，法学部や人間科学部を中心に幅広い学部の問題に取り組む必要がある。

国際教養学部

形式： 200点中英語の配点は100点。長文2，日本語要約1，自由英作文1で85分。長文は全問マーク。リスニングはその後の別時限に2題で50分（実質試験時間は17分ほど）。

必出設問
リード部付き内容一致問題（p.69）
英問英答問題（p.39）
空所補充問題（p.31）
内容一致問題（p.75）
日本語要約問題
意見論述型ライティング問題（p.238）
講義型リスニング問題（p.242）
会話型リスニング問題（p.254）など

合否の決め手 ライティングで勝負。ということは読解やリスニング問題は高得点（少なくとも8割以上）を狙いたい。

ひとこと対策 長文に関しては，特に法学部，政治経済学部や慶應大SFCの問題が有効。リスニング対策としては，英検準1級，会話に関してはNHKラジオ講座などが適している。

法学部

形式： 150点中英語の配点は60点。超長文2，文法・語法，和文英訳，自由英作文。リスニング以外のすべての形式が出題されると考えてよい。

学 部 別 対 策

必出設問
語彙問題（p.1）
文法問題（p.10）
正誤問題（p.21）
リード部付き内容一致問題（p.69）
英問英答問題（p.39）
空所補充問題（p.31）
内容一致問題（p.75）
発音問題
条件英作文問題
意見論述型ライティング問題（p.238）など

合否の決め手
超長文1題を30分前後で仕上げること，これに尽きる。飛ばし読みできるところも，あまりない。知識問題は難問が混じっているので60％正解できればよい，と割り切ること。

ひとこと対策
長文に関しては，特に国際教養学部，政治経済学部や慶應大SFCの問題が有効。前置詞や副詞を入れる問題は人間科学部の過去問で演習。ライティング問題は政治経済学部，国際教養学部，一橋大学の過去問などで練習をするとよい。

政治経済学部

形式：230点中英語の配点は90点。長文3，会話文1，自由英作文。長文は全問マーク。

必出設問
リード部付き内容一致問題（p.69）
英問英答問題（p.39）
空所補充問題（p.31）
内容一致問題（p.75）

文整序問題（p.98）
正誤問題（p.21）
語彙問題（p.1）
文法問題（p.10）
正誤問題（p.21）
会話問題（p.48）
発音問題
整序問題
意見論述型ライティング問題（p.238）など

合否の決め手　自由英作文を含めて，80％に肉薄する正答率を狙いたい。読解問題の設問がパラグラフの内容を問うものが多いので比較的とりやすいことを考えると，ライティング勝負。ライティング問題は，解答欄のスペース（約15cm×15行）からすると100語前後は書きたいところ（他学部は50〜70語）。読解問題中の語句整序は屈指の難問。

ひとこと対策　長文に関しては，特に国際教養学部，法学部や慶應大SFCの問題が有効。ライティング問題は法学部，国際教養学部，一橋大学等の設問を100語前後で仕上げる練習をするとよい。

商学部

形式：200点中英語の配点は80点。長文4，会話文1。英文和訳や和文英訳に記述あり。

必出設問　会話問題（p.48）
英文和訳問題
同意語句選択問題（p.91）

学 部 別 対 策

タイトル選択問題（p.123）
英問英答問題（p.39）
空所補充問題（p.31）
内容一致問題（p.75）
語彙問題（p.1）など

合否の決め手　正答率70％は目指したい。設問に格別な難問があるわけではないが，商学部らしくビジネスを題材にした英文の出題が多いので，内容に実感が持てない場合があり，意外に得点が上がらない。取れる問題を確実に正解すること，月並みだがそれに尽きる。焦らないことだ。

ひとこと対策　長文に関しては，教育学部や社会科学部が分量的に共通。他学部は言うに及ばず，他大学の商学部や経営学部などのビジネス系の読解問題に積極的に取り組みたい。

基幹・創造・先進理工学部

形式：360点中英語の配点は120点。長文4，語彙問題1。全問マーク。独特な形式の設問が多いのが特徴。

必出設問　語彙問題（p.1）
文法問題（p.10）
正誤問題（p.21）
英問英答問題（p.39）
空所補充問題（p.31）
内容一致問題（p.75）
文整序問題（p.98）
語句問題

合否の決め手 正答率50%を超えるのが目標。設問形式がきわめて特異だが，読解重視であることは明白。

ひとこと対策 全体を通して相当な難問。知識問題をよくも悪くも手早く終えて読解問題で正答率を稼ぎたい。全体としては正答率50%を超えることが目標だが，設問形式に惑わされず，正確に読解する習慣を養いたい。

スポーツ科学部

形式：183点中英語の配点は75点。長文3，正誤判定10。全問マーク。年度によって設問形式が変わるのが特徴。英語と国語（もしくは数学）が基準点を超えないと小論文の採点が行われない。

必出設問　語彙問題（p.1）
文法問題（p.10）
正誤問題（p.21）
英問英答問題（p.39）
空所補充問題（p.31）
同意語句選択問題（p.91）
内容一致問題（p.75）など

合否の決め手 正答率65%を目標にしたい。設問形式が変わっても，明らかに読解重視であることは明白。

ひとこと対策 相当な分量である。とは言っても，ただ字面を追うだけでは正解できる問題は少ない。本書のLesson 2と3を参考に。センター試験の問題にも積極的に取り組みたい。

学 部 別 対 策

人間科学部

形式：150点中英語の配点は50点。中文8，空所補充15，正誤判定10。全問マーク。

必出設問　リード部付き内容一致問題（p.69）
英問英答問題（p.39）
文法問題（p.10）
正誤問題（p.21）

合否の決め手　中文問題での正答率の高さが決め手になる。合計8題あり，題材も多岐にわたるので，内容がつかめなければ正解を探すだけの「探し読み」に徹して手早く処理すること。

ひとこと対策　空所補充問題と正誤判定は，過去問で出題されたものでも反復して出題されている。しっかり押さえたい。中文問題は文学部，文化構想学部に同形式の出題がある。

LESSON 1 短文問題

1 語彙・慣用句問題

早稲田大は圧倒的に読解重視！
日常の地道な語彙学習の姿勢を固める。

TRACK 01

出題学部：法学部，基幹・創造・先進理工学部，スポーツ科学部など他学部でも長文問題の中で問われる。

語彙・慣用句問題

《おすすめアプローチ》
1. 設問個所（空所や下線部）の前後だけでなく問題文全体から正解の根拠をつかむ。
2. 選択肢がある場合には，代入してみる。
3. 長文問題の中では，常にパラグラフ内での位置づけを意識する。

《得点力アップの道筋》
1. 単語集などで日本語の意味を覚えるだけではなく，英文の中での語彙力強化にも取り組む。
2. 教科書・テキスト等の基本英文は暗誦して書けるようにする。
3. 常に言い換え表現を意識する。英英辞典なども有効活用したい。

（Lesson1 問題解答は p.30 にあります）

問題 1 語彙 (理工学部出題)

Choose the best answer from a-d that best fits in the blank.

It appears that your passport is no longer (　　). You had better go and renew it.

　　a. valid　　b. implemented　　c. complied　　d. available

二本柳のひとことコメント

問題文を和訳し，消去法で正解決定。

■指示文訳：空所に最も適する答えを a～d の中から選べ。
「君のパスポートは有効期限がすでに切れているようだ。更新しに行った方がよい」
　a. 有効な　　b. 実行された　　c. 実施済みの　　d. 入手できる

問題 2 読解問題の中での語彙 (文学部出題)

Read the following passage and choose the most appropriate word for the gap.

By the age of five, most children are able to tell (　　) stories about their past experience, with setting, character, and plot. As they go through elementary school, their autobiographical memories become more subtle and elaborate.

　　a. coherent　　b. emotional　　c. original　　d. plausible

Lesson1　短文問題-1

> 二本柳のひとことコメント

後置修飾の形容詞句を参考に解答決定。

■指示文訳：以下の文章を読んで，空所に最もふさわしい言葉を選べ。
「5歳までには，ほとんどの子供たちは，自らの過去の経験について，背景，登場人物，筋立てを伴うつじつまの合った物語を語ることができる。小学校の学年が進むにつれて，子供たちの自伝的記憶はさらに緻密で手の込んだものになる」
a. つじつまの合った　　b. 感動的な　　c. 独創的な　　d. もっともらしい

問題3　読解問題の中での語彙 （文学部出題）　TRACK 04

Read the following passage and choose the most appropriate word for the gap.

Moreover, those stories carry out the (　　) of explaining to their own narrators how it is that they have become who they are today and what kind of life they expect to have in the future.

　　　　a. function　b. intention　c. possibility　d. significance

> 二本柳のひとことコメント

of 以下の具体的内容を参考に解答決定。

■指示文訳：以下の文章を読んで，空所に最もふさわしい言葉を選べ。
「その上，この物語は，その語り手が，どのようにして自分が今日の姿になったのか，そして将来どのような人生を送りたいと思っているのかを，語り手自身に説明する機能も果たす」
a. 機能　　b. 意図　　c. 可能性　　d. 意義

問題4 読解問題の中での語彙（商学部出題）

下線部の意味に最も近いものを a～d から1つ選べ。

One of the most widely accepted, commonly repeated <u>assumptions</u> in our culture is that if you exercise, you will lose weight.

  a. beliefs b. calculations c. conditions d. contradictions

二本柳のひとことコメント

文型から解答決定。
↑本文と選択肢の意味がほぼわかる程度の語彙力を。

「我々の文化の中で最も広く受け入れられ，最も一般的に繰り返されている<u>想定</u>は，運動をすれば体重が減るというものだ」
a. 信念 b. 計算 c. 条件 d. 矛盾

問題5 慣用句（法学部出題）

Choose the one way to complete this sentence that would make it grammatically INCORRECT.

Don't cut (　　) that tree just yet.
  a. down b. into c. through d. until e. up

二本柳のひとことコメント

until の用法だけでなく，**cut** を用いたイディオムの知識も必須！

■指示文訳：この文を完成させるものとして，文法的に正しくならないものを1つ選べ。
a. cut down... 「…を切り倒す」 b. cut into... 「…に切り込む」
c. cut through... 「…を切り開く，突き刺す」 e. cut up... 「…を切り裂く」

Lesson1 短文問題-1

問題6 慣用句 (法学部出題)

Choose the best item from the box with which to fill the blanks in the passage below. You may use each item only ONCE.

a. above	b. down	c. for	d. into	e. off
f. out	g. over	h. through	i. up	j. with

When I visited the doctor the other day, she told me that I was overweight, and that I should cut [1] on fatty foods. I tried to tell her that I was careful about what I ate, but was quickly cut [2] by the doctor. She measured my blood pressure, and as it was very high, she warned me that I should not let work cut [3] my leisure time. My new job in the office is always very busy, and I started to worry that I just wasn't cut [4] for that type of work. The pay, however, is very good —— a cut [5] that of the company I used to work for.

二本柳のひとことコメント

イディオムは暗記する前に意味を「分解」してみる癖をつけると意味の広がりに対応しやすくなる。知識だけで解くわけではない。

■指示文訳：以下の文章の空所を埋めるのに最も適するものを枠内の選択肢から選べ。それぞれの選択肢を2回以上用いてはならない。
「先日病院に行くと，体重超過なので脂肪分の多い食品を減らすようにと先生から言われた。食べるものには気を配っていると伝えようとしたが，すぐに先生に言葉をさえぎられた。血圧を測ってもらうと非常に高かったので，余暇に仕事を持ち込まないようにと注意を受けた。会社での新しい仕事のせいで，私は四六時中大変忙しい状態が続いており，そういうタイプの仕事に自分はまったく向いていないのではないかと気になり始めていた。

けれども，給料は大変よいのだ。以前勤めていた会社の給料よりも <u>1 ランク上</u> なのだ」

1. cut down on...　「…を減らす」
2. be cut off　　　「(話などを) さえぎられる」
3. cut into...　　　「…に割り込む［食い込む］」
4. be cut out for...　「…に適している」
5. a cut above...　「…よりいくぶん優れて／一段上で」

問題 7　読解問題の中での慣用句 （商学部出題）　TRACK 08

下線部の意味に最も近いものを a〜d から 1 つ選べ。

Mark: Do you get both Saturday and Sunday off?

Anna: <u>That goes without saying</u>, not to mention two weeks of vacation every year.

　　a. By all means　b. It depends　c. Of course　d. Very difficult

二本柳のひとことコメント

口語表現は手薄になりがち（Lesson2 参照）。

マーク：「土曜と日曜は両日とも休めるの？」
アンナ：「それは言うまでもないことだし，毎年 2 週間の休暇もあるわ」
a. ぜひどうぞ／まさにその通り　　b. それは時と場合による
c. もちろん　　　　　　　　　　　d. とても難しい

Lesson1　短文問題-1

問題 8 読解問題の中での慣用句（文学部出題）

Read the following passage and choose the most appropriate word for the gap.

It is not for his skill but for his vision that we honour Einstein; the latter could not have been obtained if he had not grasped firmly the very traditions of thought he challenged. And the same is fundamentally (　　) of Mozart, Wittgenstein, or Picasso. The genius of these great men arose from the soil of their cultural inheritance.

　　a. applicable　　b. conscious　　c. proud　　d. true

二本柳のひとことコメント

文脈判断だけでなく空所直後の前置詞にも要注意。

■指示文訳：以下の文章を読んで，空所を埋めるのに最も適した言葉を選べ。
「我々がアインシュタインを称えているのは，その技能に対してではなく洞察力に対してである。後者は，もし彼が，自ら異議を唱えていたまさにその思想の伝統をしっかり理解していなかったら得られなかっただろう。そして，同じことはモーツァルト，ヴィトゲンシュタイン，ピカソにも本質的に当てはまる。これらの偉人の才能は，彼らの文化的継承という土壌から生まれたのだ」
a. 当てはまる　　b. 意識している　　c. 誇りをもっている　　d. 当てはまる

問題 9 読解問題の中での慣用句 (教育学部出題)

下線部の意味に最も近いものを a〜e から 1 つ選べ。

Five months into Barack Obama's presidency, two researchers are <u>at odds over</u> whether a so-called "Obama effect" can bump up black students' standardized test scores and help to close the achievement gap between blacks and whites. In the days after Obama's election in November, school officials across the country reported a noticeable improvement in students' performance —— particularly in black communities —— and attributed it to Obama's success. But two studies have produced conflicting reports on the existence of such an effect —— calling into question whether inspiration alone is enough to bring quantifiable change.

  a. questioning b. investigating c. exploring
  d. disagreeing e. considering

二本柳のひとことコメント

下線部に未知の表現があっても，選択肢の代入で乗り切れ。

「バラク・オバマが大統領に就任するまでの 5 か月，いわゆる「オバマ効果」が黒人学生たちの標準テストの成績を急上昇させ，黒人と白人との間の学力格差を埋めるのに役立つかどうか<u>について</u>，2 人の研究者の<u>意見が食い違っている</u>。11 月のオバマ当選後の数日で，全米の学校職員たちが，学生たちの成績が特に黒人社会において目立って向上したことを報告し，それはオバマの当選によるものだとした。しかし，2 つの研究がそのような効果の存在に関して相反する報告を作成し，鼓舞されるだけで数量化される変化をもたらすのに十分かどうかという点に疑問を生じさせた」

a. 質問している b. 調査している c. 探求している
d. 意見が合わない e. 考えている

問題 10　整序問題の中での慣用句 （法学部出題）

Translate the Japanese prompts in this dialogue into natural English. You MUST use ALL the English words provided after each Japanese prompt, in the form and order in which they appear.

A: Where's your brother?
B: ₁(1人で東京に出かけました：left / own) last Monday.
A: ₂(いつ戻るか，わかりますか：Do / idea / might / return)?
B: He must be back ₃(遅くても明日には：tomorrow / at / very).

1.＿＿＿＿＿＿＿＿＿＿＿＿＿＿＿＿＿＿＿＿＿＿＿＿＿

2.＿＿＿＿＿＿＿＿＿＿＿＿＿＿＿＿＿＿＿＿＿＿＿＿＿

3.＿＿＿＿＿＿＿＿＿＿＿＿＿＿＿＿＿＿＿＿＿＿＿＿＿

二本柳のひとことコメント

イディオムは例文とともに英訳できるようにしておくべき。

■指示文訳：以下の会話文中の日本語の台詞を自然な英語に直せ。それぞれの日本語の台詞に続く英単語を，与えられた形，順序ですべて用いること。

LESSON 1　短文問題

2　文法・語法問題
文法もさることながら語法をしっかり！

TRACK 12

出題学部：法学部，人間科学部・スポーツ科学部など他学部でも読解問題の中で問われる。

文法・語法問題

《おすすめアプローチ》
1. 「何となく見たことがある形だ」という理由だけで，いきなり解答を選ばない。
2. 構造が複雑な問題文も多いが，極力，文全体を解釈して解答を決定するよう心がける。
3. 前置詞の有無などのような知識問題は，ハッキリしなければ考えすぎずに割り切る。

《得点力アップの道筋》
1. 選択肢のある問題では，各選択肢の正解（あるいは誤答）の根拠を説明できるようにする。
2. 動詞・名詞・形容詞・前置詞の語法は（出題が多いので）日頃から意識する。辞書を引くことを億劫がらない。
3. 読解問題では，「何となく」訳すのではなく，文構造に注意し，正確に解釈する日頃の姿勢が大切。

（Lesson1 問題解答は p.30 にあります）

Lesson1　短文問題-2

問題1　文法・語法 (スポーツ科学部出題)　TRACK 13

Choose the answer that most naturally complete the following sentence.

Herbert Simon, winner of the Nobel Prize in Economics in 1978, started working on artificial intelligence at (　　) Carnegie Mellon University in 1949.

　　a. a place calling　　b. previously known as
　　c. what is now　　d. which used to be called

二本柳のひとことコメント

空所に入るべき品詞を常に確認。

■指示文訳：以下の文に最も自然に入る答えを選べ。
「1978年のノーベル経済学賞受賞者のハーバート・サイモンは，1949年に現在のカーネギー・メロン大学（であるもの）で，人工知能に取り組み始めた」
　a. …を呼んでいる場所　　b. …として知られていた
　c. 現在…であるもの　　　d. 昔は…と呼ばれていた

問題2　文法・語法 (スポーツ科学部出題)　TRACK 14

次の文の空所を補充する語としてもっとも適切なものを，a～d から1つ選べ。

The workers want higher pay to keep up with (　　) prices.
　　a. rise　　b. risen　　c. rising　　d. rose

二本柳のひとことコメント

準動詞の理解はあいまいな点を残さないように。

「労働者たちは，上昇している物価に対応するために賃上げを望んでいる」
　a. 上昇する　　b. 上昇してしまった　　c. 上昇している　　d. 上昇した

• 11

問題3 読解問題の中での文法 (教育学部出題)

空所 [　] に入れるのに最もふさわしいものを a～e から1つ選べ。

[　] since that date no syntactical changes of consequence have taken place in either branch indicates a remarkable solidarity of structure.

a. As　b. While　c. What　d. So　e. That

二本柳のひとことコメント

4択問題では定番だが，読解問題の中でもポイントが見抜けるか。

「その時代から（アメリカ英語とイギリス英語という）2つの支流のどちらにおいても重大な構文上の変化が起きていないということは，驚くほどの構造上の結束を示している」
a. …なので　b. …する一方で　c. …すること
d. したがって　e. …ということ

発展　関係代名詞 what vs 接続詞 that

→ どちらも名詞節を導き，訳も「こと」と紛らわしい。

■ 関係代名詞 what の直後
文の要素（S, O, C）が欠けた「不完全な文」
I did what I thought was right.「私は正しいと思うことをした」

■ 接続詞 that の直後
文の要素が欠けていない「完全な文」
I don't think that she will come.「彼女は来ないと思う」

問題4 読解問題の中での文法 (文化構想学部出題)

Read the following passage and choose the most appropriate word or phrase for the gap.

There is a story from long ago of an old lady who lived in Scotland. The old woman, Mrs Duncan, lived on her own, just outside of the town, but on many evenings she would come to the town and visit some friends with whom she would (　　　) the evening playing cards and drinking whisky.

　　a. lose　　b. make　　c. spend　　d. watch

二本柳のひとことコメント

早稲田大の語法問題は標準レベルが繰り返し出題される。

■指示文訳：次の英文を読み，空所に入れる最も適切な語（句）を選べ。
「スコットランドに暮らしていた老女について昔から伝わる話がある。その老女は，ダンカンさんといい，町のすぐ外れで1人暮らしをしていたが，晩にはよく町までやって来て友人たちを訪ね，トランプをしたりウィスキーを飲んだりしてその日の晩を過ごした」
a. 失う　　b. 作る　　c. 過ごす　　d. 注意して見る

発展　spend の基本語法

■ **spend＋時間・金額＋(in) *doing*** 「…して（時間・金額）を費やす」
She spent the whole evening (in) writing a letter.
「彼女は1通の手紙を書くのにまるまるひと晩かけた」

■ **spend＋時間・金額＋on 事柄** 「…に対して（時間・金額）を費やす」
She spends a lot of money on her books.
「彼女は本代にお金をたくさん使う」

問題 5 読解問題の中での語法（商学部出題）

下線部の can と同じ用法を a〜d から 1 つ選べ。

　The basic problem is that while it is true that exercise burns calories and that you must burn calories to lose weight, exercise has another effect: it <u>can</u> stimulate hunger.

　　a. I can take the car if necessary.
　　b. In Japan people can vote when they are twenty.
　　c. It can be quite cold here in winter.
　　d. You can wear jeans at work.

二本柳のひとことコメント

辞書や文法書などを参照する際には「ひと手間」を惜しまず概観しよう。

「基本的な問題は，確かに運動することでカロリーが消費されるし，体重を減らすためにはカロリーを消費しなければならないことも事実なのだが，運動はまた別の効果ももたらすということだ。つまり，運動は食欲を刺激する<u>場合もある</u>のだ」
a. 必要があれば私はその車を利用できる。
b. 日本では 20 歳になると選挙権が得られる。
c. ここは冬になるととても寒くなることがある。
d. 職場でジーンズをはいてもいいですよ。

問題 6 前置詞・副詞 (人間科学部出題)

次の設問 1〜15 の空所を補うものとして最も適当な語を，(A)〜(K) の中から選びなさい。ただし，使われない語が含まれていることもあります。また，同じ語を繰り返して使うこともできます。空所に何も補う必要のない場合には (L) を選びなさい。

(A) against	(B) at	(C) by	(D) for
(E) in	(F) into	(G) of	(H) on
(I) over	(J) up	(K) with	(L) NO WORD

1. The committee will carefully review all proposals before deciding _____ a final plan.

2. Elizabeth is so kind that she will bend _____ backwards to help someone in need.

3. I like songs _____ good lyrics, as can be found in many recordings of the 1940s and 1950s.

4. _____ second thought, maybe I will have one more piece of that delicious pie.

5. After news of the scandal broke, Mr. Smith's future in politics was _____ doubt.

6. Several prominent studies supported _____ the need to increase the nation's birthrate.

7. The coach treated all his players _____ respect which motivated them to play as a team.

8. When children suddenly grow quiet, it can be a sign that they are getting _____ mischief.

9. Although the economy is still slow, we can see the light _____ the end of the tunnel.

10. Thousands protested as opposition leaders pressed _____ a meeting with the president.

11. Getting a basic, easy-to-use camera will be a better present _____ your brother.

12. Governments are being urged to step _____ measures to combat poverty on a global scale.

13. I don't know if the staff can keep it _____ because they've been working so much overtime.

14. It's not customary _____ people to send midsummer gifts to one another in my country.

15. People with chronic illnesses are usually _____ greater risk of contracting influenza.

Lesson1　短文問題-2

> 二本柳のひとことコメント

早稲田大学志望者は，人間科学部の前置詞問題に取り組んでおこう。

問題訳：
1. その委員会は，最終案を決定する前にあらゆる提案を慎重に再検討するだろう。
2. エリザベスは大変親切なので，困っている人がいると無理をしてでも助けようとする。
3. 1940年代や50年代の数多くの録音に見られるように，歌詞のよい歌が私は好きだ。
4. 考え直してみて，もしかすると，そのおいしいパイをもう1切れいただくかもしれません。
5. スキャンダルのニュースが発表された後，スミス氏の政治家としての将来は危ういものとなった。
6. いくつかの卓越した研究は，その国の出生率を高める必要性を支持した。
7. そのコーチは，全選手に，チームとしてプレイする気にさせるような敬意をもって接した。
8. 子供たちが突然静かになったら，それは，いたずらをしようとしている表れかもしれない。
9. 経済はいまだに減速しているけれども，終わりが見えてくる可能性もある。
10. 野党指導者たちが大統領との面会を強要したので，何千人もの人々が抗議した。
11. 必要最低限の機能がついた使いやすいカメラを買ってあげるのが，あなたの弟さんにはよりよいプレゼントになりますよ。
12. 各国政府は，地球規模の貧困と闘う対策を強化する必要に迫られている。
13. 相当残業が続いてきているので，社員がこの調子で頑張り続けることができるかどうかはわからない。
14. 私の国では，人々がお互いにお中元を贈ることは習慣となっていない。
15. 慢性的な病気を患っている人々は，一般的にインフルエンザにかかる危険もより高い。

問題 7 前置詞・副詞 （法学部出題）

Choose the most appropriate blank in which to place the given word in order to complete the sentence below.

up

As the students kept ☐A☐ wasting ☐B☐ electricity and did not give ☐C☐ any thought to the environment nor make ☐D☐ an effort to end ☐E☐ the increase of greenhouse gases, their teacher made them look ☐F☐ the issue on the Internet.

二本柳のひとことコメント

設問Ⅲ全体は難問だが，この問題は取らねば。

■指示文訳：以下の文を完成させるために，与えられた語を入れるのに最も適する空所を選べ。

「その学生たちは電気を無駄に使い続け，環境にまったく配慮せず，温室効果ガスの増加を食い止めようという努力もしなかったので，彼らの教師は，彼らにインターネットでこの問題を調べさせた」

問題 8 読解問題の中での前置詞 (文学部出題)

Read the following passage and choose the most appropriate word for the gap.

Achievement is what is achieved within a particular tradition, and it is deeply affected by that tradition even when it heads (　　) a new direction. As one critic says, only a Christian culture could have produced anti-Christian thinkers like Voltaire or Nietzsche.

a. for　　b. in　　c. to　　d. under

二本柳のひとことコメント

head for「…に向かってまっすぐ進む」は正解ではない。形だけで解答することは極力避けたい。

■指示文訳：以下の文章を読んで，空所に最もふさわしい言葉を選べ。
「（学問の）成果とは，ある特定の伝統の中で達成されるものであり，それは，たとえ新たな方向を目指していても，その伝統から深い影響を受けている。ある批評家が言っているように，ヴォルテールやニーチェのような反キリスト教の思想家を輩出することができたのはキリスト教文化だけだったであろう」

問題 9 読解問題の中での前置詞 （教育学部出題）

空所〔　　〕に入れるのに最もふさわしいものを a〜e から1つ選べ。

Between 1620 and 1800 important changes took place in the grammatical structure of English, both in Great Britain and America, but instead of drifting apart in this period of marked changes these two branches of English, at all important points, developed harmoniously together. This was the result of the universal tendency in colonial days among Americans 〔　　〕 culture to follow in speech the usage of the mother country.

　　a. in　　b. over　　c. across　　d. of　　e. under

二本柳のひとことコメント

正確に読もうとするふだんの英文に接する姿勢が問われている問題と言ってよい。

「1620年から1800年の間に、イギリスとアメリカ双方で、英語の文法構造に重要な変化が起きたが、この時期の著しい変化の中で別個のものになるのではなく、これら2つの系統の英語は、すべての重要な点で共に調和しながら発展した。このことは、教養のあるアメリカ人の間での、話し言葉においては母国の用法に従おうとする植民地時代の一般的な傾向の結果であった」

LESSON 1　短文問題

3 正誤問題
頻出事項は繰り返し出題されている！

TRACK 22

> **出題学部**：社会科学部・人間科学部など法学部・理工学部・スポーツ科学部でも出題歴あり。

正誤問題

《おすすめアプローチ》
1. 1回目は文構造に気を配りながらざっと読む（下線部が正しいという前提で読み，ひっかかるものはないか）。
2. 2回目はひとつひとつの語句に注意しながらていねいに読む（下線部が誤っているという前提で読み，文意が通じるか）。ここで解答を決定する。
3. 3回目に，2で決定した解答で文意が通じるかどうか確認する意味で読む。ここで解答が決まらなければ誤りなしとする。

《得点力アップの道筋》
1. まずは4択問題の正解の根拠を把握し，正答率を高める。
2. 1と同時並行で語法や熟語にも習熟する。
3. 早稲田大・慶應大の正誤問題（過去問）に取り組む。その際には，すべての下線部に納得し，英文の日本語訳も理解する。

（Lesson1 問題解答は p.30 にあります）

問題 1 文構造 (社会科学部出題)

次の設問の a～d のうち，誤った英語表現を含んだ部分がある場合には a～d の中の 1 つを，誤りがない場合には e を選べ。

<u>It</u> was <u>customary</u> in that country, the couple <u>decided to</u> get
 a   b   c
married only after having received the <u>permission of</u> both of
                                                  d
their entire families.　NO ERROR
                              e

二本柳のひとことコメント

1 回目のアプローチでは，まず接続詞・関係詞の使い方を中心に文と文とのつながりをチェック。

「その国の習慣に従って，そのカップルは両家の家族全員の承認を受けて初めて結婚することに決めた」

問題 2 文構造 (社会科学部出題)

次の設問の a～d のうち，誤った英語表現を含んだ部分がある場合には a～d の中の 1 つを，誤りがない場合には e を選べ。

For the <u>life of me</u>, I can't <u>figure out</u> how Jim was able to get
            a   b
such an <u>unbelievable</u> score on the math test <u>despite</u> he studied
          c   d
less than anyone in our class.　NO ERROR
                                    e

二本柳のひとことコメント

despite は正誤問題では頻出の前置詞（接続詞ではないので文と文とをつなぐことはできない）。

「クラスの誰よりも勉強しないにもかかわらず，数学のテストでどうしてジムがあんなに信じられないほどよい点数を取れたのか，どうしても理解できない」

問題 3 文構造 （社会科学部出題）　TRACK 25

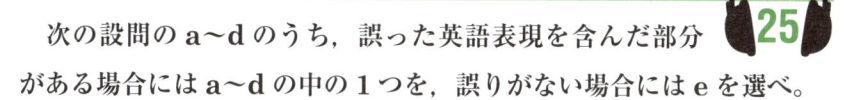

次の設問の **a〜d** のうち，誤った英語表現を含んだ部分がある場合には **a〜d** の中の **1** つを，誤りがない場合には **e** を選べ。

<u>Over the course of</u> the summer, I visited <u>a number of</u>
　　　　a　　　　　　　　　　　　　　　**b**

museums in this area that I had really wanted <u>to go</u> in the past
　　　　　　　　　　　　　　　　　　　　　　　c

but couldn't <u>because of</u> my busy study and work schedule.
　　　　　　　　d

NO ERROR
　e

二本柳のひとことコメント

1 回目のアプローチでは文と文とのつながり，及び文型判断をしよう。

「夏の間に，私は，以前に行ってみたいと思っていたが，研究や仕事の予定が忙しかったために行くことができなかったこの地区のいくつもの博物館を訪ねた」

問題 4 品詞 (人間科学部出題)

次の設問の a~d のうち，誤った英語表現を含んだ部分がある場合には a~d の中の1つを，誤りがない場合には e を選べ。

A study <u>tried to estimate</u> <u>the number of</u> <u>wrong addressed</u>
 　　　　　　　a　　　　　　　　　b　　　　　　　c

<u>envelopes</u> <u>that were returned.</u>　NO ERROR
　　　　　　　d　　　　　　　　　　　　　e

二本柳のひとことコメント

副詞→形容詞→名詞という語順も要注意。

「ある研究は，宛名が誤っていて差し戻された封筒の数を推定しようとした」

問題 5 品詞 (スポーツ科学部出題)

Identify the ONE underlined word or phrase a, b, c, or d in the sentence that should be corrected or rewritten.

My parents <u>are leaving</u> <u>on</u> <u>a</u> <u>two-weeks</u> vacation.
　　　　　　　　a　　　　　b　c　　　d

二本柳のひとことコメント

形容詞に複数形なし。

■指示文訳：設問文中の下線部 a~d のうち，正すか，書き直す必要があるものを1つ選べ。
「私の両親は2週間の休暇に出発する予定だ」

問題 6 品詞（人間科学部出題）

次の設問の a〜d のうち，誤った英語表現を含んだ部分がある場合には a〜d の中の 1 つを，誤りがない場合には e を選べ。

<u>In the wake of</u> the devastation, <u>heavy machineries</u> were
　　　a　　　　　　　　　　　　　　b
<u>put to work</u> <u>to search for</u> survivors.　NO ERROR
　　c　　　　　　d　　　　　　　　　　　　　e

二本柳のひとことコメント

問題文が難しいときほど，正解ポイントは意外と簡単（1 回目のアプローチで見つけよう）。

「廃墟のあとで，重機が生存者捜索のために働いていた」

発展　まぎらわしい可算名詞と不可算名詞

- ☐ **a bag**　　　「カバン 1 つ」
  　baggage　「手荷物全体」
- ☐ **a machine**　「1 台の機械」
  　machinery　「機械設備全体」
- ☐ **a poem**　　「1 編の詩」
  　poetry　　「詩という文学形式」
- ☐ **a table**　　「テーブル 1 台」
  　furniture　「家具，調度品，備品全体」
- ☐ **a view**　　「1 箇所からの見晴らし」
  　scenery　　「ある地域の景観全体」

問題 7 受動態 (人間科学部出題)

次の設問の a～d のうち，誤った英語表現を含んだ部分がある場合には a～d の中の 1 つを，誤りがない場合には e を選べ。

<u>Each winter</u>, a snow festival <u>is taken place</u> in Sapporo,
　　　a　　　　　　　　　　　　　b
<u>to the delight of</u> <u>residents and tourists.</u>　NO ERROR
　　　c　　　　　　　　　　d　　　　　　　　　e

二本柳のひとことコメント

能動態⇔受動態の誤りは気づきにくい。

「毎年冬になると札幌で雪祭りが行われ，市民や観光客を楽しませている」

発展　to one's ＋感情を表す名詞

□ **to *one*'s disappointment**　「A が失望したことに」
□ **to *one*'s dismay**　　　　　「A がうろたえたこと」
□ **to *one*'s joy**　　　　　　「A が喜んだことに」
□ **to *one*'s regret**　　　　　「A が残念に思ったことに」
□ **to *one*'s surprise**　　　　「A が驚いたことに」など

問題 8 準動詞 (社会科学部出題)

誤った英語表現を含んだ部分がある場合には a〜d から誤りを1つ選び、誤りがない場合には e を選べ。

<u>In a way</u> he is one of the most brilliant people I have ever
  a

<u>run into</u>, especially when <u>it comes to</u> <u>be able</u> to discuss world
 b   **c**   **d**

affairs.　NO ERROR
           e

二本柳のひとことコメント

不定詞を作る **to** なのか前置詞の **to** なのかは日頃から意識しよう。

「ある意味で彼は、私がこれまで出会った最も優秀な人々のうちの1人だ。ことに世界情勢について議論できるということになるとなおさらそうだ」

発展　「前置詞 to ＋動名詞」の要注意表現

- ☐ **(be) devoted to** *doing*　　　　　　「…することに専念している」
- ☐ **(be) used [accustomed] to** *doing*　「…することに慣れている」
- ☐ **come near to** *doing*　　　　　　　「…しそうになる」
- ☐ **look forward to** *doing*　　　　　　「…することを楽しみにする」
- ☐ **object to** *doing*　　　　　　　　　「…することに反対する」
- ☐ **when it comes to** *doing*　　　　　「…することに関して言えば」
- ☐ **with a view to** *doing*　　　　　　　「…するために」
- ☐ **What do you say to** *doing*?　　　「…するのはいかがですか」

問題 9 準動詞 (社会科学部出題)

誤った英語表現を含んだ部分がある場合には a～d から誤りを 1 つ選び，誤りがない場合には e を選べ。

It takes me <u>a lot longer</u> than <u>the other students</u> to finish my
     a   **b**

homework, mainly because I tend <u>to get distracted easily</u> and
          c

<u>end up to lose</u> interest. NO ERROR
 d   **e**

二本柳のひとことコメント

動名詞を目的語にとる動詞を覚えているか。

「私は宿題を終えるのに他の生徒よりもはるかに時間がかかる。主な理由はすぐに気が散ってしまい最後には関心がなくなってしまいがちだからだ」

発展　動名詞を目的語にとる動詞

- ☐ **admit**　　　「認める」
- ☐ **consider**　「考慮する」
- ☐ **deny**　　　「否定する」
- ☐ **escape**　　「逃れる」
- ☐ **(can/can't) help**　「避ける」
- ☐ **miss**　　　「免れる」
- ☐ **give up**　　「やめる」

- ☐ **avoid**　　「避ける」
- ☐ **enjoy**　　「楽しむ」
- ☐ **finish**　　「終える」
- ☐ **mind**　　「いやがる」
- ☐ **stop**　　　「やめる」
- ☐ **suggest**　「提案する」
- ☐ **put off**　　「延期する」など

問題 10 誤りなし（社会科学部出題）

誤った英語表現を含んだ部分がある場合には a〜d から誤りを 1 つ選び，誤りがない場合には e を選べ。

Some people say that there is more <u>profit in</u> selling services
                                                      a
than <u>there is</u> in making products, <u>although</u> I'm not sure
      b   **c**
<u>whether or not</u> that's really true.   NO ERROR
d   **e**

二本柳のひとことコメント

全 10 題中 1〜2 題「誤りなし」がある可能性が高い。

「本当に正しいことかどうかははっきりとはわからないけれども，製品を作るよりもサービスを売る方が利益になるという人がいる」

Lesson1-1　問題解答

(1) a. valid　　(2) a. coherent　　(3) a. function
(4) a. beliefs　　(5) d. until
(6) 1 — b. down　 2 — e. off　 3 — d. into　 4 — f. out　 5 — a. above
(7) c. Of course　　(8) d. true　　(9) d. disagreeing
(10) 1 He left for Tokyo on his own (last Monday.)
　　 2 Do you have any idea (as to) when he might return (?)
　　 3 (He must be back) (by) tomorrow at the very latest (.)

Lesson1-2　問題解答

(1) c. what is now　　(2) c. rising
(3) e. That　　(4) c. spend
(5) c. It can be quite cold here in winter.
(6) 1. H (on)　　2. I (over)　　3. K (with)　　4. H (on)
　　 5. E (in)　　6. L (NO WORD)　　7. K (with)　　8. F (into)
　　 9. B (at)　　10. D (for)　　11. D (for)　　12. J (up)
　　 13. J (up)　　14. D (for)　　15. B (at)
(7) F　　(8) b. in　　(9) d. of

Lesson1-3　問題解答

(1) a. It ⇒ As [As it]
(2) d. despite ⇒ (al)though [even though]
(3) c. to go ⇒ to go to
(4) c. wrong addressed envelopes ⇒ wrongly addressed envelopes
(5) d. two-weeks ⇒ two-week
(6) b. heavy machineries ⇒ heavy machines
(7) b. is taken place ⇒ takes place
(8) d. be able ⇒ being able
(9) d. end up to lose ⇒ end up losing
(10) e. (誤りなし)

LESSON 2 中文問題

1 空所補充問題
「形」と「流れ」の両面作戦で。

TRACK 01

出題学部：文学部，文化構想学部，基幹・創造・先進理工学部，その他，読解総合問題の一部としてほぼ全学部。

空所補充問題

《おすすめアプローチ》
1. まずは，選択肢の品詞を意識して空所前後との文法的結びつきやイディオム，慣用表現が作れないかを検討する。つまり「形」の検討から入る。
2. 「形」で決まらなかったら，前後の文脈から検討する。正解を導く根拠は本文中に必ずあるのだが，1つの空所にあまり時間をかけすぎないこと。
3. 選んだ解答でつじつまが合うかどうか訳して確認すること。

《得点力アップの道筋》
1. 平素から，各設問の正解に至るプロセスや理由付けを丹念に行う癖をつける。
2. 「形」で解答が決定できた場合でも，必ず文全体をざっとでも訳すこと。
3. イディオムや慣用表現なども貪欲に吸収する。

（Lesson2 問題解答は p.68 にあります）

Read the following passage and choose the most appropriate words or phrases for the gaps.
(文化構想学部出題)

It has long been believed that human babies are incapable of communicating their thoughts, simply because they cannot speak properly as adults do, and it is therefore difficult to gauge them. However, there are recent findings which contradict this hypothesis. 'Baby signing' is a system of body language developed and promoted by American child psychologists Linda Acredolo and Susan Goodwyn. The language is comprised of manual signs or gestures expressing not only nouns ('dog', 'book', 'light'), but also (1) movements ('to open', 'to play', 'to sit down') and emotions ('happy', 'sleepy', 'scary'). These signs help deepen communication between parents and their babies who have not learned to speak. How does this work? The following explanation highlights the remarkable sophistication of communication by babies.

(2), babies start talking at around eighteen months, but they show interest in communicating with their parents at a much earlier age. However, because their tongues and throats, vital for the pronunciation of actual words, are still underdeveloped, they constantly (3) the frustration of not being able to express what they want. On the other hand, at this age, babies' manual movements are fairly well developed and so they use this method of communication rather than the (4) function. By practising baby signing, the following effects result: babies' frustration is reduced; parents are more (5) about their child's needs during the nursing period; and a much deeper bond of mutual understanding is developed.

The most frequently raised concern about this system is that baby signing may (6) babies' acquisition of language and subsequently delay its development. Surprisingly, however, follow-up research suggests the contrary: baby signing encourages babies to improve their linguistic ability, as they start training their initial communication skills by signs (7) such early phases. Another survey of seven-year-old children shows that the children who used baby signing scored twelve points higher in IQ tests than those who did not.

(1) a. chemical　　b. local　　　　c. mechanical　d. physical

(2) a. Against expectations　　b. Generally speaking
　　c. In addition　　　　　　d. Surely enough

(3) a. come　　　b. face　　　　c. meet　　　　d. receive

(4) a. scientific　b. traditional　c. usual　　　　d. verbal

(5) a. confident　b. fanciful　　c. pleasant　　d. resolute

(6) a. abandon　b. bore　　　　c. discourage　d. exclude

(7) a. about　　b. during　　　c. on　　　　　d. to

■指示文訳：以下の文を読んで，空所に最も適した語，または句を選べ。

問題(1)

The language is comprised of manual signs or gestures expressing **not only** nouns ('dog', 'book', 'light'), **but also** (1) movements ('to open', 'to play', 'to sit down') and emotions ('happy', 'sleepy', 'scary').

問題文訳［38ページ］ 1 参照

  a. chemical b. local c. mechanical d. physical

二本柳のひとことコメント

空所直後の具体例（「開けること」，「遊ぶこと」，「座ること」）を表す形容詞を選択肢から選ぶ。

 a. 化学的な b. 局所的な c. 機械的な d. 身体的な

問題(2)

(2), babies start talking at around eighteen months, but they show interest in communicating with their parents at a much earlier age. **However**, because their tongues and throats...

問題文訳［38ページ］ 2 参照

  a. Against expectations b. Generally speaking
  c. In addition   d. Surely enough

二本柳のひとことコメント

空所を含む文の直後の文が **However** で始まっていることから，空所を含む文が一般的な事実であることをつかむ。

 a. 予想に反して b. 一般的に言うと c. さらに d. 確かなことに

Lesson2 中文問題-1

問題(3)

However, **because** their tongues and throats, vital for the pronunciation of actual words, are still underdeveloped, they constantly （ **3** ） the frustration of not being able to express what they want.

問題文訳［38ページ］ 3 参照

  a. come b. face c. meet d. receive

二本柳のひとことコメント

空所を含む文の前に **because** 節があるので，その結論となるように動詞を選ぶ。
 a. 来る b. 直面する c. 会う d. 受け取る

問題(4)

On the other hand, at this age, babies' manual movements are fairly well developed and so they use **this** method of communication **rather than** the （ **4** ） function.

問題文訳［38ページ］ 4 参照

  a. scientific b. traditional c. usual d. verbal

二本柳のひとことコメント

空所直前の **rather than** から，対比の構造をつかむ。
 a. 科学の b. 伝統の c. 平素の d. 言葉の

問題(5)

By practising baby signing, the following effects result: babies' frustration is reduced; parents are more (　5　) about their child's needs during the nursing period; and a much deeper bond of mutual understanding is developed.

問題文訳［38 ページ］ 5 参照

  a. confident b. fanciful c. pleasant d. resolute

二本柳のひとことコメント

ベビー・サインを実践することによる効果が列挙されている中の 1 つである，という流れをつかむ。

  a. 確信している b. 架空の c. 楽しませるような d. 断固とした

問題(6)

The most frequently raised concern about this system is that baby signing may (　6　) babies' acquisition of language and subsequently delay its development.

問題文訳［38 ページ］ 6 参照

  a. abandon b. bore c. discourage d. exclude

二本柳のひとことコメント

空所後の and 以下と共通の内容となるものを選ぶ。**SVC** の文型も有効活用したい。

  a. 捨てる b. 退屈させる c. 妨げる d. 除外する

問題(7)

Surprisingly, however, **follow-up research** suggests the contrary: baby signing encourages babies to improve their linguistic ability, as they start training their initial communication skills by signs (　7　) such early phases.

問題文訳［38ページ］ 7 参照

  a. about b. during c. on d. to

【二本柳のひとことコメント】

空所直後の **such early phases**「そのような初期の段階」が「生まれて間もない時期」という特定の期間を表していることをつかむ。

問題文訳

　人間の赤ん坊は，単に大人がするように正確に話すことができないという理由で，自らの考えを伝えることができないし，それゆえに，赤ん坊の考えを読み取ることは難しいと長く信じられてきた。しかし，この仮説と矛盾する最近の研究結果がある。「ベビー・サイン」は，アメリカの児童心理学者，リンダ・アクレドロとスーザン・グッドウィンによって開発，促進されている身体言語の体系である。 1 この言語は，名詞（「犬」，「本」，「光」）だけでなく，身体的動作（「開けること」，「遊ぶこと」，「座ること」）や感情（「うれしい」，「眠い」，「怖い」）も表現する，手による合図や身振りから成っている。これらのサインは，親とまだ話せるようになっていない赤ん坊との間の意思の疎通を深めるのに役立つ。これはどのように作用するのか。以下の説明は，赤ん坊による驚くほど洗練された意思伝達に焦点を当てたものだ。

　 2 一般的に言えば，赤ん坊は18か月頃から話し始めるが，親との意思の疎通にはそれよりずっと早い時期に興味を示す。 3 しかし，実際の言葉の発音に不可欠な舌やのどが十分発育していないので，赤ん坊は自分の望むことを表現できないという欲求不満に絶えず直面している。 4 一方，この時期，赤ん坊の手の動きは，かなり発達しているので，赤ん坊は言語機能よりもむしろこの意思伝達の方法を使う。 5 ベビー・サインを実践することによって，次のような効果が生じる。赤ん坊の欲求不満が減る，親は授乳期間中の子供が何を要求しているのかについてもっと確信を持てる，はるかに深い相互理解の絆が築ける，といったところである。

　 6 この方法について最も頻繁に生じる不安は，ベビー・サインが赤ん坊の言語の習得を妨げ，その後の言語の発育を遅らせるかもしれない，ということだ。 7 しかし，驚くべきことに，引き続き行われた調査は，正反対のことを示している。つまり，ベビー・サインは，赤ん坊が自分の言語能力を向上させるのを促す，というのである。というのは，赤ん坊は，そのような初期の段階に，手の合図によって最初の意思伝達能力を訓練し始めるからだ。7歳の子供についての別の調査は，ベビー・サインを使った子供が，ベビー・サインを使わなかった子供よりも，IQテストにおいて12ポイント高く得点したことを示している。

LESSON 2 中文問題

2 英問英答問題
パラグラフの要旨が問われる。

TRACK 09

出題学部：人間科学部，文学部，文化構想学部，その他，読解総合問題の一部として全学部。

英問英答問題

《おすすめアプローチ》
1. 英問は本文内容の「予告編」なので先読みが大原則。仮に英問で問われている内容がつかめなくても，あわてずに本文を読み始めればよい。
2. パラグラフの趣旨をつかむことを常に意識する。
3. 選択肢には判断に迷うものが含まれている場合が多いので，本文⇔選択肢の照合作業を念入りに行う。

《得点力アップの道筋》
1. 設問の問われ方はさまざまだが，パラグラフもしくは全文の趣旨を問う問題がほとんどなので，パラグラフの内容をつかむことを常に意識する。
2. 正解にいたる該当文は「正確に」把握する必要があるので，速さだけではなく，読もうと思えばいつでも正確に読めるという「解釈力」を身につけるよう平素から心がける。
3. 本文中にまったく登場しない「記述なし」の選択肢がありうることも念頭に置く。

（Lesson2 問題解答は p.68 にあります）

1. Read the following passage and answer the questions.
（文学部出題）

There are two main ways in which novels, plays, films, television, and songs have depicted the American small town. In one version, the town is a backwater, a quiet place where quiet, ordinary people get on with their lives, mostly undisturbed by the world outside. It is the kind of town to which the hero returns, coming to realize that his life in the city has been empty, lacking the true values of simplicity and goodness he can only find at home.

In the other version, the small town is quiet on the surface, but underneath we find darkness and despair. Violence, prejudice, drug addiction and alcoholism, incest, and murder, indeed serial murder, are all to be found just behind the illusion of normality this fictional small town presents. But while both versions of the small town in literature and other cultural mediations may be misleading, for an increasingly urbanized population they will represent the good or bad dream of a place elsewhere.

(1) According to the passage, the idea of the small town as represented in American culture is
   a. a place of utopian perfection where everybody is a good friend.
   b. divided between extremes of normal life and social breakdown.
   c. not welcoming or accepting of any outsiders or strangers.
   d. somewhere people from the city would like to live.

(2) The passage says that the literary idea of the small town is wrong, but
   a. as more and more people live in the city, the more it will become widely held.
   b. cities also are unreal places where people live with their dreams.
   c. there are many more murderers and drug addicts in the big cities.
   d. when people move back to the country from the city, they will realize the truth.

問題 1-(1)

According to the passage, the idea of the small town as represented in American culture is

    a. a place of utopian perfection where everybody is a good friend.

    b. divided between extremes of normal life and social breakdown.

    c. not welcoming or accepting of any outsiders or strangers.

    d. somewhere people from the city would like to live.

二本柳のひとことコメント

パラグラフの内容を意識しながら読み進めるのは，早稲田大が要求する読解の基本姿勢だ。

「本文によれば，アメリカ文化で表現されている小さな町についての考え方は」
a. 誰もがよき友人であるユートピア的な完璧さを持つ場所である。
b. 普通の生活と社会的崩壊という両極の間で分断されている。
c. よそ者や見ず知らずの者を歓迎することも迎え入れることもない。
d. 都会出身の人々が暮らしてみたくなるような場所である。

問題 1-(2)

The passage says that the literary idea of the small town is wrong, but

    a. as more and more people live in the city, the more it will become widely held.

    b. cities also are unreal places where people live with their dreams.

c. there are many more murderers and drug addicts in the big cities.
d. when people move back to the country from the city, they will realize the truth.

二本柳のひとことコメント

早稲田大の読解問題は直球勝負。結論部分は必ず問われると考えてよい。

「本文によれば，小さな町についての文学的概念は誤っているとあるが」
a. 都会で暮らす人々が増えるにつれ，その概念はますます広く共有されるようになるだろう。
b. 都会もまた人々が夢を持って暮らす非現実的な場所である。
c. 大都市には殺人者や薬物中毒者がいっそう数多く存在している。
d. 都会から田舎に戻ると，人々は真実に気づくだろう。

問題文訳

　小説，戯曲，映画，テレビ，そして歌がこれまでにアメリカの小さな町を描いてきた主な方法には2種類ある。第1の描き方では，その町は僻地で，穏やかで普通の人々が外界にほとんど煩わされることなく自分たちの暮らしを営んでいる静かな場所である。そこは，主人公が戻ってみると，都会の暮らしが空虚で，ふるさとにしか見出せない飾り気のなさや善良さが持つ本当の価値に欠けていることに気づくようになるといったような町なのだ。
　第2の描き方では，その小さな町は表面上は静かだが，その根底には暗闇と絶望が存在することに気づく。暴力，偏見，薬物依存症やアルコール中毒，近親相姦や殺人（それも実際には連続殺人）などといったすべてが，この架空の小さな町が示す正常さという幻想の真後ろに見出されうるのだ。しかし，文学や他の媒体におけるそういった小さな町の描き方は，どちらも誤解を招くかもしれない一方で，ますます都会化する住民にとって，そういった描き方はどこかよその場所に対して描く良くも悪くも夢のような話を表しているのだろう。

2. Read the following passage and answer the questions.
（人間科学部出題）

TRACK 12〜14

More college students are studying abroad than ever before and more are traveling during their summers for volunteer work, to study a foreign language, and to simply improve their resumes. However, while one might believe traveling for an entire summer is certainly not affordable it actually is more affordable than you might have imagined.

For example, there are many institutes and programs across the world that offer foreign language courses, culture immersion, internships with local businesses, and homestays for one flat fee from two to eight weeks in the summer. Rates vary depending on the program and the country, but there are many very affordable programs out there for students. In addition to this, there are some great flight offers for college students and student travel agencies that focus on providing the cheapest flights to students as possible. In light of this, it truly is affordable to study or immerse yourself in another culture for a couple of weeks or months and not spend too much money. All you have to do is a little research in order to be aware of all the services out there that will help you travel on a budget.

(1) What is NOT a reason some students study abroad?
 a. Experience another culture.
 b. Improve their job prospects.
 c. Learn a language.
 d. Save money.

(2) What can make a study abroad program more affordable?
　　a. Flat fees　　　b. Homestays
　　c. Internships　　d. Variable rates

　　　　　　　　　　　　　　　　　　　_____

(3) What is the main idea of this passage?
　　a. There are many challenges to studying abroad.
　　b. Picking the right study abroad program is hard.
　　c. Learning a foreign language is important.
　　d. Studying abroad doesn't have to be expensive.

　　　　　　　　　　　　　　　　　　　_____

問題 2-(1) 〔TRACK 12〕

What is NOT a reason some students study abroad?

   a. Experience another culture.
   b. Improve their job prospects.
   c. Learn a language.
   d. Save money.

二本柳のひとことコメント

具体的な情報の列挙に関する設問は，思い込みで解答しないこと。必ず本文中で確認を。

「一部の学生が留学する理由とならないものはどれか」
a. 異文化を経験すること。　b. 就職の可能性を高めること。
c. 言語を学ぶこと。　　　　d. お金を節約すること。

問題 2-(2) 〔TRACK 13〕

What can make a study abroad program more affordable?

   a. Flat fees   b. Homestays
   c. Internships   d. Variable rates

二本柳のひとことコメント

パラグラフの内容を意識することで解答時間は早まる。

「なぜ留学プログラムはより手ごろな価格になりうるのか」
　　a. 均一料金　　b. ホームステイ　　c. インターンシップ　　d. 変動する料金

問題 2-(3)

What is the main idea of this passage?

a. There are many challenges to studying abroad.
b. Picking the right study abroad program is hard.
c. Learning a foreign language is important.
d. Studying abroad doesn't have to be expensive.

二本柳のひとことコメント

こういう設問で確実に正解を出せる読み方をしたい。

「本文の主旨は何か」
 a. 留学するには数多くの課題がある。
 b. 適切な留学プログラムを精選するのは難しい。
 c. 外国語を学ぶことは重要だ。
 d. 留学するのに高い費用は必要ではない。

問題文訳

　これまでにないほど多くの学生が留学し，また夏の間ボランティア活動をしたり，外国語を学んだり，単に履歴書に記載する内容をよりよくすると言ったような理由で旅行している。しかしながら，夏休みの間中旅行を続ける金銭的余裕などあるわけがないと思い込んでいる人もいるかもしれないが，実際には想像していたよりも手ごろな値段なのである。

　例えば，夏期の2週間から8週間，均一料金で，外国語コース，文化の集中体験，地元企業でのインターンシップ，それにホームステイをさせる機関やプログラムは世界中にたくさんある。料金はプログラムや国によって異なるが，海外には学生にとって大変手ごろなプログラムが数多くある。これに加えて，大学生向けに提供されるフライトや，学生にできるだけ安価なフライトを供給することに特化した学生旅行代理店も存在する。こういったことを考慮すれば，2週間もしくは2か月，留学したり異文化に浸ったりして，しかもあまり費用をかけないことは十分手の届く範囲なのである。予算に見合う旅行に役立つ海外でのサービスをすべて知るために，少し調べてみるだけでよい。

LESSON 2 中文問題

3 会話問題
実は「正確な文構造把握」がメイン。

TRACK 15

出題学部：社会科学部，文学部，文化構想学部，商学部，政治経済学部，教育学部，基幹・創造・先進理工学部など。

会話問題

《おすすめアプローチ》
1. 会話文といえども文構造を意識する。特に空所直後に注意。
2. 省略や指示語は必ず復元して読み進める。
3. 発話内容を総括しながら読み進める。

《得点力アップの道筋》
1. 平素から口語表現はイディオムと捉え，形を分解して理解しておくこと。早稲田大では訳の丸暗記はほとんど役に立たない。
2. 1回の発話＝1つのパラグラフ，と捉え，何が言いたいのか総括しながら極力正確に読み進める。この視点がないと合否が分かれる設問で正解が出せない。
3. 以上の点を踏まえて，全学部の会話問題に取り組む。

（Lesson2 問題解答は p.68 にあります）

1. Choose the most appropriate answers from the list (a-k) for the gaps (1-7) in the following conversation.
（文化構想学部出題）

TRACK 16

Hiromi, an exchange student, is talking to a counselor about what classes to choose.

Counselor: Hello, Hiromi. (1) take a seat and tell me about what you would like to study?

Hiromi: Well, I'm not really sure what to take this semester, but I need to take care of some of the basic requirements.

Counselor: Your records show that you have taken care of your language requirement. (2) the sciences?

Hiromi: (3) I have been trying to avoid them.

Counselor: (4) perhaps try Prof. Redenbacher's Natural Science 101. It's very popular.

Hiromi: That sounds good. I've heard good things about it.

Counselor: (5) you take something in the social sciences, too.

Hiromi: (6) I took sociology then?

Counselor: (7) work.

Hiromi: Great. Otherwise there is no problem with my major. Thanks for the advice!

a. Have you   b. How about   c. How will
d. How would it be if   e. I recommend that
f. I'm afraid that   g. I'm sorry to   h. That would
i. They might   j. Why don't you   k. You could

(1) _____   (2) _____   (3) _____   (4) _____

(5) _____   (6) _____   (7) _____

■指示文訳：次の会話の空所（1〜7）に入れるのに最も適切な答えをリスト（a〜k）から選べ。

二本柳のひとことコメント

(1) 会話問題こそ「形」が重要。空所直後が動詞の原形であり，かつ疑問文であることから候補を絞り込み，最後に内容で解答決定。

(2) 空所直後が名詞のみであり，かつ疑問文であることから候補を絞り込み，最後に内容で解答決定。

(3) 空所直後が完全な文であることから候補を絞り込み，最後に内容で解答決定。

(4) 空所の後に動詞の原形があることから候補を絞り込み，最後に内容で解答決定。

(5) (3)に同じ。

(6) 空所直後が完全な文であり，かつ疑問文であることから候補を絞り込み，最後に内容で解答決定。会話問題こそ「形」が重要。

(7) (4)に同じ。

問題文訳

交換留学生のヒロミが，どのクラスを選ぶべきかについてカウンセラーと話している。

カウンセラー：こんにちは，ヒロミ。席に座って，何を勉強したいかについて教えてくれるかな？
ヒロミ：ええと，今学期に何を履修するべきなのかあまりよくわかっていないのですが，基礎必修科目を何科目か取る必要があります。
カウンセラー：君の成績表を見ると，言語の必修科目は単位を修得しているよ。自然科学はどうかな？
ヒロミ：あいにく自然科学は受講しないようにしてきました。
カウンセラー：よかったらレデンバッカー教授の自然科学 101 を試してみたらどうだろう。とても人気があるんだ。
ヒロミ：それはいいですね。その講義については良い評判を耳にしています。
カウンセラー：社会科学分野でも何か履修することを勧めるよ。
ヒロミ：そういうことなら，社会学を履修するというのはどうでしょうか？
カウンセラー：それでいいと思うよ。
ヒロミ：よかった。それ以外の点では，私の専攻に関しては何も問題はありません。アドヴァイスありがとうございました。

2. Read this dialogue and answer the questions below.
（政治経済学部出題）

TRACK 17〜20

Police officer: Good evening, sir. Would you mind stepping out of your car for a moment, please?

Driver: (A) Is something the matter?

Police officer: (B) on this road, aren't you?

Driver: Forty miles per hour, I think. But I'm sure I was doing less than that.

Police officer: (C), the limit here is 50, but you were doing 78 around that bend.

Driver: I find that rather hard to believe. How can you be so sure?

Police officer: I've been driving behind you for the last 12 miles. Didn't you see me in your rearview mirror?

Driver: (D) I was too busy enjoying the scenery.

Police officer: Well, I'm afraid I'm going to have to give you a speeding ticket. Please be more careful in the future.

Driver: Just a minute! If you were behind me all that time, doesn't that mean you were speeding, too?

(1) Choose the most suitable phrase from those below to fill in blank space (A).

   a. If you please.   b. It's a fact.
   c. Neither would I.   d. Not at all.   e. So it seems.

(2) Use the seven words below to fill in blank space（　B　）in the best way. Indicate your choices for the first, third, and fifth positions.

　　a. are　　b. aware　　c. limit　　d. of
　　e. speed　　f. the　　g. you

　　　　　　　　　1st：　　　　3rd：　　　　5th：　　　　

(3) Choose the most suitable phrase from those below to fill in blank space（　C　）.

　　a. All in all
　　b. As it happens
　　c. By all means
　　d. In a while
　　e. Just in case

　　　　　　　　　　　　　　　　　　　　　　　　　　

(4) Choose the most suitable phrase from those below to fill in blank space（　D　）.

　　a. I can't say I did.
　　b. I don't say I have.
　　c. I must say I do.
　　d. I should say I could.
　　e. I wouldn't say I can.

問題 2-(1)

(A) Is something the matter?

Choose the most suitable phrase from those below to fill in blank space (A).

a. If you please.　　b. It's a fact.　　c. Neither would I.
d. Not at all.　　　e. So it seems.

> **二本柳のひとことコメント**

「頻出表現」と言われているものは，イディオムと同様に分解してみよう。使う場面をイメージすること。

「空所（ A ）に入れるのに最も適切な表現を下記のものから選べ」
a. よろしければ。　　b. それは事実です。　　c. 私もしないでしょう。
d. ええ，いいですよ。　e. そうらしいですね。

発展　Would you mind V-ing?

■ **Do[Would] you mind V-ing?**
「V することを気にしますか」→「V していただけませんか」

■ **Do[Would] you mind if I V?**
「私が V することを気にしますか」→「私が V してもかまいませんか」

Certainly not. / Not at all. / Of course not.
「いいえ，気にしません」→「いいですよ」

I'd rather S didn't V.
「S に V しないでもらいたい」→「いやです」

問題 2-(2)

(B) on this road, **aren't you?**

Use the seven words below to fill in blank space (B) in the best way. Indicate your choices for the first, third, and fifth positions.

a. are b. aware c. limit d. of e. speed f. the g. you

⬛ 二本柳のひとことコメント

付加疑問＋イディオム＋直後の文で正解ゲット！

「以下の7つの語を用いて，最も適切な形で空所（ B ）を埋めよ。解答は1番目，3番目，5番目に来る語として選択したものを示せ」

問題 2-(3)

(C), the limit here is 50, but you were doing 78 around that bend.

Choose the most suitable phrase from those below to fill in blank space (C).

a. All in all   b. As it happens   c. By all means
d. In a while   e. Just in case

⬛ 二本柳のひとことコメント

前後のつながり＋口語表現＋選択肢の消去法。

「空所（ C ）に入れるのに最も適切な表現を下記のものから選べ」
a. 全体として b. あいにく c. ぜひとも d. しばらくしたら e. 念のため

問題 2-(4)

(D) **I was too busy** enjoying the scenery.

Choose the most suitable phrase from those below to fill in blank space (D).

　　a. I can't say I did.
　　b. I don't say I have.
　　c. I must say I do.
　　d. I should say I could.
　　e. I wouldn't say I can.

　二本柳のひとことコメント

空所前後の過去形に注目。

「空所（ D ）に入れるのに最も適切な表現を下記のものから選べ」
　a. 見たとは言えません。
　b. 見たことがあるとは言っていません。
　c. 見ていると言わざるを得ません。
　d. たぶん見えたはずです。
　e. 見ることができるとは言わないでしょう。

問題文訳

警察官：こんばんは。ちょっと車から出ていただけませんか？
運転手：ええ，いいですよ。何かありましたか？
警察官：この道路の制限速度はご存じですよね？
運転手：時速40マイルだと思います。でも，そんなに速度は出していなかったと思いますよ。
警察官：あいにくですが，ここの制限は50マイルなんですが，あなたはあそこのカーブのところで78マイル出ていました。
運転手：それはかなり信じがたいです。どうしてそんなに確信を持てるんですか？
警察官：私はこの12マイルの間，あなたを追走していました。バックミラー越しに私が見えませんでしたか？
運転手：見たとは言えません。景色を楽しむのにあまりにも忙しかったからです。
警察官：それでは，あいにくあなたにスピード違反の切符を切らなければならないようですね。これからはもっと注意してください。
運転手：ちょっと待ってください。もしあなたがずっと私の後ろにいたのなら，あなただってスピード違反をしていたことになりませんか？

3. 次の英文を読み，設問 1〜8 に答えよ。
(教育学部出題)

TRACK 21〜28

KEN: I think (**1**) I returned you the bike you so generously lent to me last week. To tell you the truth I've had just about as much as I can take and I think I have reached the breaking point as far as riding a bike on Tokyo streets is concerned.

ICHIRO: I thought (**2**) riding around Tokyo exploring the city and seeing the sights. Don't you like cycling?

KEN: Yes, I do, but the stereotype image of the Japanese as a polite, orderly and law-abiding people has taken some hard battering these last few days. I know ⬜ A ⬜ the hang of cycling in these conditions.

ICHIRO: You're probably just suffering from cultural shock, there's nothing to get so (**3**) about. Surely once you get used to the particular rules and exotic behaviour patterns you'll find it as easy as you found cycling in New York.

KEN: (**4**) it were just a question of the rules being a little different, but I've come sadly but surely to the pessimistic conclusion that it's not so much a question of the rules being different as the fact that there just aren't any rules at all — none, whatsoever.

ICHIRO: Come on, calm down and take life with a pinch of salt, after all it can't be so tough, I'm sure you'll regret giving up the bike.

KEN: Well, maybe you're right, (**5**) can you explain to me why Japanese cyclists ride on both sides of the road indiscriminately in flagrant defiance of any traffic code, both with or against the flow of traffic, why they refuse to signal when they turn or suddenly stop or change direction, why they never look to the side or sometimes even in front, why 　B　 or ride about on the roads and sidewalks at night without a lamp? (　6　) pedestrians have a tendency to regard cyclists as dangerous maniacs with latent suicidal tendencies.

(1) 空所（　1　）に入れるのに最もふさわしいものを a～e から 1 つ選べ。
   a. it's about deadline　　b. I must ensure
   c. the date is past when　d. it's high time
   e. the time is now that

(2) 空所（　2　）に入れるのに最もふさわしいものを a～e から 1 つ選べ。
   a. I enjoyed myself　　　b. you were enjoying yourself
   c. I had enjoyed myself　d. you must be enjoying it
   e. it was enjoyable to you

(3) 空所（　3　）に入れるのに最もふさわしいものを a～e から 1 つ選べ。
   a. panicked　b. hysterical　c. upsetted
   d. unsettled　e. over-worried

(4) 空所（ 4 ）に入れるのに最もふさわしいものをa〜eから1つ選べ。
   a. I mustn't think that   b. I should not say
   c. I wouldn't mind if   d. I do not say that
   e. I couldn't care if

(5) 空所（ 5 ）に入れるのに最もふさわしいものをa〜eから1つ選べ。
   a. but in that case   b. and so how   c. but then why
   d. since I ask when   e. if only you

(6) 空所（ 6 ）に入れるのに最もふさわしいものをa〜eから1つ選べ。
   a. It's a problem how   b. So consequently that
   c. That's reasonable when   d. No wonder why
   e. Some reason for which

(7) 空所　A　に入るように次の単語を並べ替えた場合、**2番目**と**5番目**に来る単語はどれか。a〜hからそれぞれ1つ選べ。
   a. but   b. can't   c. generalize   d. get   e. I
   f. it's   g. to   h. wrong

   2番目：＿＿＿＿　5番目：＿＿＿＿

(8) 空所　B　に入るように次の単語を並べ替えた場合、**3番目**と**6番目**に来る単語はどれか。a〜hからそれぞれ1つ選べ。
   a. carry   b. cellular   c. conversations   d. cycling
   e. on   f. phone   g. while   h. they

   3番目：＿＿＿＿　6番目：＿＿＿＿

問題 3-(1)

I think (1) I **returned** you the bike you so generously lent to me last week.

空所（ 1 ）に入れるのに最もふさわしいものを a～e から 1 つ選べ。

- a. it's about deadline
- b. I must ensure
- c. the date is past when
- d. it's high time
- e. the time is now that

二本柳のひとことコメント

空所直後の述語動詞が過去形。

- a. そろそろ締め切りだ
- b. 私は確実に…するようにしなければならない
- c. …の日付は過ぎている
- d. とっくに…する時間だ
- e. …するときは今だ

問題 3-(2)

I **thought** (2) **riding** around Tokyo exploring the city and seeing the sights.

空所（ 2 ）に入れるのに最もふさわしいものを a～e から 1 つ選べ。

- a. I enjoyed myself
- b. you were enjoying yourself
- c. I had enjoyed myself
- d. you must be enjoying it
- e. it was enjoyable to you

二本柳のひとことコメント

空所直後の **riding** が決め手！
選択肢を切るには形容詞 **enjoyable** の語法も。

a. 私は楽しんだ
b. 君は楽しんでいた
c. 私は楽しんだ
d. 君はそれを楽しんでいるに違いない
e. 君には楽しめるものだった

問題 3-(3)　TRACK 23

You're probably just suffering from cultural shock, there's nothing to get so (　3　) about.

空所（　3　）に入れるのに最もふさわしいものを a～e から 1 つ選べ。

a. panicked　　b. hysterical　　c. upsetted
d. unsettled　　e. over-worried

二本柳のひとことコメント

空所以前の発言内容から **KEN** の心理状態を総括する形容詞を選ぶ。難問。

a. うろたえた
b. ヒステリー状態の
c. 心が乱れた
d. 不安定な
e. 必要以上に心配して

問題 3-(4)

(4) **it were** just a question of the rules being a little different, but I've come sadly but surely to the pessimistic conclusion that it's not so much a question of the rules being different as the fact that there just aren't any rules at all —— none, whatsoever.

空所（ 4 ）に入れるのに最もふさわしいものを a〜e から 1 つ選べ。

    a. I mustn't think that   b. I should not say
    c. I wouldn't mind if   d. I do not say that
    e. I couldn't care if

二本柳のひとことコメント

空所直後の it were から仮定法過去。

  a. 私は…だと考えてはいけない
  b. 私は…だと言うべきではない
  c. もし…だとしても私は気にしないだろう
  d. 私は…だとは言わない
  e. もし…だとしても私は構っていられないだろう

問題 3-(5)

Well, **maybe** you're right, (5) **can you explain to me why** Japanese cyclists ride on both sides of the road indiscriminately in flagrant defiance of any traffic code, both with or against the flow of traffic, **why** they refuse to signal when they turn or suddenly stop or change direction, **why** they never look to the side or sometimes even in front, **why** B or ride about on the roads and sidewalks at night without a lamp?

空所(5)に入れるのに最もふさわしいものを a～e から1つ選べ。

  a. but in that case   b. and so how   c. but then why
  d. since I ask when   e. if only you

二本柳のひとことコメント

正確な文構造把握で正解を出す問題。ぜひ正解したい。

 a. しかしその場合には   b. それならどのようにして
 c. しかしそれならなぜ   d. いつなのか私が尋ねるので
 e. 君が…ならなあ

問題 3-(6)

(6) pedestrians have a tendency to **regard** cyclists **as** dangerous maniacs with latent suicidal tendencies.

空所(6)に入れるのに最もふさわしいものを a～e から1つ選べ。

a. It's a problem how
b. So consequently that
c. That's reasonable when
d. No wonder why
e. Some reason for which

> 二本柳のひとことコメント

空所直後の **KEN** の発言内容がここまでの発言と矛盾していないことをつかむ。空所直後の文は語彙が難しいが，発話の結論部分であることから推測する。ここも取りたい！

a. どのようにして…なのかが問題だ
b. したがって…
c. …のとき，そのことは理にかなっている
d. なぜ…なのか不思議ではない
e. …のための理屈

問題 3-(7)

Yes, I do, but the stereotype image of the Japanese as a polite, orderly, and law-abiding people has taken some hard battering these last few days. **I know** [A] **the hang of cycling** in these conditions.

空所 [A] に入るように次の単語を並べ替えた場合，**2 番目**と **5 番目**に来る単語はどれか。**a〜h** からそれぞれ 1 つ選べ。

a. but b. can't c. generalize d. get e. I
f. it's g. to h. wrong

> 二本柳のひとことコメント

選択肢中の動詞に注目＋空所前後の「形」を常に意識する。

会話問題 3-(8)

Well, maybe you're right, (but in that case) can you explain to me why **Japanese cyclists** ride on both sides of the road indiscriminately in flagrant defiance of any traffic code, both with or against the flow of traffic, why they refuse to signal when they turn or suddenly stop or change direction, why they never look to the side or sometimes even in front, why ⬚ B ⬚ or ride about on the roads and sidewalks at night without a lamp?

空所 B に入るように次の単語を並べ替えた場合，3番目と6番目に来る単語はどれか。a～h からそれぞれ1つ選べ。

a. carry　　b. cellular　　c. conversations　　d. cycling
e. on　　　f. phone　　　g. while　　　　　　h. they

二本柳のひとことコメント

選択肢中の動詞に注目＋空所前後の「形」を常に意識する。
"**while V-ing**"「V しながら」は早稲田大では頻出表現として押さえよう。

問題文訳

ケン：君が先週，気前よく貸してくれた自転車なんだけど，そろそろ返さなきゃいけない頃だね。実を言うと，僕はできうる限り耐えられることにはほぼ耐えて，東京の通りで自転車に乗ることに関する限り我慢の限界に行き着いてしまったと思うんだ。

イチロー：僕は，君が自転車に乗って東京の街を探索したり観光したりして楽しんでいるものだと思っていたよ。サイクリングが好きじゃないのかい？

ケン：いや，好きだよ。けれど，日本人が礼儀正しく，秩序を守り，法律を遵守する国民だという固定観念が，ここ数日でひどく崩れたんだ。日本人全部を一緒くたにするのはよくないことだとはわかっているけれど，こんな状況ですで自転車の乗り方なんてわかるわけがない。

イチロー：おそらく君はカルチャーショックに苦しんでいるだけで，なにもそんなにヒステリックになることはないよ。いったん特定のルールと異国の行動パターンに慣れてしまえば，きっとニューヨークでサイクリングするのと同じくらい簡単だと思うようになるよ。

ケン：単にルールが少し違っているだけという問題なら僕も気にしないんだけれど，ルールが異なっているという問題であるというより，むしろルールがまったくない，それも本当にまったくないという事実であるという悲観的な結論に，悲しいけれど確実に達したんだ。

イチロー：おいおい，落ち着いて，もっと気楽に構えなよ。そもそも人生はそんなにつらいもんじゃないよ。きっと自転車をあきらめたことを後悔するぜ。

ケン：確かに君の言う通りかもしれない。けれど，それなら説明してくれないか？日本で自転車に乗る人たちは，なぜ交通規則を目に余るほど無視して，道路の両側を見境なく，往来の流れに従ったり無視したりして乗るのか，曲がったり突然停止したり方向転換する際になぜ合図を出さないのか，脇や正面さえなぜ見ようとしないのか，自転車に乗りながらなぜ携帯電話で話をするのか，あるいは夜ライトもつけずになぜ道路や歩道を走るのか，ということを。歩行者が，自転車に乗る人たちのことを，潜在的に自殺願望傾向がある危険な狂人たちだ，とみなす傾向があるのも，不思議なことではないよ。

Lesson2-1　問題解答

(1) d. physical　　(2) b. Generally speaking　　(3) b. face
(4) d. verbal　　(5) a. confident　　(6) c. discourage　　(7) b. during

Lesson2-2　問題解答

1. (1) b. divided between extremes of normal life and social breakdown.
   (2) a. as more and more people live in the city, the more it will become widely held.
2. (1) d. Save money.　　(2) a. Flat fees
   (3) d. Studying abroad doesn't have to be expensive.

Lesson2-3　問題解答

1. (1) j. Why don't you　　(2) b. How about
   (3) f. I'm afraid that　　(4) k. You could
   (5) e. I recommend that　　(6) d. How would it be if
   (7) h. That would
2. (1) d. Not at all.　　(2) g.―b.―f. (*You* are *aware* of *the* speed limit)
   (3) b. As it happens　　(4) a. I can't say I did.
3. (1) d. it's high time　　(2) b. you were enjoying yourself
   (3) b. hysterical　　(4) c. I wouldn't mind if
   (5) a. but in that case　　(6) d. No wonder why
   (7) h.―a. (it's *wrong* to generalize, *but* I can't get)
   (8) e.―c. (they carry *on* cellular phone *conversations* while cycling)

LESSON 3　長文問題：基本編

1　リード部付き内容一致問題
処理手順を確立しよう。

TRACK 01

出題学部：全学部で出題歴あり。

リード部付き内容一致問題

《おすすめアプローチ》
1. リード部だけ先読みして，本文中で探すべき情報をつかむ。
2. リード部に該当する箇所を探す意識で本文を読み進める。その際，細かい表現だけでなくパラグラフ内の論旨展開，またパラグラフ相互の関係を常に意識すること。
3. 該当する箇所と思われる表現が出てきたらチェックしておく。
4. パラグラフ通読，もしくは全文通読後，該当すると思われる箇所について，本文⇔選択肢の検討を慎重に行い，解答となる選択肢を決定する。

《得点力アップの道筋》
1. 本文は，平素から前後の文との関係を把握しながら読み進める。
2. 練習段階では，該当箇所⇔選択肢の照合作業には時間をかけて納得するまで取り組む。それが本番での速さにつながる。
3. 以上の点を踏まえて，全学部のリード部付き内容一致問題や英問英答問題に取り組む。

（Lesson3 問題解答は p.134, 135 にあります）

問題 1 （政治経済学部出題）

When cars run on electric power they not only save fuel and cut emissions but also run more quietly. Ordinarily, people might welcome quieter cars on the roads. However, as the use of hybrid and electric vehicles grows, a new concern is growing, too: pedestrians and cyclists find it hard to hear them coming, especially when the cars are moving slowly through a busy town or maneuvering in a parking lot. Some drivers say that when their cars are in electric mode people are more likely to step out in front of them. The solution, many now believe, is to fit electric and hybrid cars with external sound systems.

Choose the most suitable answer from those below to complete the following sentence.

One problem concerning the use of hybrid and electric vehicles is that they

    a. contribute most to heavy traffic in busy towns.
    b. have trouble moving around in a parking lot.
    c. make it hard for drivers to hear external sounds.
    d. make too little noise to be easily noticed.
    e. save fuel but increase emissions.

Lesson3　長文問題：基本編-1

二本柳のひとことコメント

リード部を先読みして，該当箇所を手早く見つけよう。逆接表現の直後の文は，早稲田大のお気に入りの設問箇所だ。

「自動車が電力で動くと，燃料の節約になり，排気ガスの排出量を削減するだけでなく，より静かに走行するようになる。普通なら，人々は路上での騒音の少ない自動車を歓迎するところだろう。ところが，ハイブリッドカーや電気自動車の利用が増えるにつれて，新たな懸念も生じつつある。歩行者や自転車に乗っている人は，そういった車が近づいてくる音が聞こえづらいのだ。特に交通量が多い町中を低速で走行しているときや，駐車場内で車を動かしているときはなおさらだ。自分の車が電力で走行しているときは，目の前に人が出てくる可能性がより高くなる，と語るドライバーもいる。解決策としては，電気自動車やハイブリッドカーに音を出す装置を取り付けることだと，今では多くの人が考えている」

■指示文訳：次の文を完成させるのに最も適切な答えを以下から選べ。
「ハイブリッドカーや電気自動車の使用に関する問題点の1つは，それらが…ということだ」
　a. 交通量が多い町中で渋滞の最大の原因となる。
　b. 駐車場内で動き回るのに苦労する。
　c. ドライバーが外部の音を聞き取るのが大変である。
　d. あまりにも音を立てないので，なかなか気づかれない。
　e. 燃料の節約にはなるが，排気ガスの排出量は増加する。

✓ word check !

- emissions　排気ガスの排出量
- electric vehicle　電気自動車
- pedestrian　歩行者
- step out　（人が）出てくる
- fit ... with ～　…に～を取り付ける
- heavy traffic　渋滞
- hybrid vehicle　ハイブリッドカー
- concern　懸念
- maneuver　（車を）動かす
- solution　解決策
- contribute to ～　～の原因となる

問題 2 （国際教養学部出題）

It may seem that, in making the assumption that the coffeehouse sprang logically from the commercial need to sell the prepared beverage, we are overlooking another obvious possibility. One still finds in Istanbul and the cities of the Levant street vendors who sell everything from kebabs and grilled fish to sour cherry juice and even water. Why was this type of sale not applied to coffee as well? Coffee, quite simply, has to be prepared and consumed in a particular manner, one that rules out a completely mobile operation. Coffee, particularly in the form in which it was and is drunk in the Middle East, must be served and drunk hot. European accounts emphasize that Arabs and Turks liked their brew very hot. If coffee is to be served at such a temperature, a strolling coffee vendor would not be able merely to prepare it in large quantities ahead of time and carry it around, selling it as he went, without some sort of elaborate apparatus for keeping it warm. Similarly, the customer cannot merely have a steaming cup of coffee put in his hands and be expected to swallow it down. Turkish coffee, when first poured, is full of powdery grounds which, left undisturbed, settle in about a minute into a thick mud at the bottom of the cup, leaving an inch and a half or so of clear coffee on top. This may well be what accounts for the fact that the Turks sip their coffee more slowly. All this is best accomplished with a stationary and relatively protected place of consumption. Coffee demands that you take your time.

（中　略）

Lesson3　長文問題：基本編-1

　In the long run what kept the coffeehouse jammed was the fact that its facilities for sitting and having a cup offered the perfect setting for socializing with one's fellow patrons. This role of the coffeehouse as a center of social intercourse was clearly what fueled the controversy surrounding coffee. The moral question had nothing to do with what one drank in the coffeehouse, but rather with social anxieties concerning why one came, with whom one associated, and what one did alone or in groups in these places.

Choose the best way to complete the following sentence.

The passage suggests that, in the Middle East, coffee
　　a. has been at the center of debates concerning morality.
　　b. is consumed quickly while hot.
　　c. is frequently sold by street vendors.
　　d. is sold like tea and cherry juice.

　二本柳のひとことコメント

該当文を要約したり，本文全体との関係で総括させるのも，早稲田大のお気に入りの設問だ。

　「用意された飲み物を売るという商業的必要性からコーヒーハウスが必然的に生まれたという推測をすると，明らかな可能性をもう1つ見過ごすことになるかもしれないように思われる。今でもイスタンブールやレヴァント地方には，ケバブや焼き魚からすっぱいサクランボのジュースや水まで，ありとあらゆるものを売っている露天商人の姿がある。なぜこうした売り方がコーヒーにも使われなかったのだろうか？　きわめて単純なことだが，コーヒーは，特別な入れ方で飲まなければならず，その入れ方のせいで，完全に移動式で販売することは除外されてしまう。コーヒーは，特に中東で昔も今も飲まれている形式で

は，熱くして出し，飲まなければならない。ヨーロッパ人の説明によると，アラブ人やトルコ人は非常に熱く入れて飲むのを好んでいたことが強調されている。もしコーヒーがそのような温度で出されなければならないとしたら，保温するための何らかの精巧な器具でもなければ，前もって大量に入れておき，持って回りながら売って歩くことなどできなかっただろう。同様に，客も，単に湯気のたっているコーヒーカップを両手に持ち，飲み干すことなどまずできない。トルココーヒーは，注ぎたてのときはざらざらした粉がいっぱいで，そっとしておくと1分ほどでカップの底に沈んで厚い泥のようにたまり，その上に1インチ半ほどのコーヒーの上澄みが残る。これで，トルコ人がコーヒーをよりゆっくりするという事実の説明がおそらくつくだろう。こういったことはすべて，固定した比較的保護された飲み場所でこそ最もうまく行うことができる。コーヒは，ゆっくり時間をかけることを求めているのだ。　　（中略）

　結局，コーヒーハウスを繁盛させたのは，腰掛けてコーヒーを1杯飲むための施設が，仲間の客たちとの絶好の交流の場を提供したという事実だった。社交の中心としてのコーヒーハウスのこういった役割は，明らかにコーヒーにまつわる論争に火を注ぐものだった。道徳性に関する問題は，コーヒーハウスで飲むものには何の関係もなく，むしろなぜ人はコーヒーハウスにやって来るのか，誰と付き合っているのか，そしてこういった場所で1人きりもしくは集団で何をしているのか，といったことに関する社会的不安に関わるものだった」

■指示文訳：次の文を完成させるのに最も適切なものを選べ。
　「中東ではコーヒーは，…と，本文は示唆している」
　a. 道徳性に関する論争の的だった。
　b. 冷めないうちにすばやく飲み干される。
　c. 露店の物売りによって販売されることが多い。
　d. お茶やチェリージュースのように売られている。

✓ word check !

- assumption　推測
- vendor　物売り
- rule out 〜　〜を除外する
- account　説明
- elaborate　精巧な
- be accomplished　達成される
- in the long run　結局
- facility　施設
- social intercourse　社交
- overlook 〜　〜を見過ごす
- apply to 〜　〜に適用する
- operation　作業
- strolling　ぶらついている
- apparatus　器具
- sip 〜　〜を少しずつ飲む
- stationary　固定された
- socialize　交流する
- controversy　論争

LESSON 3 長文問題：基本編

2 内容一致問題
選択肢は無理に先読みしなくてもよい。

TRACK 04

出題学部：全学部で出題歴あり。

内容一致問題

《おすすめアプローチ》
1. 選択肢が英文の場合，無理に先読みしなくてもよい。本文を少なくとも半分程度読み進め，本文内容がある程度つかめてからでよい。
2. 選択肢を先読みする場合，キーワード（名詞中心）をチェックしてから本文の該当箇所を探す。ただし，この方法を用いても時間がかかりすぎる場合には，1のやり方に戻ること。
3. 該当すると思われる箇所に到達したら，本文⇔選択肢の検討を慎重に行い，解答となる選択肢を決定する。ただし，基本は消去法である。

《得点力アップの道筋》
1. 自分なりの処理手順を確立する。
2. 練習段階では時間をかけて該当箇所を見つけ，判断理由を突き詰める。
3. 以上の点を踏まえて，全学部の内容一致問題に取り組む。

（Lesson3 問題解答は p.134, 135 にあります）

問題 1 （商学部出題）

You have heard it for years: to lose weight, go to the gym. But while physical activity is crucial for good health, it doesn't always melt off the weight — in fact, it can add some. Here is why.

One of the most widely accepted, commonly repeated assumptions in our culture is that if you exercise, you will lose weight. I exercise all the time obsessively, but my weight remains the same 74 kg it has been most of my adult life. I still have stomach fat that hangs over my belt when I sit. Why isn't all the exercise wiping it out?

The basic problem is that while it is true that exercise burns calories and that you must burn calories to lose weight, exercise has another effect: it can stimulate hunger. That causes us to eat more, which in turn can negate the weight loss benefits we just acquired. Exercise, in other words, does not necessarily help us lose weight. It may be even making it harder.

People who regularly exercise are at significantly lower risk for all manners of diseases — those of the heart in particular. They less often develop cancer, diabetes and many other illnesses. In addition, exercise improves your mental health and cognitive ability. A study found that older people who exercise at least once a week are 30% more likely to maintain cognitive function than those who exercise less. But the past few years of obesity research show that the role of exercise in weight loss has been widely overstated.

After we exercise, we often yearn for sugary calories like those in muffins or in sports drinks. A standard bottle of sports drink contains 130 calories. If you are hot and thirsty after a 20-minute run in summer heat, it is easy to drink that bottle in 20 seconds, in which case the calorie output and the calorie intake are probably the same. From a weight loss perspective, you would have been better off sitting on the sofa knitting.

Ultimately, the problem is about not exercise itself but the way we have come to define it. Many obesity researchers now believe that very frequent, low-level physical activity — the kind humans did for tens of thousands of years before the leaf blower was invented — may actually work better for us than the occasional bouts of exercise you get as a gym member.

In short, it is what you eat, not how hard to try to work it off, that matters more in losing weight. You should exercise to improve your health, but be warned: intense spurts of vigorous exercise could lead to weight gain.

注　diabetes：糖尿病　　　cognitive：認知的　　　obesity：肥満

次の 1〜5 について，本文の内容に合うものは T の欄に，合わないものは F の欄に記せ。

1. Pushing people to more physical exercise actually contributes to our obesity problem.
2. Physical exercise is good for lowering the risk of many illnesses.
3. Physical exercise may strengthen various aspects of cognitive functioning.
4. If you are more physically active, you might get hungry and drink and eat more.
5. Regular activity during our waking hours does not benefit our health much.

T : _____

F : _____

Lesson3　長文問題：基本編-2

> 二本柳のひとことコメント

1. 下線部が本文中に記述なし。思い込みで判断してはならない。判断が易しくない選択肢。

<u>Pushing people to more physical exercise</u> actually <u>contributes to our obesity problem.</u>
「人々にもっと体を動かして運動するように強いることは，実際には肥満の問題の一因となっている」

2. 以下を言い換えただけなので早稲田大レベルでは平易な選択肢。

Physical exercise is good for lowering the risk of many illnesses.
「運動は，多くの病気にかかる可能性を低くするのに役立っている」

> People who regularly exercise are at significantly **lower risk** for all manners of **diseases** ― those of the heart in particular.

問題文訳［81ページ］ **2** 参照

3. 以下参照。❶の具体的説明が❷となっており，それらをまとめたのが選択肢の表現。これまた早稲田大の定番。

Physical exercise may strengthen various aspects of cognitive functioning.
「運動は，認知機能のさまざまな側面を強化するかもしれない」

> ❶ In addition, **exercise improves your mental health and cognitive ability.** ❷ A study found that **older people who exercise at least once a week are 30% more likely to maintain cognitive function** than those who exercise less.

問題文訳［81ページ］ **3** 参照

4. ❶原因→❷結果，その具体例が❸。

If you are more physically active, you might get hungry and drink and eat more.
「もし肉体面でより積極的であれば，空腹になって飲食の量も増加するかもしれない」

> ❶ The basic problem is that while it is true that exercise burns calories and that you must burn calories to lose weight, **exercise has another effect: it can stimulate hunger.** ❷ **That causes us to eat more,** which in turn can negate the weight loss benefits we just acquired.
>
> 問題文訳［81 ページ］ **4-①** 参照

> ❸ If you are hot and thirsty after a 20-minute run in summer heat, it is easy to drink that bottle in 20 seconds, in which case the calorie output and the calorie intake are probably the same.
>
> 問題文訳［81 ページ］ **4-③** 参照

5. 以下が該当文だが選択肢とは肯定⇔否定が逆。内容に一致しない選択肢としては判断が楽なので必ず正解したい。

Regular activity during our waking hours does not benefit our health much.
「起きている時間に行う規則的な活動は，人間の健康にあまり利益をもたらさない」

> Many obesity researchers now believe that **very frequent**, low-level physical **activity** — the kind humans did for tens of thousands of years before the leaf blower was invented — **may actually work better** for us than the occasional bouts of exercise you get as a gym member.
>
> 問題文訳［81 ページ］ **5** 参照

問題文訳

　長年にわたって，次のような言葉を耳にしている。「減量するにはジムに行きなさい」。しかし，肉体的活動は健康にとって必要不可欠ではあるが，そうしたからといって必ずしも体重が減るとは限らないのだ。——それどころか実際にはいくらか体重が増える場合もある。理由は以下のとおりだ。

　われわれの文化の中で最も広く受け入れられ，最もふつうに繰り返されている思い込みは，運動すれば体重が減るというものだ。私はとりつかれたように常に運動しているが，体重はずっと74キロで変わらず，これは成人してからのほとんどの期間変化していない。それでも，座るとベルトに覆いかぶさるほど腹回りには脂肪がついている。四六時中運動していてなぜ脂肪が落ちないのだろうか。

　4-① 基本的な問題は，確かに運動すればカロリーが消費されるし，減量するためにはカロリーを消費しなければならないのは間違いないのだが，運動は別の効果ももたらすということだ。つまり，運動は食欲を刺激する可能性があるのだ。そのため，より多く食べてしまい，それによって手に入れたばかりの体重減少という恩恵を，逆に帳消しにしてしまう可能性もある。言い換えると，運動は，必ずしも減量に役立つとは限らない。運動することで，減量がいっそう難しくなってしまうかもしれないのだ。

　2 定期的に運動する人たちは，あらゆる種類の病気，特に心臓病にかかる可能性が明らかに低い。彼らは，ガンや糖尿病，それにその他多くの病気になる頻度が低い場合が多い。
　3 さらに，運動は精神面での健康や認知能力を向上させる。ある研究で判明したのは，最低でも週に1回運動する高齢者は，それほど運動しない高齢者よりも，認知機能を維持する可能性が30%高い，ということだ。しかし，過去数年間の肥満に関する調査は，体重減少における運動の役割がはなはだしく誇張されてきたことを示している。

　運動した後は，マフィンやスポーツドリンクの中に含まれるもののような，糖分を含んだカロリーが無性に欲しくなることが多い。普通のスポーツドリンク1本は130カロリーである。4-③ 夏の暑さの中で20分走った後，身体が熱くなり，のどが渇いていれば，1本を20秒で簡単に飲んでしまうが，その場合，消費カロリーと摂取カロリーはおそらく同じ数値である。体重減少という観点からは，ソファーに座って編み物をしている方がよいだろう。

　結局，問題は運動そのものではなく，運動がどう定義されるようになったかにある。5 現在，たいへん頻繁に行う軽い肉体的活動，つまり落ち葉を吹き飛ばす機械が発明される以前に人類が何万年もの間やっていたようなことのほうが，ジムの会員として時々ひとしきり運動するよりも，実際には効果があるのかもしれない，と信じている肥満研究者は多い。

　要するに，減量する際により重要なのは，何を食べるかであり，どれだけ懸命にそれを運動で消費しようとするかではないのだ。健康を増進するために運動はするべきだが，注意しなければならないこともある。それは，激しい運動を一気に猛烈に行うと体重が増えてしまうことにもなりかねない，ということである。

✅ word check !

- crucial　必要不可欠な
- assumption　思い込み
- stomach　腹
- negate 〜　〜を帳消しにする
- not necessarily 〜　必ずしも〜とは限らない
- significantly　明らかに
- yearn for 〜　〜が欲しくなる
- calorie intake　摂取カロリー
- define 〜　〜を定義する
- vigorous　激しい
- melt off 〜　〜が減る
- obsessively　とりつかれたように
- stimulate 〜　〜を刺激する
- benefit　恩恵
- overstate 〜　〜を誇張する
- calorie output　消費カロリー
- perspective　観点
- matter　重要である

問題 2 (教育学部出題)

A probe from NASA designed to seek out potentially life-bearing planets around other stars was being readied for work after being launched from Cape Canaveral. It is designed to find the first Earth-size planets in habitable zones — orbiting stars at a distance where water could pool on their surface. It is not capable of detecting life itself, but it should be able to spot planets capable of bearing life. Such a discovery would be an important event which astronomers hope would show that small rocky planets such as Earth are common and would encourage other missions to study them in detail.

A professor of planetary science said Kepler was far more than just another science probe. "Kepler's mission is to find mankind's place in the universe. If we find planets with orbits similar to that of Earth then there is a chance they, too, could harbour life," he said. The Kepler probe, from its position following the Earth in its orbit around the sun, is designed to spot the tiny "twinkles" made by stars as their orbiting planets pass in front of them, a movement known as transiting.

Kepler will focus on one star-rich area of the sky in the constellations Cygnus and Lyra. Over the next six years it will simultaneously measure variations in the brightness of more than 100,000 stars, searching for the tiny decreases in light output that might signify a transiting planet. An ultra-sensitive 95 megapixel camera will be used. The camera can detect the virtually imperceptible dimming of a car headlight when a fly crosses it.

The mission is riddled with technical difficulties. Transits, for example, are seen only when a planet's orbit is aligned with the line of sight from Earth. The chances of any distant planet having such an alignment are less than 1%. In addition, an Earth-size planet transiting a star similar in size to the sun will cause a change in brightness of only 84 parts per million — less than $1/100^{th}$ of 1%. Kepler's photometer, the light-detecting instrument at its heart, had to be among the most sensitive ever deployed to detect such tiny fluctuations.

Such methods have already helped to locate more than 300 large planets outside the solar system. Most of those are extreme places with crushing gravity resulting from their great size and roasting temperatures caused by orbiting close to their stars. Kepler will be looking for planets that are much smaller and which lie in the so-called Goldilocks zone, cool enough for liquid water to exist but not so cold that it freezes. "We will monitor a wide range of stars from small cool ones, where planets must circle closely to stay warm, to stars bigger and hotter than the sun, where planets must stay well clear to avoid being roasted," said the principal investigator for the mission. "If Kepler can find such planets, then the next generation of satellites can examine their atmospheres to find gases like oxygen that suggest life has emerged," said another scientist.

本文の内容と合致するものを **a〜h** から **2つ**選べ。

a. It is well known that small rocky planets are commonly found in the universe.
b. Kepler can only find possible life-bearing planets, but not any actual evidence which suggests life.
c. Kepler has already been launched and is ready to start work.
d. Kepler is capable of detecting a tiny fluctuation such as a change in brightness less than 0.001%.
e. Kepler is similar to other science probes in that it is capable of detecting life.
f. Kepler resembles other science probes in that it can spot planets capable of bearing life.
g. Most of the large planets so far found are located in the so-called Goldilocks zone.
h. When stars are bigger and hotter, their planets must orbit closer to stay warm.

_____ , _____

> 二本柳のひとことコメント

a. 文中の **would** に注目。まだ現実になっていない。仮定法は内容一致問題の頻出文法項目。

It is well known that small rocky planets are commonly found in the universe.
「小さくて岩石の多い惑星が宇宙では一般的に存在することは，よく知られている」

> Such a discovery **would** be an important event which astronomers hope **would** show that small rocky planets such as Earth are common and **would** encourage other missions to study them in detail.

問題文訳［89ページ］ **a** 参照

b. 下記の文の言い換え。正解しなければいけない。

Kepler can only find possible life-bearing planets, but not any actual evidence which suggests life.
「ケプラーは，生命を産む可能性がある惑星を発見することだけはできるが，何であれ生命を暗示する実際の証拠は見つけることができない」

> It is not **capable** of detecting life itself, but it **should be able to** spot planets capable of bearing life.

問題文訳［89ページ］ **b** 参照

c. 下記の文の言い換え。これも正解しなければ。

Kepler has already been launched and is ready to start work.
「ケプラーはすでに打ち上げられており，作動する準備は整っている」

> A probe from NASA designed to seek out potentially life-bearing planets around other stars **was being readied for work after being launched** from Cape Canaveral.

問題文訳［89ページ］ **c** 参照

d. 「1%の100分の1」とは0.01%である。数値のすり替えも誤りの選択肢の定番。

Kepler is capable of detecting a tiny fluctuation such as a change in brightness less than 0.001%.
「ケプラーは，0.001％以下の明るさの変化のような，微小な変動を探知することができる」

> In addition, an Earth-size planet transiting a star similar in size to the sun will cause a change in brightness of only 84 parts per million — less than **1/100th of 1%**.

問題文訳［89ページ］ d 参照

e. 選択肢と反対の内容であることに注目。

Kepler is similar to other science probes in that it is capable of detecting life.
「ケプラーは，生命を見つけることができるという点で，その他の科学探査機と似ている」

> It is **not capable** of detecting life itself, but it should be able to spot planets capable of bearing life.

問題文訳［89ページ］ e 参照

f. 下線部についての記述は，本文中のどこにもない。このような「本文中に記述なし」という選択肢を確実に切れる読み方を心がけたい。

Kepler <u>resembles other science probes</u> in that it can spot planets capable of bearing life.
「ケプラーは，生命を産むことができる惑星を見つけることができるということにおいて，その他の科学探査機と似ている」

g. 2つの文をごちゃ混ぜにした「でっち上げ」の誤り。これも学部を問わず早稲田大の定番の誤り選択肢。

Most of the large planets so far found are located in the so-called Goldilocks zone.
「これまで発見された大きな惑星のほとんどは，いわゆるゴルディロックスゾーンに位置している」

> Most of those are extreme places with crushing gravity resulting from their **great size** and roasting temperatures caused by orbiting close to their stars. Kepler will be looking for planets that are **much smaller** and which lie in the so-called **Goldilocks zone**, cool enough for liquid water to exist but not so cold that it freezes.

問題文訳［89ページ］ **g** 参照

h. 選択肢 g と同様「でっち上げ」。ひっかかりやすい選択肢。思い込みで判断せず，必ず本文を目で見て確認。

When stars are bigger and hotter, their planets must orbit closer to stay warm.
「恒星がより大きく高温になるとき，その惑星は，暖かさを保つために接近して軌道を回らなくてはならない」

> "We will monitor a wide range of stars **from small cool ones, where planets must circle closely to stay warm, to stars bigger** and hotter than the sun, where planets must stay well clear to avoid being roasted," said the principal investigator for the mission.

問題文訳［89ページ］ **h** 参照

問題文訳

c 太陽系以外の恒星の周囲にある，生命を産む可能性を秘めた惑星を探し出すために設計されたNASAの探査機は，ケープ・カナヴェラルから打ち上げられ，その後，作動する準備が整えられていた。それは，生命居住可能領域で最初の地球サイズの惑星を見つけるように設計されている。その惑星とは，少し離れて恒星の周りを回り，表面に水をためることができるものだ。b・e 探査機は，生命そのものを見つけることはできないが，生命を産むことができる惑星を特定することはできるはずである。a そのような発見は，重要な出来事になるだろうし，それは，天文学者が望んでいることだが，地球のような岩石の多い小さな惑星はどこにでもあることを示し，他のミッションがそういった惑星を詳細に研究する励みとなるだろう。

ある惑星学の教授は，ケプラーは単なる科学探査機の1台をはるかに超えたものであると言った。「ケプラーのミッションは，宇宙に人間が住める場所を見つけることである。もし私たちが地球とよく似た軌道を持つ惑星を発見すれば，そこも生命の住みかとなる可能性がある」と，彼は言った。ケプラー探査機は，太陽を回る地球の軌道上で地球の後を追いかけているその位置から，軌道上の惑星が恒星の前を通過する際，恒星が発する微小な「またたき」を検出することができるように設計されている。その動きは天体面通過として知られているのだが。

ケプラーは，白鳥座と琴座の中にある，恒星が多く集まった上空の1つの場所に焦点を合わせる。今後6年以上は，惑星の通過を示している可能性のある微小な減光を探して，10万以上の恒星の光度の変化を同時に計測することになるだろう。95メガピクセルの超高感度カメラが使用されるだろう。そのカメラは，ハエが横切った際の車のヘッドライトの，実際には感知できない減光を検出することができる。

このミッションは技術的な困難に満ちている。例えば，天体面通過というのは，惑星の軌道が地球からの視線と直線で結ばれているときにしか見えない。どんな距離の惑星もそのような位置にある可能性は1％以下である。d さらに，太陽と同じくらいの大きさの恒星を横切っている地球サイズの惑星は，輝度の点で，わずか100万分の84の変化が起きるだけである。これは，1％の100分の1以下の割合である。光を感知する計器をその心臓部に持つケプラーの光度計は，そのようなわずかな変動を感知するため，これまで配備されたものの中で，最も感度の高いものの1つでなければならなかった。

このような手法はすでに，太陽系の外にある300以上の大きな惑星を探し当てるのに役立っている。g それらの惑星のほとんどは，その巨大さのために生じる，押しつぶされるような重力と，恒星に接近した軌道を持つために生じる，焼けつくような温度を持つ極端な場所である。ケプラーは，それらよりもはるかに小さくて，液体の水が存在するのに十分な涼しさであるが，それが凍るほど寒くはない，いわゆるゴルディロックスゾーンにある惑星を探す予定である。h 「私たちは，惑星が暖かさを保つために接近して回らなければなら

ないような，小さくて低温の恒星から，惑星が焼けつくことを回避するために十分距離をおく必要があるような，太陽よりも大きくて高温の恒星まで，幅広い範囲の恒星を観測するつもりです」と，このミッションの主任研究員は語った。「もしケプラーが，そのような惑星を発見することができれば，次世代の人工衛星は，生命が出現したことを暗示する酸素のような気体を発見するために，その惑星の大気を調査することができるのです」と，別の科学者は言った。

✓ word check !

- probe　探査機
- habitable zone　生命居住可能領域
- detect ～　～を見つける
- astronomer　天文学者
- encourage ～ to *do*　～が…するように励ます
- in detail　詳細に
- simultaneously　同時に
- signify ～　～を示す
- imperceptible　感知できない
- be riddled with ～　～に満ちている
- be aligned with ～　～と直線で結ばれている
- deploy ～　～を配備する
- locate ～　～を探し当てる
- gravity　重力
- principal investigator　主任研究員
- seek out ～　～を探し出す
- orbit ～　～の軌道を回る
- spot ～　～を特定する
- planetary science　惑星学
- variation　変化
- ultra-sensitive　超高感度の
- dim　薄暗くなる
- fluctuation　変動
- crush ～　～を押しつぶす
- monitor ～　～を観測する
- atmosphere　大気

LESSON 3 長文問題：基本編

3 同意語句選択問題
主に文脈判断と選択肢代入で解答決定。

出題学部：全学部で出題歴あり。

TRACK 07

同意語句選択問題

《おすすめアプローチ》
1. 下線部の意味がわからなくても，文脈上のさまざまな意味決定手法（代用表現・パラグラフの要旨など）を用いて意味を探る。早稲田大の問題は，これで意味が決定できる場合が多い。
2. 下線部の意味が決定できなければ，「プラス」や「マイナス」などのイメージだけでも押さえる。
3. 最終的には各選択肢を代入して，解答を決定する。

《得点力アップの道筋》
1. いくら語彙力をつけても，雑な読み方で「速さ」ばかり追求していては「何となく書いてあることは理解できる」段階までは到達しても，合否が分かれる設問の「正答率」は上がらない。未知の表現が登場したら，本文中で内容決定ができないか考察してみること。平素の堅実な読解姿勢が正答率に如実に反映する。
2. 同意語句選択問題の正解根拠を自ら説明できるように復習する。
3. 以上の点を踏まえて，全学部の同意語句選択問題に取り組む。

（Lesson3 問題解答は p.134, 135 にあります）

問題 1 単語の同意語句選択 (法学部出題)

One way to determine the extent to which free speech should be guaranteed would be to take into consideration the cultural and historical context. Some legal scholars point to such differences between Europe and the United States as the reason for the differences in their perspectives. For example, Dieter Grimm, a former justice in the *Bundesverfassungsgericht* [the German Constitutional Court], explains and justifies the criminalization, in Germany, of saying the Holocaust did not happen, as a message to its Jewish population that "atrocities like these should never happen again under the responsibility of the German state." It could be argued that the United States can afford to give greater tolerance to such views that deny the Holocaust than can Germany, where such tolerance would raise memories of the state's involvement in the genocide.

Choose the best way to complete the sentence, which relates to the underlined word in the passage.

Here "atrocities" means
- a. bad decisions.
- b. chronic forgetfulness.
- c. cruel acts.
- d. subtle differences.
- e. unfair punishments.

Lesson3　長文問題：基本編-3

二本柳のひとことコメント

下線部直後の **like these** に注目。代名詞や指示語は常に復元して読み進める。

「言論の自由を保証すべき程度を決定する1つの方法は，文化的および歴史的背景を考慮に入れることである。ヨーロッパとアメリカにおけるそういった差異が，それぞれの考え方の差異の根拠である，と指摘する法学者もいる。たとえば *Bundesverfassungsgericht*〔ドイツ憲法裁判所〕の元判事，ディーター・グリムは，ホロコーストは起きなかったと発言することを違憲としていることを，「このような残虐行為がドイツ国家の責任下で二度と起こってはならない」という，ユダヤ系市民に対するメッセージであると説明し，正当化している。ホロコーストを否定するような見解に対しては，ドイツよりもアメリカのほうが寛大な態度を示す余裕があると言えるかもしれない。というのも，ドイツではこのようなことを許容すれば，国家があの大量殺戮に加担したという記憶を呼び覚ましてしまうだろうからだ」

■指示文訳：文章中の下線部を引いた単語に関係のある文を完成させるのに最も適切なものを選べ。

「ここでの"atrocities"の意味は」
 a. 悪い決断。　　b. 慢性的な物忘れ。　　c. 残虐な行為。
 d. 微妙な差異。　　e. 不当な処罰。

✓ word check !

・guarantee〜　〜を保証する

・take into consideration〜　〜を考慮に入れる

・context　背景　　　　　　　・legal scholar　法学者

・justice　判事　　　　　　　・justify〜　〜を正当化する

・population　市民　　　　　　・responsibility　責任

・tolerance　寛大な態度　　　　・involvement　加担

・genocide　大量殺戮

問題2 イディオムの同意語句選択（スポーツ科学部出題） 〔TRACK 09〕

Read the following passage and answer the question.

Mark is not alone. Though his situation is difficult, he feels what millions of workers feel: *fear*. But this fear isn't the fear that we typically think of when we talk about losing a job during an economic downturn and then having to wait until the economy picks up.

The phrase picks up in the paragraph is closest in meaning to _____.
 a. blames b. chooses c. improves d. singles out

二本柳のひとことコメント

下線部の前の then に注目。イディオムは「分解」して考える癖をつけよう（p.5, Lesson1-1(6)参照）。

■指示文訳：以下の文を読んで問いに答えよ。
「マーク（人名）だけではない。彼の置かれている状況は困難なものだが，何百万人もの労働者が感じていることを彼も感じている。すなわち「恐怖感」だ。しかし，この恐怖感は，景気後退の間に職を失い，次に，経済が回復するまで待たなければならないことについて語るときに，われわれが典型的に思い浮かべるような恐怖感ではない」

「文中の picks up の意味は…に最も近い」
 a. 非難する b. 選択する c. 改善する d. 選択する

★ **pick up** 「(ちくりと刺して) 拾い上げる」
 ⇒（上昇するというプラスイメージで）「回復する，立ち直る」

問題3 イディオムの同意語句選択（商学部出題）

So I made the call, left a message — "If this is the Rose who..." — and two hours later, my phone rang. I remembered the voice immediately. I remembered why I liked her. We picked up where we'd left off almost 40 years ago.

下線部の意味にもっとも近いものを a〜d から選べ。

a. concentrated on
b. ended up
c. remained together
d. started again

二本柳のひとことコメント

同じイディオムが繰り返し出題される場合がある。他学部の過去問にも貪欲に取り組みたい。

「(学生時代に船上で出会って，その後も心から離れないローズの居所がわかって) それで私は電話をかけ，メッセージを残した。──『もしこちらが…ローズさんのお宅なら』──すると2時間後，我が家の電話が鳴った。私はその声をすぐに思い出した。私はなぜ彼女のことが好きなのかを思い出した。私たちは，40年近く前に終わりになったところから，また出発した」
a. …に集中した　　b. 最後は…になった
c. 一緒にとどまった　d. 再び始めた

問題 4 文の同意選択 (商学部出題)

With the economy in recession, the first thing people cut from their budgets is non-essential items, and leisure travel obviously falls into this category. As a result, hotels have seen their occupancy rates decline significantly. Yet, as we know, "necessity is the mother of invention" and budget-conscious travelers have begun to look at innovative ways to pursue their love of travel, while at the same time reducing their lodging costs. Home-exchange allows people to do exactly that and also lets them save in other ways as well. For example, many people exchange cars and museum passes as part of the deal.

下線部の意味にもっとも近いものを a〜d から 1 つ選べ。
   a. bad fortune makes the world go round
   b. people become creative when the circumstances force them to adapt
   c. people have to save money when the economy is bad
   d. people need to become more productive in times of trouble

Lesson3　長文問題：基本編-3

> 二本柳のひとことコメント

格言だからといってあわてない。逆接表現の直後の文であることに注目。下線部より後に具体的説明あり。パラグラフの内容も踏まえて，選択肢dを切れるか，が少々難問。

「経済が後退するとともに，人々が最初に家計から削るものは，必要のない品目であり，レジャー旅行も明らかにこの範疇に入ってくる。その結果，各ホテルは，稼働率が著しく低下するという経験をした。しかしながら，ご存じのとおり，「必要は発明の母」であり，家計を気にする旅行者は，宿泊費を減らすと同時に旅行に対する愛情を追求するための革新的な方法を考え始めた。自宅交換を行うことで，人々はまさにそうすることができ，また，それ以外の点でも節約が可能になるのである。たとえば，取り決めの一部として自動車や美術館の入場券を交換するのだ」

a. 不運が世の中を動かしている
b. 環境が人に適応するよう強いると，人は創造的になる
c. 人は景気が悪いときは，貯金しなければならない
d. 人は困ったときに，より創造的になる必要がある

✓ word check !

- recession　後退
- item　品目
- innovative　革新的な
- budget　家計
- occupancy rates　稼働率
- pursue 〜　〜を追求する

LESSON 3　長文問題：基本編

4 文整序問題
パラグラフを自ら作る意識で。

TRACK 12

出題学部：政治経済学部，教育学部，基幹・創造・先進理工学部など。

文 整序問題

《おすすめアプローチ》
1. 各選択肢に目を通し，冠詞，指示語や接続語などの順序の決め手となりそうな表現をチェック。選択肢のいずれかに逆接表現が含まれているものがあれば，その選択肢を突破口にして順序を組み立てる。
2. 逆接表現を含む選択肢がなければ，各選択肢を抽象→具体という組み合わせでつなげることを中心に考える。
3. 早稲田大の文整序問題は，空所前後の文やパラグラフの内容が，正解の決め手となる場合がほとんどなので，空所後も読んで最終解答する。

《得点力アップの道筋》
1. まず，センター試験第3問を，年度を問わず正解の根拠を押さえながら解き，全問正解できるようにすること。解き方の基本は早稲田大入試と変わらない。
2. 日常の読解で論説文の各パラグラフの流れ（前後の文との関係など）を捉えるように心がけること。
3. 以上の点を踏まえて，最終的には各学部の同形式の設問に取り組むこと。

（Lesson3 問題解答は p.134, 135 にあります）

Lesson3 長文問題：基本編-4

問題 1 (基礎・創造・先進理工学部出題)

TRACK 13

Paragraph A below consists of four sentences 1-4 which are not in the correct order. Rearrange the sentences and choose the correct order from a-d.

[A] 1. Environmental agencies implemented plans to reduce emissions, and these were somewhat successful: Between 1980 and 1999, sulfur dioxide (SO_2) emissions decreased by roughly 40 percent in the United States and approximately 65 percent in Europe.

2. Most of this acidity was produced in the industrialized nations of the Northern Hemisphere — the United States, Canada, Japan, and most of the countries of Eastern and Western Europe.

3. Despite these efforts, however, massive damage was done to ecosystems around the world.

4. During the course of the 20th century, acid rain came to be recognized as a leading threat to the stability and quality of the Earth's environment.

a. 1-4-3-2   b. 4-3-2-1   c. 4-2-1-3   d. 1-2-3-4

■指示文訳：以下の段落［A］は 1〜4 の 4 つの文から成っているが，正しい順序になっていない。各文を並べ替えて，その正しい順序を a〜d から選べ。

> 二本柳のひとことコメント

1. **全体が具体例であることに着目。「酸性化に対する対策」であると要約できるか。**

「環境保護機関は排出物を削減する計画を実行に移し，いくらか成功した。1980 年から 1999 年の間に，二酸化硫黄（SO_2）の排出量がアメリカで約 40％，ヨーロッパで約 65％減少したのである」

> Environmental agencies **implemented plans to reduce emissions,** and these were **somewhat successful**: Between 1980 and 1999, **sulfur dioxide（SO_2）emissions decreased** by roughly 40 percent in the United States and approximately 65 percent in Europe.

2. **指示語を含んだ this acidity「この酸性化」に着目。4 で述べられている酸性雨が及ぼす影響を受けている。4→2 とつながる。**

「こういった酸性化の大半は北半球の工業国——アメリカ，カナダ，日本，そして東西ヨーロッパの大部分の国々——で引き起こされた」

> Most of **this acidity** was produced in the industrialized nations of the Northern Hemisphere — the United States, Canada, Japan, and most of the countries of Eastern and Western Europe.

3. **however**「しかしながら」という〈逆接〉を表す語が含まれているので，最初に注目すべき選択肢。**these efforts**「これらの努力」とあるので，1 の内容を受けていることがわかる。1→3 とつながる。

「しかしながら，このような努力にもかかわらず，甚大な損害が世界中の生態系に及ぼされた」

> Despite **these efforts**, **however**, **massive damage** was done to ecosystems around the world.

4. 実際には，4→2 と 1→3 が組み合わさった段階で選択肢を見れば，自ずと解答は確定する。速やかに正解したい設問。

「20 世紀の間に，酸性雨は，地球環境の安定と質に対する主要な脅威とみなされるようになった」

> **During the course of the 20th century**, **acid rain** came to be recognized as a leading threat to the stability and quality of the Earth's environment.

✓ word check !

- environmental agency　環境保護機関
- ecosystem　生態系
- threat　脅威
- implement ～　～を実行する
- acid rain　酸性雨

発展 〈逆接〉表現を含む文の特徴

　逆接表現の後にはいわゆる〈筆者の主張〉がくることになっているが，具体的にどの部分にくるのかは，その逆接表現の品詞によって異なるのでしっかり確認すること。

(1) **等位接続詞：but, 文頭の yet, and yet**

　　Ｓ Ｖ ～ 等位接続詞 Ｓ' Ｖ' …
　　等位接続詞のあとに〈主張〉が述べられる。

(2) **従属接続詞：although, as, even if, even though, though, whereas, while**

　　従属接続詞 Ｓ' Ｖ' ～，Ｓ Ｖ …　⎫
　　Ｓ Ｖ ～，従属接続詞 Ｓ' Ｖ' …　⎬ 主節で〈主張〉が述べられる。
　　Ｓ，従属接続詞 Ｓ' Ｖ' …，Ｖ ～　⎭

(3) **副詞（句）：all the same, 文頭で at the same time, conversely, however, instead（of this）, nevertheless, on the contrary, oppositely, still, though など**

　　副詞（句）は，文頭，文中などさまざまな位置に置かれるが，いずれにせよ主節で〈主張〉が述べられる。

(4) **前置詞（句）：despite, for all, in spite of, notwithstanding, with all など**

　　前置詞（句）も，文頭，文尾などさまざまな位置に置かれるが，いずれにせよ主節で〈主張〉が述べられる。

問題 2 （政治経済学部出題）

　Women with jobs have more money to pay corporations to do their cooking, yet all American women now allow corporations to cook for them when they can.

　(　　　　) The same process of peacetime conversion that industrialized our farming ― giving us synthetic fertilizers made from the chemicals used to develop weapons ― also industrialized our eating.

Choose the most suitable order of sentences from those below to fill in the blank space.

a. After World War Ⅱ, the food industry labored mightily to sell American women on all the processed-food wonders it had invented to feed soldiers.

b. As Laura Shapiro recounts in *Something from the Oven: Reinventing Dinner in 1950s America*, the food industry ― in an effort to promote this "instant everything" ― strived to "persuade millions of Americans to develop a lasting taste for meals that were very much like field rations."

c. Such processing methods had resulted in canned meals, freeze-dried foods, dehydrated potatoes, powdered orange juice and coffee ― instant everything.

d. Those corporations have been trying to persuade Americans to let them do the cooking since long before large numbers of women entered the workforce.

　　　　　　　　　　＿＿＿　→　＿＿＿　→　＿＿＿　→　＿＿＿

■指示文訳：以下の文を，空所を埋めるのに最も適切な順序に並べ替えよ。

> 二本柳のひとことコメント

a. 文全体が具体例であることに着目。After World War Ⅱ「第二次世界大戦後」が d の since long before large numbers of women entered the workforce「多数の女性が労働力に加わるずっと以前から」の具体例であることに気づけば d→a とつながる。

「第二次世界大戦後，兵士に食糧を供給するために発明した加工食品というすばらしいものをすべてアメリカ人女性に売りこもうと，食品業界は懸命に努力した」

> After World War Ⅱ, the food industry labored mightily to sell American women on all the processed-food wonders it had invented to feed soldiers.

b. 指示語を含んだ this "instant everything"「この『なにからなにまでインスタント食品』」に注目。c の instant everything「なにからなにまでインスタント食品」を指していることは明確なので c→b とつながる。

「ローラ・シャピロが『オーヴンの中から：1950 年代のアメリカにおけるディナー改革』の中で詳しく述べているように，食品業界は——この『なにからなにまでインスタント食品』を広めようと努力する中で——『何百万人ものアメリカ人に野戦食と非常によく似ている食事を永続的に好きになるよう説得』しようと励んだ」

> As Laura Shapiro recounts in *Something from the Oven: Reinventing Dinner in 1950s America*, the food industry — in an effort to promote this "instant everything" — strived to "persuade millions of Americans to develop a lasting taste for meals that were very much like field rations."

c. 指示語を含んだ文頭の **Such processing methods**「そのような加工方法」に注目。**a** の **all the processed-food wonders it had invented to feed soldiers**「兵士に食糧を供給するために発明した加工食品というすばらしいもの」を指していることに気づけば，**a→c** とつながる。

「そのような加工方法は，缶詰の食事，フリーズドライ食品，乾燥ポテト，粉末のオレンジジュースやコーヒーといった——なにからなにまでインスタント食品——を作り出してきた」

> **Such processing methods** had resulted in canned meals, freeze-dried foods, dehydrated potatoes, powdered orange juice and coffee — instant everything.

d. 指示語を含んだ文頭の **Those corporations**「それらの企業」に注目。直前の第１パラグラフ最終文に２か所登場する **corporations**「企業」を指していることに気づけば，この選択肢 **d** が先頭にくることがわかる。本設問は，実際には第２パラグラフ冒頭におかれているので，直前の第１パラグラフとの関係を念頭におく必要がある。

「それらの企業は，多数の女性が労働力に加わるずっと以前から，調理の作業は自分たちに任せてくれるようにアメリカ人を説得しようとしてきた」

> **Those corporations** have been trying to persuade Americans to let them do the cooking since long before large numbers of women entered the workforce.

問題文訳

　仕事を持つ女性は，企業に調理を肩代わりさせるのに支払うお金をより多く持っているが，今ではアメリカ人女性全員が，自分で調理ができるのに，企業に調理させているのである。それらの企業は，多数の女性が労働力に加わるずっと以前から，調理の作業は自分たちに任せてくれるようにアメリカ人を説得しようとしてきた。第二次世界大戦後，兵士に食糧を供給するために発明した加工食品というすばらしいものをすべてアメリカ人女性に売り込もうと，食品業界は懸命に努力した。そのような加工方法は，缶詰の食事，フリーズドライ食品，乾燥ポテト，粉末のオレンジジュースやコーヒーといった——なにからなにまでインスタント食品——を作り出してきた。ローラ・シャピロが『オーヴンの中から：1950年代のアメリカにおけるディナー改革』の中で詳しく述べているように，食品業界はこの『なにからなにまでインスタント食品』を広めようと努力する中で——『何百万人ものアメリカ人に野戦食と非常によく似ている食事を永続的に好きになるよう説得』しようと励んだ。兵器の開発に使用された化学薬品で作られた合成肥料を与えることで，我々の農業を工業化した平時の転換と同じプロセスが，我々の食事も工業化した。

✓ word check！

- food industry　食品業界
- processed-food　加工食品
- promote 〜　〜を促進する，広める
- strive　励む
- persuade 〜 to *do*　〜に…するよう説得する

問題 3 （政治経済学部出題）

Systems to do this are already being developed. Lotus Engineering, the consultancy of a British sportscar maker, recently signed an agreement with a producer of audio systems to commercialize one. Lotus has worked on a number of hybrid and electric vehicles, and it was while these were being used in its factory that the engineers thought they would be safer if they made a noise.

(　　　　)

It is possible to create a different sound within a car from the one that is heard outside, says Colin Peachey, a chief engineer with Lotus. Manufacturers could create their own sounds according to how they perceive their models. Drivers of electric cars might in the future even be able to select different engine sounds, and maybe download them as we currently do with ringtones for our cellphones.

Choose the most suitable order of sentences from those below to fill in the blank space.

a. Adding external speakers allows pedestrians to hear the noise, too.
b. Lotus modified its system so that it could produce sounds that change with speed, providing a familiar audible "feedback" to drivers of vehicles with a silent engine.
c. Sound canceling works by analyzing any unwanted frequencies and then producing counteracting ones.
d. The system Lotus uses was originally developed for a different reason: to cancel out excess noise inside a car.

_____ → _____ → _____ → _____

■指示文訳：以下の文を，空所を埋めるのに最も適切な順序に並べ替えよ。

二本柳のひとことコメント

a. 文末の **too**「…もまた」という〈追加〉を表す語に注目。「誰か人間が音を聞く」という内容が **a** の前にも書かれていることがわかる。

> Adding external speakers allows pedestrians to hear the noise, too.
> 「外部スピーカーを取りつけることで，歩行者もその音を聞き取ることができる」

b.「ドライバーが車の音を聞く」という内容の文なので，**a** と共通点があることから，**b→a** とつながる。さらに，この組み合わせは，空所の直後のパラグラフで述べられている「車内で発生させることができるさまざまな音」という具体例につながっていくことも気づかなければならない。

> Lotus modified its system so that it could produce sounds that change with speed, providing a familiar audible "feedback" to drivers of vehicles with a silent engine.
> 「ロータスは速度によって変化する音が出せるようにシステムを調整し，静かなエンジンを搭載した車のドライバーに，聞きなれた音を『フィードバック』するようにした」

c. 文全体の内容が，**d** の **to cancel out excess noise**「（車内部の）過剰な騒音を相殺すること」の具体的説明であるとわかるので，**d→c** とつながる。

> Sound canceling works by analyzing any unwanted frequencies and then producing counteracting ones.
> 「望ましくない振動数を分析し，それに対抗する振動数を発生させることによって音を消すことが可能になる」

d. 空所直前のパラグラフの内容が，「ハイブリッドカーや電気自動車の静音化に対するロータス社の考え方」が述べられており，**d→c** がその具体的な取り組みとなるので，**d→c** の組み合わせが先にくることになる。本問は，前後のパラグラフとのつながりがポイントとなる難問。

Lesson3　長文問題：基本編-4

The system Lotus uses was originally developed for a different reason: to cancel out excess noise inside a car.
「ロータスが使用するシステムは，もともとは異なる理由で開発された。それは，車内部の過剰な騒音を相殺するというものだ」

発展　〈追加〉表現を含む文の特徴

➡ 文字通り，情報を〈追加〉するのであるが，さまざまな〈追加〉が考えられるので，前の文と比べてどういう点が〈追加〉されているのか平素から意識すること。

■ 副　詞（句）：**also, as well, besides, further, furthermore, in addition, moreover, too, what is more** など
■ 前置詞（句）：**besides, in addition to** など

問題文訳

　こうする（電気自動車の音をほんの少しだけ大きくする）システムは，すでに開発中である。イギリスのスポーツカー製造メーカーのコンサルタント会社である，ロータス・エンジニアリングは，ある音響システムメーカーと，システムを商品化する契約に最近署名した。ロータスは数多くのハイブリッドカーや電気自動車の作業に取り組んできた経験があり，工場でそういった車を使用中に，エンジニアたちは車から音が出ればより安全になるだろう，と考えたのだった。
　<u>ロータスが使用するシステムは，もともとは異なる理由で開発された。それは，車内部の過剰な騒音を相殺するというものだ</u>。望ましくない振動数を分析し，それに対抗する振動数を発生させることによって音を消すことが可能になる。ロータスは速度によって変化する音が出せるようにシステムを調整し，静かなエンジンを搭載した車のドライバーに，聞きなれた音を「フィードバック」するようにした。外部スピーカーを取りつけることで，歩行者もその音を聞き取ることができる。
　車外で聞こえるのとは異なる音を車内で作り出すことは可能だ，とロータスのチーフ・エンジニアであるコリン・ピーチーは言う。メーカーは，自社モデルに抱くイメージに合わせて独自の音を作り出すことができるようになるだろう。電気自動車のドライバーは将来さまざまなエンジン音を選び，現在私たちが携帯電話の着信音で行っているように，選んだエンジン音をダウンロードすることができるようになるかもしれない。

✅ **word check !**

- commercialize〜　〜を商品化する
- perceive〜　〜を知覚する，イメージを抱く
- vehicle　車
- counteract〜　〜に対抗する
- cancel out　〜を相殺する
- manufacturer　メーカー
- modify〜　〜を調整する
- frequency　振動数
- develop〜　〜を開発する
- excess　過剰な

LESSON 3 長文問題：基本編

5 文補充問題
普段からパラグラフの流れをつかむ読み方を。

TRACK 16

出題学部：文学部，文化構想学部など（スポーツ科学部でも出題歴あり）。

文補充問題

《おすすめアプローチ》
1. 各選択肢に目を通し，それぞれの主題をつかむとともに，冠詞，指示語や接続語などの順序の〈決め手となりそうな表現〉の有無をチェック。
2. 各パラグラフを，空所の前には〈どんな内容が述べられているか〉，空所の後には〈どんな内容が述べられているか〉を把握する意識で通読し，該当する選択肢をピックアップする。ここがこの設問最大のポイント！
3. 主に〈一般論→具体的説明〉という流れを重視して，解答を決定する。

《得点力アップの道筋》
1. センター試験第3問を，年度を問わず正解の根拠を押さえながら解き，全問正解できるようにすること。解き方の基本は早稲田大入試と変わらない。
2. 日常の読解で論説文の各パラグラフの流れ（前後の文との関係など）を捉え，指示語の指示内容をおさえるなどといった堅実な読解を心がける。この問題形式も文脈判断重視で取り組む。
3. 以上の点を踏まえて，最終的には文学部，ならびに文化構想学部の過去問に取り組むこと。

（Lesson3 問題解答は p.134, 135 にあります）

文補充問題 (文学部出題)

Choose the most appropriate sentences from the following list a-h for the gaps in the text (1- 7).

a. Indeed it is thought that the full extent of Smiley's criminal activity may never be known.

b. Many of the maps and books stolen from Yale were sold in secret to private collectors in America and Europe.

c. Noticing one man in particular, who was looking at some old books containing maps, the librarian checked the library register to find the man's name.

d. The librarian was suspicious that such a rare and valuable book should just be brought in from the street.

e. The rewards, if the thief is successful, can be immense; books and maps of rarity will often be worth hundreds of thousands of dollars.

f. Three of the maps were identified as coming from the books Smiley had been looking at that day in the Yale library.

g. We recognize book thieves as criminals of a particularly nasty kind, since they attack property which should be available to everybody.

h. Without such study, our knowledge of history, of literature, and of the human past would diminish and disappear.

Late one morning in June 2005, a library worker at Yale University Library noticed a small metal blade on the floor of the Rare Book reading room. She picked up the blade, which had come from a craft knife, and looked around the room. (1) She then used the Internet to discover that the man, named Edward Forbes Smiley, was a dealer in old maps; the librarian felt that something was wrong, and called the campus police and the security department, who watched the man on video surveillance.

When Smiley left the library some four hours later, he was stopped by the police, who found that he was in possession of seven maps, all of them extremely old, rare, and valuable. (2) Though he asserted his innocence at first, he later admitted to the theft, and a year later pled guilty in court to stealing 97 maps from libraries in Boston, Chicago, New York, and London, with an estimated value of 3 million dollars. Promising to pay compensation of 2.3 million dollars for the maps which had not been recovered, he was given the relatively light sentence of three years' imprisonment.

However, many librarians and scholars believed that Smiley had been responsible for the theft, and permanent loss, of many more items than the 97 with which he had been charged. In many cases, collections and books containing maps are not fully catalogued, and a missing page or sheet may not be detected for many years. (3)

Unfortunately, the theft of rare books, prints, and maps is not an uncommon event, to the great dismay of everyone concerned with scholarship and cultural heritage. While art works such as paintings and rare objects can be placed in conditions of relative security, with alarms and cameras surrounding them, it is part of the nature of books and maps that they should be available to scholars and readers who wish to study them. In the reading rooms of major universities and big private research foundations throughout the world, thousands of researchers engage every day in the study of the past through close attention to the details of printed and written objects. （ 4 ） And it has been the purpose of libraries since the earliest times to give any person with a legitimate interest access to the materials needed for research and study.

Access leads to crime, however, and with the value put on many written and printed works, it seems almost too inviting to the criminal. （ 5 ） Fortunately, a heightened sense of security, and the introduction of computerized cataloguing systems, are helping librarians to keep a check on readers and the items they consult. Moreover, the spread of the Internet has allowed instant checks to be made when questionable items surface. Just last year, for example, a man walked into a major research library in Washington, D.C., carrying a book of Shakespeare's plays, printed in 1623, which he wanted to have evaluated. The man claimed that he had bought the book, which is probably worth about 5 million dollars, in Cuba. （ 6 ） An Internet search was quickly made and emails established that the book had been stolen from Durham University, in

England, some ten years previously. While that particular case is still under investigation, it is hoped that the book will soon be restored to its rightful owners, and be made available once again to readers who need to study it.

Librarians and people who use libraries also hope that better security and a sense of ethics will also lead to a decrease in the numbers of more ordinary, but nevertheless essential, books which suffer from accidental or intentional damage. Thoughtless readers who mistreat books, those who mark or write in books, and those who cut or tear pages out all make libraries more expensive, and directly affect other readers. (**7**) In the same way, those who damage or destroy books commit a grave offense against all readers now and in the future.

1. _____   2. _____   3. _____   4. _____

5. _____   6. _____   7. _____

■指示文訳：本文の空所（1〜7）に入れるのに最も適切な文を以下の（a〜h）から選べ。

> 二本柳のひとことコメント

● **1 の決め手となる表現**　（選択肢 c.）：<u>one</u> man→（空所後）：<u>the</u> man．

Late one morning in June 2005, a library worker at Yale University Library noticed a small metal blade on the floor of the Rare Book reading room. She picked up the blade, which had come from a craft knife, and **looked around the room.** (　1　) **She then used the Internet to discover that the man, named Edward Forbes Smiley,** was a dealer in old maps; the librarian felt that something was wrong, and called the campus police and the security department, who watched the man on video surveillance.

問題文訳［121 ページ］ **1** 参照

《一般論→具体的説明の流れ》

（空所前）：looked around the room「部屋を見渡した」
→（選択肢 c.）：Noticing one man in particular「特にある男に目が留まり」．
（選択肢 c.）：the librarian checked the library register to find the man's name「図書館員はその男の名前を見つけるために利用者名簿を調べた」
→（空所後）to discover that the man, named Edward Forbes Smiley...「その男は，名前をエドワード・フォーブス・スマイリーといい，…であることを知った」

● **2 の決め手となる表現**　（空所前）：<u>seven</u> maps→（選択肢 f.）：Three of <u>the</u> maps．

When Smiley left the library some four hours later, he was stopped by the police, who found that he was in possession of seven maps, all of them extremely old, rare, and valuable. (　2　) Though he asserted his innocence at first, he later admitted to the theft, and a year later pled guilty in court to stealing 97 maps from libraries in Boston, Chicago, New York,

> and London, with an estimated value of 3 million dollars. Promising to pay compensation of 2.3 million dollars for the maps which had not been recovered, he was given the relatively light sentence of three years' imprisonment.

問題文訳［121 ページ］ **2** 参照

《一般論→具体的説明の流れ》

When Smiley left the library some four hours later, he was stopped by the police, who found that he was in possession of seven maps, all of them extremely old, rare, and valuable. ＋（選択肢 f.）: Three of the maps were identified as coming from the books Smiley had been looking at that day in the Yale library.「約 4 時間後，スマイリーが図書館を後にしたとき，警官に止められると，警官は，彼が地図を 7 枚持っているのを発見した。それらの地図は，すべて極めて古く，希少で，価値のあるものだった。地図のうちの 3 枚は，スマイリーがその日イェール大学図書館で見ていた本からのものであることが判明した」→（空所後）: the theft「その窃盗」

●3 の決め手となる表現　（選択肢 a.）: Indeed「実際のところ」

> However, many librarians and scholars believed that Smiley had been responsible for the theft, and permanent loss, of many more items than the 97 with which he had been charged. In many cases, collections and books containing maps are not fully catalogued, and **a missing page or sheet may not be detected for many years.** (　3　)

問題文訳［121 ページ］ **3** 参照

《一般論→具体的説明の流れ》

（空所前）: a missing page or sheet may not be detected for many years.「脱落したページやシートが何年も発見されていないことがある」
→（選択肢 a.）: the full extent of Smiley's criminal activity may never be known「スマイリーの犯罪活動の全容は決して知られることはないだろう」

> 発展　「実際に」を意味する表現を含む文の特徴

- ■ 訂正：誤った前言を，具体例などを用いて訂正する場合に用いる。**But** などの逆接表現などと用いることが多い。
- ■ 強調：前言を，具体例などを用いて強調する場合に用いる。

　　副詞（句）：actually, indeed, in effect, in fact, in reality, practically, really など

● 4 の決め手となる表現　（空所前）：the study of the past →（選択肢 h.）：such study.

> 　Unfortunately, the theft of rare books, prints, and maps is not an uncommon event, to the great dismay of everyone concerned with scholarship and cultural heritage. While art works such as paintings and rare objects can be placed in conditions of relative security, with alarms and cameras surrounding them, it is part of the nature of books and maps that they should be available to scholars and readers who wish to study them. In the reading rooms of major universities and big private research foundations throughout the world, thousands of researchers engage every day in **the study of the past through close attention to the details of printed and written objects.** (　4　) And it has been the purpose of libraries since the earliest times to give any person with a legitimate interest access to the materials needed for research and study.

問題文訳［121ページ］　4 参照

《一般論→具体的説明の流れ》

（空所前）：the study of the past through close attention to the details of printed and written objects「印刷物や文書の細部に細心の注意を払っての過去の研究」→（選択肢 h.）：our knowledge of history, of literature, and of the human past「歴史，文学，そして人類の過去に関する知識」

Lesson3　長文問題：基本編-5

- **5 の決め手となる表現**　特になし。灰色の網かけ部分が一般論，それ以外が具体的説明。
- **6 の決め手となる表現**　a major research library in Washington, D.C.「ワシントンD.C.のある大きな研究図書館」→（選択肢 d.）：The librarian「その図書館員」，<u>a</u> book of Shakespeare's plays「シェークスピアの戯曲の本」→<u>the</u> book「その本」→（選択肢 d.）：<u>such</u> a rare and valuable book「そのような希少価値のある本」

Access leads to crime, however, and **with the value put on many written and printed works, it seems almost too inviting to the criminal.** (　5　) Fortunately, a heightened sense of security, and the introduction of computerized cataloguing systems, are helping librarians to keep a check on readers and the items they consult. Moreover, the spread of the Internet has allowed instant checks to be made when questionable items surface. Just last year, for example, a man walked into **a major research library in Washington, D.C.,** carrying **a book of Shakespeare's plays,** printed in 1623, which he wanted to have evaluated. The man claimed that he had bought **the book,** which is probably worth about 5 million dollars, in Cuba. (　6　) An Internet search was quickly made and emails established that the book had been stolen from Durham University, in England, some ten years previously. While that particular case is still under investigation, it is hoped that the book will soon be restored to its rightful owners, and be made available once again to readers who need to study it.

問題文訳［121ページ］　**6**　参照

《一般論→具体的説明の流れ》

（空所前）：with the value put on many written and printed works, it seems almost too inviting to the criminal「多くの書面や印刷による作品には価値があるために，犯罪者にはあまりにも魅力的なのだ」→（選択肢 e.）：The rewards, if the thief is successful, can be immense; books and maps of rarity will often be worth hundreds of thousands of dollars.「もし窃盗が成功すれば，その報酬は測り知れないものとなりうる。希少な書物や地図であれば，何十万ドルもの価値がある場合も多い」

● **7の決め手となる表現** （空所後）: In the same way「同様に」。灰色の網かけ部分が一般論，それ以外が具体的説明。

> Librarians and people who use libraries also hope that better security and a sense of ethics will also lead to a decrease in the numbers of more ordinary, but nevertheless essential, books which suffer from accidental or intentional damage. Thoughtless readers who mistreat books, those who mark or write in books, and those who cut or tear pages out all make libraries more expensive, and directly affect other readers. (7) **In the same way,** those who damage or destroy books commit a grave offense against all readers now and in the future.

問題文訳［121ページ］ 7 参照

問題文訳

a. 実際に，スマイリーの犯罪活動の全容は決して知られることはないだろう，と考えられている。
b. イェール大学から盗まれた地図と本の多くは，アメリカや欧州の個人収集家に秘密裏に売却されていた。
c. 地図が載っている数冊の古い本を見ている男に特に目が留まり，図書館員はその男の名前を見つけようと利用者名簿を調べた。
d. 図書館員は，そのような希少価値のある本が単に街から持ち込まれるのは怪しいと思った。
e. もし窃盗が成功すれば，その報酬は測り知れないものとなりうる。希少な書物や地図であれば，何十万ドルもの価値がある場合も多い。
f. 地図のうちの3枚は，スマイリーがその日イェール大学図書館で見ていた本からのものであることが判明した。
g. 我々は，本の泥棒は特に卑劣な犯罪者だと認識している。というのは，彼らは誰にでも利用可能でなければならない財産を攻撃するからだ。
h. そのような研究がなければ，歴史，文学，そして人類の過去に関する知識は減少し，消滅してしまうだろう。

Lesson3　長文問題：基本編-5

■1■　2005年6月のある日の昼近く，イェール大学図書館の館員が，希少本閲覧室の床に小さな金属製の刃物が落ちているのに気づいた。彼女はその刃物を拾ってみると，それはクラフトナイフをもとに作られたものだった。そして彼女は部屋を見渡した。地図が載っている数冊の古い本を見ている男に特に目が留まり，図書館員はその男の名前を見つけようと利用者名簿を調べた。そしてインターネットを使って，その男は，名前をエドワード・フォーブス・スマイリーといい，古地図の販売業者であることを知った。図書館員はどこかおかしいと思い，大学の警備員と保安部に連絡し，彼らはその男を監視カメラで見張った。

■2■　約4時間後，スマイリーが図書館を後にしたとき，警官に止められると，警官は，彼が地図を7枚持っているのを発見した。それらの地図は，すべて極めて古く，希少で，価値のあるものだった。地図のうちの3枚は，スマイリーがその日イェール大学図書館で見ていた本からのものであることが判明した。彼は当初無罪を主張したが，後に盗んだことを認め，その1年後には法廷で，ボストン，シカゴ，ニューヨーク，ロンドンの図書館から推定価格300万ドルの地図を97枚盗んだことについて罪を認めた。すでに取り返すことができなくなった地図の賠償金230万ドルを支払う約束をし，彼は懲役3年の比較的軽い刑の判決を下された。

■3■　しかしながら，多くの図書館員や学者たちは，スマイリーが，起訴された97枚の地図以上にはるかに多くの品目の窃盗及び永久喪失に関与していた，と考えていた。多くの場合，地図を含んでいる所蔵物や書籍は完全な目録が作成されておらず，脱落したページやシートが何年も発見されていないことがあるのだ。実際に，スマイリーの犯罪活動の全容は決して知られることはないだろう，と考えられている。

■4■　学問の研究や文化遺産に携わっているすべての人にとって非常にがっかりすることであるが，残念ながら，希少な本，印刷物，それに地図の窃盗は珍しいことではない。絵画や希少品のような芸術作品は，警報器やカメラで囲み，比較的安全な状況におくことも可能であるが，本や地図には性質上，研究したいと思っている学者や読者に利用してもらうという部分がある。世界中の主要な大学や大きな私的研究財団の閲覧室では毎日，何千もの研究者たちが，印刷物や文書の細部に細心の注意を払って過去の研究に従事している。そのような研究がなければ，歴史，文学，そして人類の過去に関する知識は減少し，消滅してしまうだろう。また，正当な関心を持つ人には誰にでも調査や研究に必要な資料を利用してもらうのが，設立当初から図書館の目的だったのである。

■5■　しかし，利用できる権利が犯罪を招くし，また，多くの書面や印刷による作品には価値があるために，犯罪者にはあまりにも魅力的なのだ。もし窃盗が成功すれば，その報酬は測り知れないものとなりうる。希少な書物や地図であれば，何十万ドルもの価値がある場合も多い。幸運にも，防犯意識の高まりや，コンピュータ化された目録作成システムの導入は，図書館員が利用者や利用者の閲覧物をチェックするのを容易にしている。さらに，インターネットの普及のおかげで，疑わしい物品が浮かびあがった場合，一瞬にしてチェックすることが可能になった。たとえば，ちょうど昨年のことであるが，ある男が1623年に印刷されたシェークスピアの戯曲の本を持ってワシントンD.C.のある大きな研究図書館へやってき

●121

た。その本を査定するつもりだったのである。その男は，恐らくおよそ500万ドルの価値があるその本をキューバで買ったと主張した。図書館員は，そのような希少価値のある本が単に街から持ち込まれるのは怪しいと思った。早速インターネットで検索され，その本は約10年前に英国のダラム大学から盗まれたものであることが数通の電子メールによって確かめられた。その事例はまだ調査中であるが，その本がすぐに正当な所有者に返還されて，再び研究に必要とする読者が利用できるようになることが望まれる。

■7 図書館員や図書館利用者はまた，さらなる防犯体制と倫理観によって，希少本と比べるとありふれているが，それでも欠かすことのできない本が，偶発的あるいは意図的な被害を受ける件数がもっと減ることになればと願っている。本を乱暴に扱ったり，本に印や書き込みをしたり，ページを切り取ったり破り取ったりする軽率な読者はみな，図書館をさらに費用のかかるものにし，他の読者に直接的に影響を与えている。我々は，本の泥棒は特に卑劣な犯罪者だと認識している。というのは，彼らは誰にでも利用可能でなければならない財産を攻撃するからだ。同様に，本を損傷したりだめにしたりする人は，現在及び未来のすべての読者に対して重大な罪を犯しているのである。

✓ word check !

- register　登録簿，名簿
- nasty　卑劣な
- diminish　減少する
- security department　保安部
- be in possession of ～　～を所有している
- assert ～　～を主張する
- estimated value　推定価格
- sentence　判決
- dismay　落胆
- research foundation　研究財団
- evaluate ～　～を評価する，査定する
- restore ～　～を返還する
- suffer from ～　～で損害，被害を受ける
- affect ～　～に影響を与える
- commit a offense　罪を犯す
- immense　莫大な
- property　財産
- blade　刃物
- video surveillance　監視カメラ
- plead guilty　罪を認める
- compensation　賠償金
- charge ～　～を告発する
- heritage　遺産
- surface　～が浮上する
- under investigation　調査中
- sense of ethics　倫理観
- in the same way　同様に

LESSON 3 長文問題：基本編

6 タイトル選択問題
問題文全体の主題をつかむ。

TRACK 18

出題学部：全学部で出題歴あり。

タイトル選択問題

《おすすめアプローチ》
1. 各段落内の論理展開をつかみながら読み，その段落の〈主題〉をつかむ。
2. パラグラフ相互の関係を意識しながら最後まで読み進める。
3. 通読した結果，〈本文の主題〉を表している選択肢を「消去法」で見つける。消去する視点として，〈具体例のみをタイトル化した選択肢〉，〈本文に書かれていない情報をタイトル化した選択肢〉などを意識する。

《得点力アップの道筋》
1. センテンスレベルの和訳だけでなくパラグラフ内の位置づけを常に意識する。
2. また，各パラグラフ相互の関係も考えること。これは，全文通読後に行い，練習段階では，自分でタイトルをつけてみること。
3. 誤りの選択肢の理由づけにこだわり，納得すること。実際には，消去法を駆使することになる。

（Lesson3 問題解答は p.134, 135 にあります）

問題 1（人間科学部出題）

　When you think of solar power, you probably think of photovoltaic panels. But there is another way to make electricity from sunlight, which arguably has even brighter prospects. In the past few months BrightSource Energy, based in California, has signed the world's two largest deals to build new solar-power capacity. The company will soon begin constructing the first in a series of 14 solar-power plants that will collectively supply more than 2.6 gigawatts of electricity — enough to serve about 1.8 million homes. But to accomplish this feat BrightSource will not use photovoltaic cells, which generate electricity directly from sunlight and currently constitute the most common form of solar power. Instead, the company specializes in "concentrating solar-thermal technology" in which mirrors concentrate sunlight to produce heat. That heat is then used to create steam, which in turn drives a turbine to generate electricity.

　Solar-thermal power stations have several advantages over solar-photovoltaic projects. They are typically built on a much larger scale, and historically their costs have been much lower. Compared with other renewable sources of energy, they are probably best able to match a utility's electrical load, says Nathaniel Bullard of New Energy Finance, a research firm. They work best when it is hottest and demand is greatest. And the heat they generate can be stored, so the output of a solar-thermal plant does not fluctuate as wildly as that of a photovoltaic system. Moreover, since they use a turbine to generate electricity from heat, most solar-thermal plants can be easily and inexpensively supplemented with natural-gas boilers, enabling them to perform as reliably as a fossil-fuel power plant.

What is the best title for this passage?

　a. California's Solar Power Problem
　b. New Power Plants to be Built
　c. Solar Power Alternative Shows Promise
　d. The History of Solar Power Plants

■指示文訳：この文章のタイトルとして最もふさわしいものはどれか。

二本柳のひとことコメント

第1パラグラフ〈テーマ〉→第2パラグラフ〈具体的説明〉！

　a. カリフォルニアの太陽光発電が抱える問題点
　b. 建設されるべき新たな発電所
　c. 太陽光発電代替手段の将来性
　d. 太陽光発電所の歴史

問題文訳

　太陽光発電について考える際には，おそらく太陽光発電パネルを思い浮かべるだろう。だが，日光から電気を作る方法はもう1つあり，こちらのほうが見通しが明るいとさえ言ってよいだろう。過去数か月間に，カリフォルニアに本拠があるブライトソース・エナジー社は，太陽光発電設備を新設する世界最大の2つの契約に署名した。間もなく同社は，14基の太陽光発電所の1基目の建設に着手し，全体で2.6ギガワット以上の電力――180万世帯に供給できるだけの電力――を供給することになる。だが，この離れ業をやってのけるために，ブライトソース社は光電池を使わない。光電池は日光から直接発電するもので，現在最も一般的な形の太陽光発電である。その代わりに，同社は，鏡で日光を集中させて熱を生み出す「集中太陽熱技術」を専門に扱う。その熱は蒸気発生に使われ，それが次にタービンを動かして発電するのである。

　太陽熱発電所には，太陽光電池プロジェクトに比べて利点がいくつかある。一般的にかなり大規模に建設され，歴史的に見て，コストははるかに少なくてすむ。他の再生可能エネルギーに比べて，それらはおそらく電力事業の電気負荷に最善の組み合わせとなることができる，とリサーチ会社ニュー・エナジー・ファイナンスのナサニエル・ブラードは言う。それらは気候が最も暑く，需要が最大になるときに最もよく機能する。それにそれらが生み出す熱は貯えることができるので，太陽熱発電所の出力は光電池システムほど大きく変動しない。さらに言えば，それらは熱からタービンを使って発電するため，ほとんどの太陽熱発電所は天然ガスボイラーで簡単かつ安価に電気を補充することが可能なので，化石燃料発電所と同じくらいの信頼度で性能を発揮できるのである。

✓ word check！

- photovoltaic panel　太陽光発電パネル
- electricity　電気
- prospect　見通し
- deal　契約
- generate 〜　〜を起こす
- specialize in 〜　〜を専門に扱う
- in turn　次に
- solar-thermal power station　太陽熱発電所
- firm　会社
- fluctuate　変動する
- be supplemented with 〜　〜で補充される
- fossil-fuel　化石燃料

問題 2 （教育学部出題）

　Five months into Barack Obama's presidency, two researchers are at odds over whether a so-called "Obama effect" can bump up black students' standardized test scores and help to close the achievement gap between blacks and whites. In the days after Obama's election in November, school officials across the country reported a noticeable improvement in students' performance — particularly in black communities — and attributed it to Obama's success. But two studies have produced conflicting reports on the existence of such an effect — calling into question whether inspiration alone is enough to bring quantifiable change.

　In a study conducted during the 2008 election, Dr. Ray Friedman of Vanderbilt University found that black students achieved higher scores on standardized tests when they were reminded of Obama's achievements before the test. Their higher scores narrowed the gap between black and higher-scoring white students, suggesting a tangible effect of Obama's presidency. Friedman said the students who earned higher scores likely overcame "stereotype threat" — a fear that one's performance will confirm an existing negative stereotype of a group with which one identifies, resulting in psychological discomfort. Friedman has claimed that blacks are far more likely to score below their potential when asked to identify their race on a test — or when they are told an exam will measure innate abilities, like intelligence. But when role models from the same social group are present before a test is administered, "it tends to take away stereotype threat losses" — resulting in higher scores, according to Friedman. "When Obama broke through the barrier in such a public and important way, it helped black test takers achieve their full potential," Friedman said of the study. "The question is — will that effect persist?" While Friedman said America's first black president's influence as a positive role model likely helped raise scores, "no one's claiming that Obama is going to make people who have never studied geometry suddenly pass geometry." Friedman tested 400 subjects — in separate groups of 100 — at four different phases of the election cycle: before the Democratic convention; after Obama's acceptance speech on Aug. 28; midway between the speech and the presidential election; and after Obama's victory in November. In the first test, the average score for whites was 12.14 of 20, while the average score for blacks was 8.79 of 20. After Obama won the presidency, whites scored 11.9 and blacks scored 9.83. When Obama's political success was most apparent — after his convention speech and after his Nov. 4 victory — Friedman found that blacks' scores rose while whites' scores dropped slightly, statistically narrowing the gap.

But Friedman's findings have been challenged by another study that found no evidence of an "Obama effect" on black students' standardized test scores. Dr. Joshua Aronson of New York University, who conducted a study in June 2008 after Hillary Clinton conceded and Obama secured the nomination, found "absolutely no results" to support Friedman's findings.

Aronson tested a diverse sample of 160 college-aged students from various groups — over half of whom were black. Aronson said he had expected to detect a noticeable effect in test performance, but he found none — suggesting that black students might not identify with Obama's success. "Past research really suggests that the best role models aren't the ones who are innately gifted individuals," Aronson said. "He's certainly breaking down barriers, but he's doing it with exceptional talent, which most people think that they don't have. He might not be the best role model in terms of having people say, 'Wow, if he can do it, so can I' " he said.

Some education experts say it's too early to know whether Obama's inspiration has had a tangible effect in classrooms across the country. And some claim that even if such an effect exists, it is impossible to measure. Tom Ewing, director of press relations at Educational Testing Service, said that while there is some evidence to suggest improvement in school performance among black students, "it's too recent of a phenomena" to know if Obama deserves extra credit.

この文章のタイトルとして最もふさわしいものをa〜eから1つ選べ。

a. Obama's presidency helped black students score higher on tests.
b. Researchers debate an 'Obama effect' on black students' test scores.
c. School officials attributed a significant boost in black students' test scores to Obama's victory.
d. Obama's inspiration encouraged black students to work harder in classrooms.
e. Education experts expect Obama's success to help black students improve academic skills.

二本柳のひとことコメント

二項対立の典型的な4段構成！

第1パラグラフ〈テーマ：オバマ効果の有無について論争がある〉
→第2パラグラフ〈具体的説明①：オバマ効果があるという立場〉
→第3パラグラフ〈具体的説明②：オバマ効果はないという立場〉
→第4パラグラフ〈結論：どちらの立場が正しいのか結論を出すには早急すぎる〉。

a. オバマの大統領就任は，黒人学生のテスト成績を上げることに役立った。
b. 黒人学生のテスト成績に与えた『オバマ効果』について，研究者たちが論争している。
c. 学校職員たちは，黒人学生のテスト成績の著しい向上はオバマの勝利によるものだと考えた。
d. オバマによって刺激をうけ,黒人学生は教室でより一生懸命勉強するようになった。
e. 教育の専門家たちは，オバマの成功が，黒人学生の学力向上に役立つことを期待している。

Lesson3　長文問題：基本編-6

問題文訳

　バラク・オバマが大統領に就任するまでの5か月，いわゆる「オバマ効果」が黒人学生たちの標準テストの成績を急上昇させ，黒人と白人との間の学力格差を埋める助けとなるかどうかについて，2人の研究者の意見が食い違っている。11月のオバマ当選後の数日で，全米の学校職員たちが，学生たちの成績が特に黒人社会において目立って向上したことを報告し，それはオバマの当選によるものだとした。しかし，2つの研究がそのような効果の存在に関して相反する報告を作成し，鼓舞されるだけで数量化される変化をもたらすのに十分かどうかという点に疑問を生じさせた。

　2008年の選挙期間中に行われたある研究で，ヴァンダービルト大学のレイ・フリードマン教授は，黒人学生たちが，テスト前にオバマの偉業を思い出すと，より高得点をとるということを発見した。彼らのより高い得点は，黒人学生と好成績の白人学生との間の格差を縮め，オバマが大統領になったことの確かな効果を示したのである。フリードマンの話によると，より高い得点を取った学生たちはおそらく，「固定観念に対する恐怖」――つまりある人の成績が，その人が一体感を感じている集団に関して存在する否定的な固定観念を裏付けてしまうのではないかという恐怖感で，その結果，人は心理的な不安感を抱くようになる――を克服したとのことだ。フリードマンは，黒人たちが，テストで自らの人種を明らかにするように求められたときや，テストが知能のような先天的な能力を測るものであると言われたときに，彼らの潜在能力を下回る成績をとる傾向がはるかに強いということを主張している。しかし，テストが行われる前に，同じ社会集団から手本となる人が現れているときは，「そのことによって固定観念に対する恐怖による失点が生じなくなる傾向にあり」，結果として，より高い得点をとる，とフリードマンは言う。「オバマが非常に公的な場で，そして重要な手段で障壁を突破したとき，それは黒人の受験者が最大の可能性を発揮するのに役立った」，とフリードマンはその研究について話した。「問題は，その効果は持続するのか，ということである」。フリードマンは，アメリカ初の黒人大統領の影響は，有益な手本としておそらく成績を上げるのに役に立ったのだろうと述べる一方，「オバマが，幾何学を勉強したことのない人を突然幾何学のテストに合格させるとは，誰も言っていない」とも言う。フリードマンは，400人を被験者として――100の異なるグループに分けて――選挙期間中の4つの異なる段階でテストを行った。つまり，民主党大会の前，8月28日のオバマ指名受諾演説の後，演説と大統領選挙の中間，そして11月のオバマ勝利の後である。最初のテストでは，白人の平均的な成績は20点（満点）のうち12.14点であり，一方，黒人の平均的成績は20点のうち8.79点であった。オバマが大統領選挙に勝った後，白人は11.9点の成績で，黒人の成績は9.83点だった。オバマの政治的な成功が最も明らかになったとき――彼の党大会での演説と11月4日の勝利の後――フリードマンは，白人の成績がわずかに落ちた一方で，黒人の成績が上がり，統計的に格差を縮めたと理解した。

　しかし，フリードマンの発見は，黒人学生の標準テストの成績において「オバマ効果」の

証拠が見つからなかった別の研究によって異議を唱えられている。ニューヨーク大学のジョシュア・アロンソン博士は，ヒラリー・クリントンが身を引いてオバマが指名を獲得した後，2008年6月に，ある研究を行ったのであるが，フリードマンの発見を支持するような「結果はまったくない」ということがわかった。アロンソンは，様々なグループから選んだ160人のさまざまな大学生の被験者——その半分以上は黒人だった——に対してテストを行った。アロンソンは，テスト結果に明らかな効果を見つけることを期待していたのだったが，何も見つけられなかった，と言った。そしてそのことは，黒人学生がオバマの成功に自分を重ね合わせていないのかもしれない，ということを示唆している。「過去の研究は，確かに，最高のお手本となる人物は先天的に才能のある人ではない，ということを示唆している」とアロンソンは言った。「オバマは確かに障壁を破っているが，彼は，ほとんどの人々が自分は持っていないと考える特別な才能をもってそれを行っている。彼は，人々に『わぁ，もし彼ができるなら，私にもできる』と言わしめるかという点では，最高のお手本ではないのかもしれない」と彼は言った。

　オバマによる刺激が，全国の教室に確かな影響を与えたかどうかを知るには早すぎる，と言う教育専門家もいる。そして，そのような効果が存在するとしても，測ることは不可能だ，と主張する者もいる。教育試験サービスの広報部長であるトム・ユーイングは，黒人学生の間での成績向上を示唆する証拠もある一方で，オバマが特別な信頼に値するかどうかを知るには，「あまりにも最近の現象である」と述べた。

✅ word check !

- researcher　研究者
- be at odds over 〜　〜のことで意見が食い違う
- bump up 〜　〜を急上昇させる
- achievement gap　学力格差
- attribute ... to 〜　…を〜によるものとする
- conflicting　相反する
- suggest 〜　〜を示す
- tangible　確かな
- stereotype　固定観念
- performance　成績
- confirm 〜　〜を裏付ける
- psychological　心理的な
- potential　潜在能力
- identify 〜　〜を明らかにする
- innate　潜在的な
- intelligence　知能
- administer 〜　〜を執り行う
- break through 〜　〜を突破する
- persist　持続する
- phase　段階
- the Democratic convention　民主党大会
- while 〜　〜の一方で
- statistically　統計的に
- concede　身を引く
- nomination　指名
- diverse　多様な
- noticeable　明らかな
- in terms of 〜　〜という点では

Lesson3-1 問題解答

(1) d. make too little noise to be easily noticed.
(2) a. has been at the center of debates concerning morality.

Lesson3-2 問題解答

(1) 1: F 2: T 3: T 4: T 5: F
(2) b, c

Lesson3-3 問題解答

(1) c. cruel acts. (2) c. improves (3) d. started again
(4) b. people become creative when the circumstances force them to adapt

Lesson3-4 問題解答

(1) c. 4 - 2 - 1 - 3
(2) d. - a. - c. - b.
(3) d. - c. - b. - a.

Lesson3-5 問題解答

(1) c. Noticing one man in particular, who was looking at some old books containing maps, the librarian checked the library register to find the man's name.
(2) f. Three of the maps were identified as coming from the books Smiley had been looking at that day in the Yale library.
(3) a. Indeed it is thought that the full extent of Smiley's criminal activity may never be known.
(4) h. Without such study, our knowledge of history, of literature, and of the human past would diminish and disappear.
(5) e. The rewards, if the thief is successful, can be immense; books and maps of rarity will often be worth hundreds of thousands dollars.

(6) d. The librarian was suspicious that such a rare and valuable book should just be brought in from the street.
(7) g. We recognize book thieves as criminals of a particularly nasty kind, since they attack property which should be available to everybody.

Lesson3- 6　問題解答

(1) c. Solar Power Alternative Shows Promise
(2) b. Researchers debate an 'Obama effect' on black students' test scores.

LESSON 4　長文問題：実践編

使用学部：教育学部，商学部，社会科学部，スポーツ科学部など。

1 次の英文を読み，下記の設問に答えよ。
（商学部出題）

TRACK 01〜07

　At the main international airport for Mexico City, the first thing to notice is that the path from the baggage claim is lined with smiling employees guiding passengers to their taxis or connecting flights. The second is that they are all in wheelchairs. Since the opening of a new terminal in November 2007, the airport has (　A　) some 60 disabled, bilingual workers to serve as Mexico's face to the world. Their presence delights both passengers, who frequently offer congratulations and ask to take their picture, and their superiors. "They're professional, attentive, always in a good mood, and never miss work," says Hector Velazquez, the airport's director.

　Mr Velazquez says he first thought of seeking out disabled staff after being impressed by the performance of Jazmin Martinez, a young labour lawyer suffering from severe arthritis. He instructed an airport firm to take on 20 graduates of a physical and psychological training programme for the handicapped, and then tripled the number upon seeing the results. The workers say they are (　B　) by the public exposure — and by their respectable $550 a month salaries. "If you don't have a job, you sit at home all day thinking about what hurts," says Ms Martinez. "Now, we're independent, and people can see that our physical condition doesn't matter. They don't look at you as some strange creature any more."

Another winner is the Mexican government, now at the head of the disabled-rights movement in the developing world. In 2005 it established a council to co-ordinate its efforts across state agencies. Since then, the government has (C) a number of initiatives, including installing wheelchair ramps in 26,000 schools, and providing subsidised loans for housing for the disabled. According to the council, the proportion of government buildings accessible to the handicapped will increase from 40% to 90% by 2012, and all hospitals will include sign-language interpreters by the same date.

Unhappily, the example [airport / by / is / rare / set / the]. Employment among the disabled, who represent nearly 10% of Mexico's population, is less than half that of the rest of society, and in the public sector just 0.4% of workers are disabled, according to the National Council for People with Disabilities. Perhaps the most promising avenue for progress is the example of the airport employees: Jesus Briones, one of Terminal 2's wheelchair workers, says businessmen passing through (D) ask him about hiring his counterparts.

注　arthritis　関節炎

(1) 空所（ **A** ）〜（ **D** ）を埋めるのに最も適当な語を1〜4からそれぞれ1つ選べ。
　(A)　1. handled　　2. hired　　3. rented　　4. staffed
　(B)　1. embarrassed　2. shocked　3. thrilled　4. warned
　(C)　1. imitated　　2. launched　3. modified　4. shelved
　(D)　1. confidently　2. politely　3. practically　4. routinely

　　　　　　　　　　　　　　　　　　　　　　_____

(2)【　　　】内の単語を，前後の意味から考えて正しい順序に並べ替えよ。

　　　　　　　　　　　　　　　　　　　　　　_____

(3) 次の1〜4について，本文の内容に最も合うものをa〜dからそれぞれ1つ選べ。
　1. Why do disabled workers serve as Mexico's face to the world?
　　a. Passengers cannot help noticing their wheelchairs.
　　b. They are among the first people seen by arriving passengers.
　　c. They are delighted to have their pictures taken.
　　d. They can communicate with passengers in their own language.

　　　　　　　　　　　　　　　　　　　　　　_____

　2. Why don't passengers see the disabled staff as strange creatures?
　　a. They are made aware that disabled staff can do the same work as able-bodied staff.
　　b. They are reassured by the constant congratulations.

c. They are too busy with baggage, transfers and taxis to notice.
   d. They realize that the staff members are friendly and bilingual.

   _____

3. How has the Mexican government benefitted from the use of disabled staff?
   a. It has been able to reduce labour costs.
   b. It has filled jobs that average workers are unwilling to do.
   c. It has increased the number of tourists visiting Mexico.
   d. It is now seen as a leader in helping and supporting the disabled.

   _____

4. Why do businessmen show an interest in the airport's disabled workers?
   a. They are eager to coordinate the efforts of state agencies.
   b. They know that only 0.4% of the public sector consists of disabled workers.
   c. They see them as a promising avenue for progress.
   d. They would like to employ some of them in their own companies.

   _____

(Lesson4 問題解答は p.179 にあります)

問題(1)

空所（　A　）〜（　D　）を埋めるのに最も適当な語を1〜4からそれぞれ1つ選べ。

(A)　1. handled　　2. hired　　3. rented　　4. staffed
(B)　1. embarrassed　2. shocked　3. thrilled　4. warned
(C)　1. imitated　2. launched　3. modified　4. shelved
(D)　1. confidently　2. politely　3. practically　4. routinely

二本柳のひとことコメント

(A) 空所前の文から明らか。本文が障害者の「雇用」をテーマにしていることにも着目したい。

1. …を扱った　2. …を雇った　3. …を賃借りした　4. …に職員を配置した

At the main international airport for Mexico City, the first thing to notice is that the path from the **baggage claim** is lined with smiling employees guiding passengers to their taxis or connecting flights. The second is that **they are all in wheelchairs.** Since the opening of a new terminal in November 2007, **the airport has （　A　） some 60 disabled, bilingual workers** to serve as Mexico's face to the world.

問題文訳［147ページ］　A▶参照

Lesson4　長文問題：実践編-1

（B） 空所直後には「人前に出たり，月給550ドルというまずまずの給与を支払われる」という内容が述べられており，かつ同じ第2パラグラフの最後には「今では私たちは自立していて，私たちの肉体的状態は問題ではないのだとわかってもらえます。奇妙な生き物だという目で見られることは，もはやありません」とある。以上のことからプラスイメージの選択肢が正解となる。常にパラグラフ全体に気を配る読解姿勢を堅持すれば，平易な設問。

1. 困惑して　　2. ショックを受けて　　3. わくわくした　　4. 警告される

> The workers say they are (　**B**　) by the public exposure —— and by their **respectable** $550 a month salaries. "If you don't have a job, you sit at home all day thinking about what hurts," says Ms Martinez. "Now, we're independent, and people can see that our physical condition doesn't matter. **They don't look at you as some strange creature any more.**"

問題文訳［147ページ］　**B** 参照

（C） パラグラフのテーマがメキシコ政府の障害者雇用促進の積極姿勢であることに着目。

1. まねした　　2. …を始めた　　3. 修正した　　4. 棚上げした

> **Another winner is the Mexican government, now at the head of the disabled-rights movement in the developing world.** In 2005 it established a council to co-ordinate its efforts across state agencies. Since then, the government has (　**C**　) **a number of initiatives,** including installing wheelchair ramps in 26,000 schools, and providing **subsidised** loans for housing for the disabled. According to the council, the proportion of government buildings accessible to the handicapped will increase from 40% to 90% by 2012, and all hospitals will include sign-language interpreters by the same date.

問題文訳［147ページ］　**C** 参照

(D) 設問文のエピソードは，障害者の雇用の将来性を感じさせるものであることに注目。

1. 確信を持って　　2. 礼儀正しく　　3. 実際的に　　4. 日常的に

> **Perhaps the most promising avenue** for progress is the example of the airport employees: Jesus Briones, one of Terminal 2's wheelchair workers, **says businessmen passing through** （　D　）**ask him about hiring his counterparts**.

問題文訳［147 ページ］ **D** 参照

問題(2)

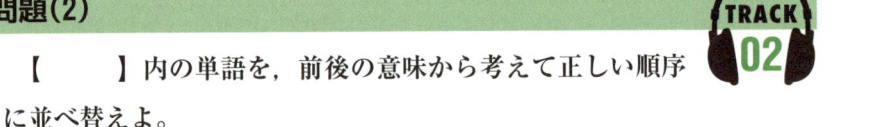

【　　】内の単語を，前後の意味から考えて正しい順序に並べ替えよ。

二本柳のひとことコメント

直前の **the example** にかかる修飾語句を考える。

> Unhappily, **the example** 【airport / by / is / rare / set / the】. Employment among the disabled, who represent nearly 10% of Mexico's population, is less than half that of the rest of the society, and in the public sector just 0.4% of workers are disabled, according to the National Council for People with Disabilities.

Lesson4　長文問題：実践編−1

問題(3)

次の 1〜4 について，本文の内容に最も合うものを a〜d からそれぞれ 1 つ選べ。

1. Why do disabled workers serve as Mexico's face to the world?
    a. Passengers cannot help noticing their wheelchairs.
    b. They are among the first people seen by arriving passengers.
    c. They are delighted to have their pictures taken.
    d. They can communicate with passengers in their own language.

二本柳のひとことコメント

以下参照。第 1 パラグラフには，障害を持つ空港職員の働きぶりが具体的に述べられている。

「なぜ障害を持つ職員が，世界に向けてのメキシコの顔として働いているのか」
a. 乗客が彼らの車椅子に気づかずにはいられないから。
b. 彼らは，到着する乗客たちが最初に目にする人の 1 人だから。
c. 彼らは，写真を撮られて喜んでいるから。
d. 彼らは，自分自身の言葉で乗客たちと意思を伝え合うことができるから。

At the main international airport for Mexico City, **the first thing to notice is that the path from the baggage claim is lined with smiling employees guiding passengers to their taxis or connecting flights.** The second is that they are all **in wheelchairs.**

2. Why don't passengers see the disabled staff as strange creatures?
   a. They are made aware that disabled staff can do the same work as able-bodied staff.
   b. They are reassured by the constant congratulations.
   c. They are too busy with baggage, transfers and taxis to notice.
   d. They realize that the staff members are friendly and bilingual.

二本柳のひとことコメント

以下参照。第2パラグラフには，その働きぶりによって周囲の認識が変わっていく経緯が述べられている。

「なぜ乗客は，障害を持つ職員を奇妙な生き物とみなさないのか」
a. 障害を持つ職員が，健常者の職員と同様の仕事ができると気づかされるため。
b. 彼らは，絶えず賛辞を送られることで安心するから。
c. 彼らは，手荷物や乗り換えやタクシーに忙しすぎて，気づかないから。
d. 彼らは，そうした職員が親切で2か国語を話せることがわかるから。

> **"Now, we're independent, and people can see that our physical condition doesn't matter.** They don't look at you as some strange creature any more."

Lesson4　長文問題：実践編−1

3. How has the Mexican government benefitted from the use of disabled staff?
   a. It has been able to reduce labour costs.
   b. It has filled jobs that average workers are unwilling to do.
   c. It has increased the number of tourists visiting Mexico.
   d. It is now seen as a leader in helping and supporting the disabled.

二本柳のひとことコメント

第3パラグラフは，メキシコ政府が障害者支援政策を積極的に推進している様子が述べられている。

「メキシコ政府は，障害を持つ職員を使うことでどのような利点があったか」
a. 政府は，人件費を削減することができた。
b. 政府は，普通の労働者がやりたがらない仕事を埋め合わせてきた。
c. 政府は，メキシコを訪れる旅行者の数を増やしてきた。
d. 政府は，今では，障害者援助・支援における主導的立場にあると考えられている。

> Another winner is the Mexican government, now **at the head of** the disabled-rights movement in the developing world.

4. Why do businessmen show an interest in the airport's disabled workers?
   a. They are eager to coordinate the efforts of state agencies.
   b. They know that only 0.4% of the public sector consists of disabled workers.
   c. They see them as a promising avenue for progress.
   d. They would like to employ some of them in their own companies.

二本柳のひとことコメント

最終パラグラフは，障害者雇用の将来性について肯定的に述べられている。
「なぜビジネスマンたちは空港の障害者職員に興味を持つのか」
a. 彼らは，政府機関の努力を熱心に調整したがっているから。
b. 彼らは，公共部門における障害者職員の割合が0.4％に過ぎないことを知っているから。
c. 彼らは，障害者職員を前進に向けた有望な道だと考えているから。
d. 彼らは，障害者の一部を自分の会社に雇いたいと思っているから。

> Perhaps the most promising avenue for progress is the example of the airport employees: Jesus Briones, one of Terminal 2's wheelchair workers, says businessmen passing through (routinely) ask him about hiring his counterparts.

✓ word check !

- attentive　注意深い，思いやりのある
- instruct ~　~に指示する
- proportion　割合
- promising　有望な
- miss ~　~をし損なう
- respectable　まずまずの
- sector　部門
- hire ~　~を雇う

Lesson4　長文問題：実践編-1

問題文訳

A メキシコシティーの主要な国際空港で，最初に気づくのは，手荷物引渡し所から続く通路に，タクシーや接続便へと乗客を誘導する微笑を浮かべた職員たちが並んでいるということだ。2番目に気づくのは，彼らが全員車椅子に乗っているということだ。2007年11月の新ターミナル開港以来，この空港は，世界に対するメキシコの顔として勤務し，障害を持ち2か国語を話す職員を約60名採用してきた。彼らがいるおかげで，頻繁に賛辞を送ったり，写真を撮ることを頼んだりする乗客と，彼らの上司の双方が大喜びしている。「彼らはプロであり，思いやりがあり，常に陽気であり，決して仕事を休むことがありません」と空港の社長のヘクター・ベラスケスは言う。

ベラスケス氏は当初，労働問題を扱う若い弁護士で重度の関節炎を患っているジャスミン・マルチネスの業績に感銘を受けた後，障害を持った職員を捜すことを思いついたと言っている。彼は，障害者向けの身体的，心理学的訓練プログラムを修了した20名を採用するよう空港会社に指示したが，その後結果を見るや，その数を3倍にしたのである。**B** そうして職員になった人たちは，人前に出たり，月給550ドルというまずまずの給与を支払われることで，わくわくしていると言っている。「仕事がなければ，どこが痛むのか考えながら，1日中家で座っていますよ」とマルチネスさんは言う。「今では私たちは自立していて，私たちの肉体的状態は問題ではないのだとわかってもらえます。奇妙な生き物だという目で見られることは，もはやありません」

C もう1人の勝者はメキシコ政府であり，現在，発展途上世界では，障害者の権利運動の先頭に立っている。2005年に，政府は国の機関相互の努力を連携させるために，協議会を設立した。それ以来，政府は，26,000の学校に車椅子用のスロープを設置したり，障害者のために住宅ローンの補助をすることを含め，多くの構想に着手してきた。協議会によると，障害者にも利用可能な政府の建物の割合は，2012年までに40％から90％に増加し，同じ期日までにすべての病院に手話通訳者がおかれる予定である。

残念なことに，空港によって示された例はまれなものである。全国障害者協議会によると，メキシコの人口の約10％を占める障害者に対する雇用は，社会のその他の人々の数値の半分にも満たず，公共部門においては，障害を持つ労働者は全体の0.4％にすぎない。**D** ことによると，前進に向けての最も有望な道は，空港で雇用されている人たちの例であろう。第2ターミナルの車椅子の職員の1人であるジーザス・ブライオンズは，通り過ぎるビジネスマンたちが，決まって自分と同じような障害者の雇用について尋ねてくる，と述べている。

2 次の英文を読んで下の問いに答えよ。
（社会科学部出題）

Why should Asian families be such powerful agents of influence? Here I need to step back a bit and note some very great differences between Asian and Western societies. Asians are much more inter-dependent and collectivist than Westerners, who are much more independent and individualist. These East-West differences go back at least twenty-five-hundred years to the time of Confucius and the ancient Greeks.

Confucius emphasized strict observance of proper role relations as the foundation of society, the relations being primarily those of emperor to subject, husband to wife, parent to child, elder brother to younger brother, and friend to friend. Chinese society, which was the prototype of all East Asian societies, was an agricultural one. In these societies, especially those that depend on irrigation, farmers need to cooperate with one another because cooperation is essential to economic activity. Such societies also tend to be very hierarchical, with a tradition of power flowing from the top to the bottom. Social bonds and constraints are strong. The most important part of Chinese society in particular is the extended family unit. Obedience to the will of the elders was, and to a substantial degree still is, an important bond linking people to one another.

This traditional role of the family is still a powerful factor in the relations of second- and even third-generation Asian Americans and their parents. I have had Asian American students tell me that they would like to go into psychology or philosophy but that it is not possible because their parents want them to be a doctor or an engineer. For my European American students, their parents' preferences for their occupations are about as relevant to them as their parents' taste in art.

The Greek tradition gave rise to a fundamentally new type of social relations. The economy of Greece was based not on large-scale agriculture but on trade, hunting, fishing, herding, piracy, and small agribusiness enterprises such as wine making and olive oil production. None of these activities required close, formalized relations among people. The Greeks, as a consequence, were independent and had the luxury of being able to act without being bound so much by social constraints. They had a lot of freedom to express their talents and satisfy their wants. The individual personality was highly valued and considered a proper object of commentary and study. Roman society continued the independent, individualistic tradition of the Greeks, and after a long period in which the European peasant was probably little more individualist than his Chinese counterpart, the Renaissance and then the Industrial Revolution took up again the individualist strain of Western culture and even accelerated it.

（1） According to this article, which **TWO** of the following are true?
　　a. It is said that the Greeks generally prefer to do things together with other people.
　　b. For the most part Westerners rely on others and fail to act on their own.
　　c. China was a farming society whose members found it necessary to help one another.

d. In ancient Greece the people of advanced age were usually disregarded and neglected.

e. Asian societies rarely tended to stress fairness and economic equality.

f. The societies of Greece and Rome had similar views concerning the individual.

g. Asian Americans do not follow the traditional custom of strong family ties.

h. The foundation of Greek society is quite similar in many ways to that of China.

_____

(2) According to this article, which one of the following is **NOT** true?

a. In East Asia farmers seldom had to worry about an adequate supply of water.

b. Individualism has been a prominent feature in the societies of the West.

c. The Greeks were never totally restrained by the pressures and controls of society.

d. In East Asia personal decisions often depend on the wishes and desires of parents.

e. The foundations of Greek society and Chinese society were fundamentally different.

_____

(3) Which one of the following could best be used in place of the phrase the prototype of ?

a. the final basis for

b. the previous example of

c. the major component for
　　d. the main measure of
　　e. the original model of

(4) According to this article, which one of the following best describes the society of China?
　　a. individualistic, agricultural, and traditional
　　b. collectivistic, hierarchical, and familial
　　c. interdependent, flexible, and influential
　　d. cultural, independent, and constrained
　　e. restrained, cooperative, and proud

(5) Which one of the following best describes the main point of this article?
　　a. Hunters and gatherers tend to be much more interdependent than traditional farmers.
　　b. Europeans find it easier than Chinese to adapt to unfamiliar and contrasting societies.
　　c. Asian-Americans will become more and more Asian as time slowly progresses.
　　d. Ancient differences between countries will gradually become more meaningless.
　　e. Cultural differences between East and West are closely related to historical factors.

（Lesson4　問題解答は p.179 にあります）

問題(1)

According to this article, which TWO of the following are true?

    a. It is said that the Greeks generally prefer to do things together with other people.
    b. For the most part Westerners rely on others and fail to act on their own.
    c. China was a farming society whose members found it necessary to help one another.
    d. In ancient Greece the people of advanced age were usually disregarded and neglected.
    e. Asian societies rarely tended to stress fairness and economic equality.
    f. The societies of Greece and Rome had similar views concerning the individual.
    g. Asian Americans do not follow the traditional custom of strong family ties.
    h. The foundation of Greek society is quite similar in many ways to that of China.

■指示文訳：本文によれば，次のうちどの2つが正しいか。

二本柳のひとことコメント

a. ギリシャ人の個人主義的性格が述べられているので，不一致。本問では，選択肢の配列が本文の記述順とは一致していないので，注意が必要である。

It is said that the Greeks generally prefer to do things together with other people.
「ギリシャ人は一般に，他人と一緒に物事を行うほうを好むと言われている」

> None of these activities required close, formalized relations among people. The Greeks, as a consequence, were independent and had the luxury of being able to act without being bound so much by social constraints. They had a lot of freedom to express their talents and satisfy their wants. The individual personality was highly valued and considered a proper object of commentary and study.

問題文訳［163ページ］ **a** 参照

b. 西洋人が自立している，と述べられているので，不一致。

For the most part Westerners rely on others and fail to act on their own.
「たいていの場合，西洋人は他人を頼り，自分で行動できない」

> Asians are much more inter-dependent and collectivist than Westerners, who are much more independent and individualist. These East-West differences go back at least twenty-five-hundred years to the time of Confucius and the ancient Greeks.

問題文訳［163ページ］ **b** 参照

c. 同趣旨のことが述べられているので，一致。

China was a farming society whose members found it necessary to help one another.
「中国は，お互いに助け合うことが必要だとわかっている人々から成る農耕社会であった」

> Chinese society, which was <u>the prototype of</u> all East Asian societies, **was an agricultural one**. In these societies, especially those that depend on irrigation, farmers need to cooperate with one another because cooperation is essential to economic activity.

問題文訳［163ページ］ **c** 参照

d. 本文中には古代ギリシャの高齢者に関する記述がないので，不一致。

In ancient Greece the people of advanced age were usually disregarded and neglected.
「古代ギリシャでは，高齢者は普通，注意を払われず無視された」

e. 本文中には公平さと経済的平等についての記述がないので，不一致。

Asian societies rarely tended to stress fairness and economic equality.
「アジア社会は，公平さと経済的平等を強調することはめったになかった」

f. 同趣旨のことが述べられているので，一致。

The societies of Greece and Rome had similar views concerning the individual.
「ギリシャ社会とローマ社会は，個人に関して同じような見方をしていた」

> **Roman society continued the independent, individualistic tradition of the Greeks**, and after a long period in which the European peasant was probably little more individualist than his Chinese counterpart, the Renaissance and then the Industrial Revolution took up again the individualist strain of Western culture and even accelerated it.

問題文訳［163ページ］ **f** 参照

g. アジア系アメリカ人においては今でも家族が強力な要素である，とあり，更にその具体例があげられているので，不一致。

Asian Americans do not follow the traditional custom of strong family ties.
「アジア系アメリカ人は，家族の強い絆という伝統的習慣に従わない」

> **This traditional role of the family is still a powerful factor** in the relations of second- and even third-generation Asian Americans and their parents. I have had Asian American students tell me that they would like to go into psychology or philosophy but that it is not possible because their parents want them to be a doctor or an engineer.

問題文訳［163ページ］ **g** 参照

Lesson4　長文問題：実践編-2

h. 中国社会の土台は役割関係だ，とあり，

The foundation of Greek society is quite similar in many ways to that of China.
「ギリシャ社会の土台は，中国社会の土台と多くの点できわめてよく似ている」

> Confucius emphasized **strict observance of proper role relations** as the foundation of society, the relations being primarily those of emperor to subject, husband to wife, parent to child, elder brother to younger brother, and friend to friend.

問題文訳［163ページ］ h-① 参照

一方，以下には，ギリシャ社会が新しい社会関係を生み出した，とある。両者に一致点がないので，不一致。

> The Greek tradition gave rise to a fundamentally new type of social relations.

問題文訳［163ページ］ h-② 参照

問題(2)　TRACK 09

According to this article, which one of the following is NOT true?

a. In East Asia farmers seldom had to worry about an adequate supply of water.

b. Individualism has been a prominent feature in the societies of the West.

c. The Greeks were never totally restrained by the pressures and controls of society.

d. In East Asia personal decisions often depend on the wishes and desires of parents.

e. The foundations of Greek society and Chinese society were fundamentally different.

● 155

■指示文訳：本文によれば，次のうちどれが正しくないか。

> 二本柳のひとことコメント

a. 灌漑に依存している，とは書かれているが，めったに心配することはなかった，とは述べられていないので，不一致。

In East Asia farmers seldom had to worry about an adequate supply of water.
「東アジアでは，農業従事者が水の十分な供給について心配することはめったになかった」

> **In these societies, especially those that depend on irrigation, farmers need to cooperate with one another** because **cooperation is essential to economic activity.**

b. 同趣旨のことが述べられているので，一致。

Individualism has been a prominent feature in the societies of the West.
「個人主義は，西洋社会の顕著な特徴であり続けている」

> Asians are much more inter-dependent and collectivist than Westerners, who are much more independent and individualist. These East-West differences go back at least twenty-five-hundred years to the time of Confucius and the ancient Greeks.

c. 同趣旨のことが述べられているので，一致。

The Greeks were never totally restrained by the pressures and controls of society.
「ギリシャ人は，社会の圧力と支配によって完全に抑制されていたというわけでは決してなかった」

> The Greeks, as a consequence, were independent and had the luxury of being able to act **without** being bound **so much** by social constraints.

d. 中国社会が今でも相当な程度に年長者の意思に従順である，と書かれており，アジア系アメリカ人の家族の絆の強さが具体例と共に述べられているので，一致。

In East Asia personal decisions often depend on the wishes and desires of parents.
「東アジアでは，個人的決定は親の要望や欲求に左右されることが多い」

> The most important part of Chinese society in particular is the extended family unit. Obedience to the will of the elders was, and to a substantial degree still is, an important bond linking people to one another.
>
> This traditional role of the family is still a powerful factor in the relations of second- and even third-generation Asian Americans and their parents. I have had Asian American students tell me that they would like to go into psychology or philosophy but that it is not possible because their parents want them to be a doctor or an engineer.

e. 中国社会の土台は役割関係だ，とあり，一方，ギリシャ社会が新しい社会関係を生み出した，とある。両者に一致点がないので，一致。

The foundations of Greek society and Chinese society were fundamentally different.
「ギリシャ社会と中国社会の土台は根本的に異なっていた」

> Confucius emphasized strict observance of proper role relations as the foundation of society, the relations being primarily those of emperor to subject, husband to wife, parent to child, elder brother to younger brother, and friend to friend.

> The Greek tradition gave rise to a fundamentally new type of social relations.

問題(3)

Which one of the following could best be used in place of the phrase <u>the prototype of</u>?

a. the final basis for
b. the previous example of
c. the major component for
d. the main measure of
e. the original model of

二本柳のひとことコメント

社会科学部の同意語句選択問題は難問が多い。

「下線部の語句(the prototype of)の代わりに用いるのに最も適しているのは次のどれか」
a. …への最終基盤　　b. …の先例　　c. …の主要要素
d. …への主要な手段　e. …の原型

問題(4)

According to this article, which one of the following best describes the society of China?

a. individualistic, agricultural, and traditional
b. collectivistic, hierarchical, and familial
c. interdependent, flexible, and influential
d. cultural, independent, and constrained
e. restrained, cooperative, and proud

Lesson4　長文問題：実践編-2

■指示文訳：本文によれば，次のうちどれが中国社会を最もよく表しているか。

> 二本柳のひとことコメント

a. 以下の文より individualistic は西洋社会の記述なので，不適当。

individualistic, agricultural, and traditional
「個人主義的，農業的，伝統的な」

> Asians are much more inter-dependent and collectivist than Westerners, who are much more independent and individualist.

b. 以下の文より，適当。

collectivistic, hierarchical, and familial
「集団的，階層的，家族的な」

> Asians are much more inter-dependent and collectivist than Westerners, who are much more independent and individualist.

> Such societies also tend to be very hierarchical, with a tradition of power flowing from the top to the bottom.

> The most important part of Chinese society in particular is the extended family unit.

c. flexible に関する記述がないので，不適当。

interdependent, flexible, and influential
「相互依存的，柔軟な，影響力がある」

d. 以下より independent は西洋社会の記述なので，不適当。

cultural, independent, and constrained
「文化的，自立的，制約された」

> Asians are much more inter-dependent and collectivist than Westerners, who are much more independent and individualist.

e. proud に関する記述がないので，不適当。

restrained, cooperative, and proud
「制約された，協力的な，誇り高い」

問題(5)

Which one of the following best describes the main point of this article?

a. Hunters and gatherers tend to be much more interdependent than traditional farmers.
b. Europeans find it easier than Chinese to adapt to unfamiliar and contrasting societies.
c. Asian-Americans will become more and more Asian as time slowly progresses.
d. Ancient differences between countries will gradually become more meaningless.
e. Cultural differences between East and West are closely related to historical factors.

■指示文訳：本文の主旨を最もよく表しているのは次のうちどれか。

> 二本柳のひとことコメント

a. 相互依存の度合いについての比較に関する記述がないので，不適当。

Hunters and gatherers tend to be much more interdependent than traditional farmers.
「狩猟者や採集者は，伝統的な農業従事者よりもはるかに相互依存している傾向がある」

b. 順応性についての比較に関する記述がないので，不適当。

Europeans find it easier than Chinese to adapt to unfamiliar and contrasting societies.
「ヨーロッパの人々は，中国人よりも，なじみの薄い対照的な社会に順応するのがたやすいとわかっている」

c. アジア的云々に関する記述がないので，不適当。

Asian-Americans will become more and more Asian as time slowly progresses.
「アジア系アメリカ人は，時がゆっくりと進行するにつれて，ますますアジア的になる」

d. 相違が今後どうなっていくのかは本文中に書かれていないので，不適当。

Ancient differences between countries will gradually become more meaningless.
「国と国との間の昔からある相違は，次第に無意味になっていくだろう」

e. 以下の文より適当。パラグラフの内容をつかみ，他の選択肢を着実に切っていきたい。

Cultural differences between East and West are closely related to historical factors.
「東西間の文化の相違は，歴史的要因と密接に関わっている」

Why should Asian families be such powerful agents of influence? Here I need to step back a bit and note some very great differences between Asian and Western societies. Asians are much more inter-dependent and collectivist than Westerners, who are much more independent and individualist. These East-West differences go back at least twenty-five-hundred years to the time of Confucius and the ancient Greeks.

Roman society continued the independent, individualistic tradition of the Greeks, and after a long period in which the European peasant was probably little more individualist than his Chinese counterpart, the Renaissance and then the Industrial Revolution took up again the individualist strain of Western culture and even accelerated it.

✓ word check !

- observance　遵守
- hierarchical　階級制度の，階層的な
- obedience　従順
- relevant　関連のある
- commentary　論評，評価
- irrigation　灌漑
- constraint　強制，制約
- substantial　相当な
- give rise to ～　～を生み出す
- strain　素質，傾向，気質

Lesson4　長文問題：実践編-2

問題文訳

　いったいなぜ，アジア人の家族はそれほど強力な影響力を及ぼしあっているのだろうか。ここで私は少し距離を置いて，アジア社会と西洋社会との非常に大きな違いにいくつか触れなければならない。**b** アジア人は西洋人よりもはるかに相互に依存しあい，集団主義的である。そして西洋人はアジア人よりもはるかに自立しており，個人主義的である。このような東洋と西洋との違いは，孔子や古代ギリシャ人の時代にまで，少なくとも 2500 年前にさかのぼる。

　h-① 孔子は，社会の基盤として適切な役割関係の厳守を強調した。その役割関係とは，主に，皇帝と臣下，夫と妻，親と子，兄と弟，そして友人同士の関係であった。**c** 東アジア社会全体の原型であった中国社会は，農耕社会であった。こういった社会，特に灌漑に依存するような社会では，協力し合うことが経済活動に欠かせないため，農業従事者は互いに協力し合う必要がある。そのような社会はまた，権力という伝統が上から下へと伝わることで，非常に階層的になる傾向がある。社会的な制約や絆は強力である。特に中国社会の最も重要な部分は，拡大家族という単位である。年長者の意思に従順であることは，人々を互いに結びつける重要な絆であったし，相当な程度に現在でもそうである。

　g 家族が持つこういった伝統的役割は，2 世，そして 3 世でさえアジア系アメリカ人とその親との関係において，今なお強力な要素である。自分は心理学か哲学の道に進みたいのだが，親は医師か技師になってもらいたいと思っているので，それは無理だ，とアジア系アメリカ人の学生に言われたことがある。ヨーロッパ系アメリカ人の私の学生にとっては，自分の職業に対する親の好みは，親自身の芸術の好みとほとんど同じ程度の意味しかもたない。

　h-② ギリシャの伝統は，根本的に新しい種類の社会的関係を生み出した。ギリシャ経済は大規模農業ではなく，交易，狩猟，漁業，牧畜，海賊行為や，ワイン造りやオリーブ油製造などの小規模な農業関連事業に基づいていた。**a** これらの活動は，いずれも人々の間の緊密で形式張った関係を必要としなかった。その結果，ギリシャ人は自立し，社会的制約にさほど縛られずに活動できる贅沢を手にした。彼らは，自らの才能を発揮し，欲求を満たせるだけの大いなる自由を手にしたのである。個人の人格は大いに価値あるものとされ，評価や研究にふさわしい対象とみなされた。**f** ローマ社会もギリシャ人の自立した個人主義的な伝統を受け継ぎ，ヨーロッパの農民がおそらく中国の農民とさほど変わらず個人主義的ではなかった長い期間を経た後，ルネサンスとその後の産業革命が，再び西洋文化の個人主義的気質を奪いかえして，それを加速させさえした。

3 次の英文を読み，設問1～10に答えよ。
（教育学部出題）

In early American English the prevailing type of expression was southern British, the language of the southern half of England and at the same time the literary language of the United Kingdom, [1] at first the literary language of England and that of America had the same general character. In the eighteenth century came Scotch-Irish immigrants in large numbers, also many from the north of England. The speech of these newcomers was, of course, northern British, a (2)<u>conservative</u> form of English preserving older sounds and expressions. The new settlers naturally went to the newer parts of the country west of the old colonies. Their presence there in large numbers influenced American English in certain respects. While the younger, southern British form of English remained intact for the most part on the Atlantic seaboard and in large measure also in the south generally, the modified form of it, characterized by older, northern British features, became established everywhere in the north except along the Atlantic seaboard.

On the other hand, the new things and the new needs of the New World called forth a large number of new words and new expressions. Moreover, the abounding, freer life of the New World created a new slang. Even conservative Scotch-Irish had something new to offer —— *will* in the first person of the future tense instead of literary *shall*. These differences in vocabulary and idiom will always distinguish the English-speaking peoples, but will not separate them. They have already stood a severe test. Between 1620 and 1800 important changes took place in the grammatical structure of English, both in Great Britain and America, but [4] drifting apart in this period of marked changes these two branches of English, at all important points, developed harmoniously together. This was the result of the universal tendency in colonial days among Americans [5] culture to follow in speech the usage of the mother country. The colonies had little literature of their own and were largely dependent in matters of culture upon the Old World. If it had not been for this general tendency of American culture, the language of the New World might have drifted away from that of England, for as can be seen by American popular speech, there is a very strong tendency [6] English on American soil to cling to the older forms of the language. About 1800 the structure of literary English had virtually attained its present form in both territories and was in both essentially the same. That since that date no syntactical changes of (7)<u>consequence</u> have taken place in either branch indicates a remarkable solidarity of structure. The English-speaking people are held together by their priceless common heritage —— the English language in its higher forms in science and literature. Constant contact with these forces will keep the different peoples in touch with one another. The same English life pulsates everywhere, insuring in spite of the different conditions a similarity, [8] a oneness, of evolution.

(1) 空所 [1] に入れるのに最もふさわしいものを a〜e から1つ選べ。
   a. despite   b. in that   c. as if   d. so that   e. because

_____

(2) 下線部（2）の語で最も強く発音する母音と同じ母音を持つものを a〜e から1つ選べ。
   a. sign   b. fur   c. dot   d. dim   e. gape

_____

(3) 本文の内容と合致するものを a〜e から1つ選べ。
   a. The English language of those who came later to America had younger features of the language.
   b. The older form of English was influenced and modified by the younger one in America.
   c. The English spoken by the people who came earlier to America preserved older features of the language.
   d. People who settled in the newer parts of America spoke an older form of English.
   e. The new form of English modified on the American soil spread in the East Coast regions of America.

_____

(4) 空所 [4] に入れるのに最もふさわしいものを a〜e から1つ選べ。
   a. by way of   b. instead of   c. on account of
   d. on top of   e. in the form of

_____

(5) 空所 [**5**] に入れるのに最もふさわしいものを a〜e から 1 つ選べ。

a. in　　b. over　　c. across　　d. of　　e. under

_____

(6) 空所 [**6**] に入れるのに最もふさわしいものを a〜e から 1 つ選べ。

a. to　　b. in　　c. towards　　d. for　　e. with

_____

(7) 下線部（**7**）の語はどのような意味で使われているか，最もふさわしいものを a〜e から 1 つ選べ。

a. result　　b. motivation　　c. significance
d. sufficiency　　e. consideration

_____

(8) 空所 [**8**] に入れるのに最もふさわしいものを a〜e から 1 つ選べ。

a. like　　b. if not　　c. as much as
d. for the most part　　e. from the direction of

_____

(9) 本文の内容と**合致しないもの**を a～e から 1 つ選べ。

　　a. American English did not drift apart from British English due to the inclination of American culture to follow British ways of speaking.

　　b. American English still tends to preserve the older forms of English.

　　c. American English can be distinguished from British English because it has vocabulary and idioms different from those of British English.

　　d. American English and British English developed in the same direction even after experiencing significant changes in the grammatical structure of the language.

　　e. American English had a strong tendency to create new words and new expressions because American people had little literature of their own.

　　　　　　　　　　　　　　　　　　_____

　　　　　　　　　（Lesson4 問題解答は p.179 にあります）

問題(1)

空所 [1] に入れるのに最もふさわしいものを a～e から1つ選べ。

 a. despite b. in that c. as if d. so that e. because

二本柳のひとことコメント

典型的な因果関係。

a. …にもかかわらず b. …という点で c. まるで…のように
d. その結果… e. なぜなら…だから

> ★ In early American English the prevailing type of expression was southern British, the language of the southern half of England and at the same time the **literary language of the United Kingdom,** [1] **at first the literary language of England and that of America had the same general character.**

問題文訳［177 ページ］ 1 参照

問題(2)

下線部（2）の語で最も強く発音する母音と同じ母音を持つものを a～e から1つ選べ。

 a. sign b. fur c. dot d. dim e. gape

二本柳のひとことコメント

平易な発音問題。

a. [sáin] b. [fə́:r] c. [dá:t, dɔ́t] d. [dím] e. [géip]

> The speech of these newcomers was, of course, northern British, a (2)<u>conservative</u> form of English preserving older sounds and expressions.

問題文訳［177 ページ］ 2 参照

問題(3)

本文の内容と合致するものを a〜e から 1 つ選べ。

TRACK 16

a. The English language of those who came later to America had younger features of the language.
b. The older form of English was influenced and modified by the younger one in America.
c. The English spoken by the people who came earlier to America preserved older features of the language.
d. People who settled in the newer parts of America spoke an older form of English.
e. The new form of English modified on the American soil spread in the East Coast regions of America.

> 二本柳のひとことコメント

a. 次ページの❶参照。典型的な〈反対〉パターン。
b. ❹参照。情報の〈すりかえ〉。
c. 前ページ★と❶参照。これまた〈反対〉。
d. ❶・❷を総括した正解選択肢。
e. ❹参照。情報の〈すりかえ〉。

本問は，設問の位置から考えても第 1 パラグラフについての設問であることは明白である。

a. アメリカに後からやってきた人々が話す英語は，その言語のより新しい特徴を持っていた。
b. 英語の古い形は，アメリカでは，より新しい形に影響を受け，変化した。
c. より早期にアメリカにやって来た人々によって話される英語は，その言語のより古い特徴を保っていた。
d. アメリカのより新しい地域に入植した人々は，より古い形の英語を話した。
e. アメリカの地で変化した新しい形の英語は，アメリカの東海岸地域に広がった。

❶ The speech of these newcomers was, of course, northern British, a conservative form of English preserving older sounds and expressions. ❷ The new settlers naturally went to the newer parts of the country west of the old colonies. ❸ Their presence there in large numbers influenced American English in certain respects. ❹ While the younger, southern British form of English remained intact for the most part on the Atlantic seaboard and in large measure also in the south generally, the modified form of it, characterized by older, northern British features, became established everywhere in the north except along the Atlantic seaboard.

問題文訳［177 ページ］ ❸ 参照

問題(4)

空所［ 4 ］に入れるのに最もふさわしいものを a〜e から 1 つ選べ。

  a. by way of b. instead of c. on account of
  d. on top of e. in the form of

二本柳のひとことコメント

空所直後の **drifting apart**「バラバラに離れてしまう（こと）」に対し，その後の主節では，**developed harmoniously**「調和して発展した」とあることから，逆の内容であることがわかる。

 a. …経由で b. …する代わりに c. …のために d. …の上に e. …の形で

Between 1620 and 1800 important changes took place in the grammatical structure of English, both in Great Britain and America, but ［ 4 ］ **drifting apart** in this period of marked changes these two branches of English, at all important points, **developed harmoniously together**.

問題文訳［177 ページ］ ❹ 参照

問題(5)

空所［ 5 ］に入れるのに最もふさわしいものを a～e から1つ選べ。

　　a. in　　b. over　　c. across　　d. of　　e. under

二本柳のひとことコメント

不可算名詞の **culture** には「教養」という意味があり，**Americans of culture**「教養あるアメリカ人」となる。

> This was the result of the universal tendency in colonial days **among Americans** [5] **culture** to follow in speech **the usage of the mother country**.

問題文訳［177 ページ］ 5 参照

問題(6)

空所［ 6 ］に入れるのに最もふさわしいものを a～e から1つ選べ。

　　a. to　　b. in　　c. towards　　d. for　　e. with

二本柳のひとことコメント

空所直後の English on American soil は，その後の to cling の意味上の主語であり，to 不定詞の意味上の主語は for で表す。なお，**for English on American soil to cling to the older forms of the language** は，直前の **a very strong tendency** の内容を表しており，「アメリカの地に根付いた英語が，その言語の古い形式に執着するという非常に強い傾向」となる。

Lesson4　長文問題：実践編-3

> The colonies had little literature of their own and were largely dependent in matters of culture upon the Old World. If it had not been for this general tendency of American culture, the language of the New World might have drifted away from that of England, for as can be seen by American popular speech, **there is a very strong tendency [　6　] English on American soil to cling to the older forms of the language.**

問題文訳［177ページ］ 6 参照

問題(7)

下線部（7）の語はどのような意味で使われているか，最もふさわしいものを a〜e から 1 つ選べ。

　　a. result　　b. motivation　　c. significance
　　d. sufficiency　　e. consideration

二本柳のひとことコメント

以下参照。不可算名詞の **consequence** には「重要性」という意味があり，**changes of consequence**「重要な変化」となる。

a. 結果　　b. 動機づけ　　c. 重要性　　d. 十分　　e. 考慮

> That since that date no syntactical **changes of** (7)**consequence** have taken place in either branch indicates a remarkable solidarity of structure.

問題文訳［177ページ］ 7 参照

問題(8)

空所 [8] に入れるのに最もふさわしいものを a〜e から1つ選べ。

　　a. like　　b. if not　　c. as much as
　　d. for the most part　　e. from the direction of

二本柳のひとことコメント

空所前の **a similarity**「類似性」と空所後の **a oneness**「単一性，同一性」から考える。

a. …のように　　b. …でないにしても　　c. …と同じくらい
d. 大部分は　　e. …の方角から

> The same English life pulsates everywhere, **insuring** in spite of the different conditions **a similarity**, [8] **a oneness**, of evolution.

問題文訳［177ページ］ 8 参照

Lesson4　長文問題：実践編-3

問題(9)

本文の内容と合致しないものを a～e から1つ選べ。

a. American English did not drift apart from British English due to the inclination of American culture to follow British ways of speaking.

b. American English still tends to preserve the older forms of English.

c. American English can be distinguished from British English because it has vocabulary and idioms different from those of British English.

d. American English and British English developed in the same direction even after experiencing significant changes in the grammatical structure of the language.

e. American English had a strong tendency to create new words and new expressions because American people had little literature of their own.

二本柳のひとことコメント

a.「合致しないもの」を選ぶ点に注意。次ページの❼に一致する。
b. ❾の後半に一致する。
c. ❹参照。選択肢の配列が本文の記述とは異なっている。
d. ❻に一致する。
e. ❶参照。「独自の文学を持たなかったから」とは書いていない。

a. アメリカ英語は，アメリカ文化にイギリス英語の話し方に従うという傾向があったため，イギリス英語からは離れなかった。
b. アメリカ英語は，今なお，古い形態の英語を残す傾向にある。
c. アメリカ英語は，イギリス英語とは異なる語彙やイディオムを持っているので，イギリス英語と区別することができる。
d. アメリカ英語とイギリス英語は，その文法的な構造において著しい変化を経た後でさえも，同じ方向に発展して言った。
e. アメリカ人は<u>独自の文学をほとんど持っていなかったので</u>，アメリカ英語には新しい言葉や表現を作り出す強い傾向があった。

❶ On the other hand, the new things and the new needs of the New World called forth a large number of new words and new expressions. ❷ Moreover, the abounding, freer life of the New World created a new slang. ❸ Even conservative Scotch-Irish had something new to offer —— *will* in the first person of the future tense instead of literary *shall*. ❹ These differences in vocabulary and idiom will always distinguish the English-speaking peoples, but will not separate them. ❺ They have already stood a severe test. ❻ Between 1620 and 1800 important changes took place in the grammatical structure of English, both in Great Britain and America, but [instead of] drifting apart in this period of marked changes these two branches of English, at all important points, developed harmoniously together. ❼ This was the result of the universal tendency in colonial days among Americans [of] culture to follow in speech the usage of the mother country. ❽ The colonies had little literature of their own and were largely dependent in matters of culture upon the Old World. ❾ If it had not been for this general tendency of American culture, the language of the New World might have drifted away from that of England, for as can be seen by American popular speech, there is a very strong tendency [for] English on American soil to cling to the older forms of the language.

問題文訳

1 初期のアメリカ英語において，広く行きわたっていた表現の形は，南部イギリス英語，つまりイングランドの南半分の言語であり，同時にイギリスの文語でもあった。その結果，当初は，イギリスとアメリカの文語は同じ一般的な特徴を持っていた。18世紀には，スコットランド系アイルランド人の移民たちが数多くやってきて，同様にイングランド北部からも大勢やってきた。**2・3** こういった新しくやってきた人たちの言語は，言うまでもなく，イギリス北部の英語で，それはより古い発音と表現を守っている保守的な形の英語であった。その新しい入植者たちは，自然と以前からの入植地より西のアメリカの新しい土地へ向かった。そこに彼らが大勢存在したことが，いくつかの点で，アメリカ英語に影響を及ぼした。より新しいイギリス南部の英語の形は，大西洋沿岸のほとんどの地域，および南部全般においても大体は，そのままの形で残っていたのに対し，より古いイギリス北部の英語の特徴を持った，変形した英語は，大西洋沿岸以外の北部全域で定着した。

他方で，新世界の新しい物事や新しい要求が，数多くの新語や新しい表現を生んだ。さらに，豊かでより自由な新世界での生活は，新しい俗語を生んだ保守的なスコットランド系アイルランド人でさえ，新しいものを提供した。文語の shall の代わりに，未来時制の第1人称に will を用いるようになったのだ。これらの語彙やイディオムにおける違いは，英語を話す諸国民を絶えず区別するが，切り離すわけではない。こういった違いは，すでに過酷な試練に耐えてきたのである。**4** 1620年から1800年の間に，イギリスとアメリカの両方において，英語の文法構造に重要な変化が起こったが，著しい変化が生じたこの時期にバラバラに離れてしまうのではなく，これら2つの英語の支流は，すべての重要な点において，互いに調和して発展したのである。**5** このことは，言葉においては母国の慣用に従うという，植民地時代における教養あるアメリカ人の間に共通する一般的傾向の結果であった。**6** 植民地は，独自の文学をほとんど持っておらず，文化ということに関しては旧世界に大いに依存していた。もしこのアメリカ文化の一般的傾向がなかったとしたら，新世界の言語はイングランドの言語から離れていったかもしれない。というのは，アメリカの大衆的な話し言葉に見られるように，アメリカの地に根付いた英語には，その言語の古い形式に執着するという非常に強い傾向があるからである。およそ1800年頃，英語の文語体の構造は，両方の領土内において，実質的に現在の形式に到達しており，どちらも本質的には同じであった。**7** その日以来，どちらの支流でも重大な構文上の変化が起こっていないということは，驚くほど構造が一致しているということを示している。英語を話す人々は，彼らの計り知れない共有財産，つまり，科学と文学における高次の形態の英語によって結びついているのである。このような力と絶え間なく接触することが，異なった国民を互いに接触させ続けていくだろう。**8** 状況が異なっているにもかかわらず，同一ではないにしても，進化の類似性を保ちながら，同じ英語の命がいたる所で脈動しているのである。

✓ word check !

- prevailing　広く行き渡っている
- character　特徴
- respect　点
- feature　特徴
- cling to ～　～に執着する
- solidarity　団結，一致
- insure ～　～を保つ，請け負う
- literary language　文語
- conservative　保守的な
- intact　そのままの形で
- drift apart　離れていく
- syntactical　構文上の
- pulsate　脈動する

Lesson4- 1　問題解答

(1) (A) 2. hired　(B) 3. thrilled　(C) 2. launched　(D) 4. routinely
(2) set by the airport is rare
(3) 1. b. They are among the first people seen by arriving passengers.
　　2. a. They are made aware that disabled staff can do the same work as able-bodied staff.
　　3. d. It is now seen as a leader in helping and supporting the disabled.
　　4. d. They would like to employ some of them in their own companies.

Lesson4- 2　問題解答

(1) c. China was a farming society whose members found it necessary to help one another.
　　f. The societies of Greece and Rome had similar views concerning the individual.
(2) a. In East Asia farmers seldom had to worry about an adequate supply of water.
(3) e. the original model of
(4) b. collectivistic, hierarchical, and familial
(5) e. Cultural differences between East and West are closely related to historical factors.

Lesson4- 3　問題解答

(1) d. so that　(2) b. fur
(3) d. People who settled in the newer parts of America spoke an older form of English.
(4) b. instead of　(5) d. of　(6) d. for　(7) c. significance
(8) b. if not
(9) e. American English had a strong tendency to create new words and new expressions because American people had little literature of their own.

LESSON 5 超長文問題

使用学部：法学部，国際教養学部，政治経済学部など。

1 Answer the questions below after reading the following passage.
（国際教養学部出題）

TRACK 01〜08

　Human intelligence is a puzzle. Although using IQ scores as a measurement of intelligence is controversial, some scientists believe we can use them to argue that intelligence is higher, on average, in some places than in others. And it seems to have been rising in recent decades. Why these two things should be true is also controversial. Recently, however, a group of researchers at the University of New Mexico have suggested the same explanation for both: the effect of infectious disease[1]. If they are right, it suggests that the control of such diseases is crucial to a country's development in a way that had not been understood before. Countries that have a lot of parasites[2] and pathogens[3] not only suffer the weakening effects of disease on their workforces, but also on the personal development of individuals.

　Christopher Eppig and his colleagues make their suggestion in the *Proceedings of the Royal Society*. They note that the brains of newly-born children require 87% of those children's metabolic[4] energy. In five-year-olds the figure is still 44% and even in adults the brain — a mere 2% of the body's weight — uses about a quarter of the body's energy. Any competition for this energy is likely to damage the brain's development, and parasites and pathogens compete for it in various ways. Some feed on the host's body directly to reproduce. Some, particularly those that live in the stomach, can prevent a person absorbing food. And all parasites and pathogens provoke the host's immune system[5] into activity, which prevents valuable energy from being used for more productive purposes.

There is a clear relationship between a country's disease burden and the average IQ scores of its people. The higher the country's disease burden, the lower the average IQ scores of its people. This is an example of an inverse correlation. To calculate the disease burden, the researchers used data from the World Health Organization (WHO). The WHO has developed the concept of a "disability-adjusted life year" (DALY), which is a measure of overall disease burden. The DALY measures not only potential years of life lost due to early death, but also years of healthy life lost by a person as a result of their being in a condition of poor health or disability.

The WHO is able to calculate the DALYs which are lost as a result of the impact of 28 infectious diseases. These data exist for 192 countries. The IQ scores came from work carried out earlier this decade by Richard Lynn, a British psychologist, and Tatu Vanhanen, a Finnish political scientist, who analyzed IQ studies from 113 countries, and from subsequent work by Jelte Wicherts, a Dutch psychologist.

At the bottom of the list of average IQ scores is Equatorial Guinea, followed by St Lucia. Cameroon, Mozambique and Gabon tie at third from bottom. These countries are also among those that have the highest infectious disease burden. At the top of the list of countries with the highest average IQ score is Singapore, followed by South Korea. China and Japan tie in third place. These countries all have relatively low levels of disease. America, Britain and a number of European countries follow behind the leaders.

The correlation between disease burden and lower IQ scores is about 67%, and the possibility that this strong statistical relationship occurred by chance is less than one in 10,000. Researchers are always trying to identify strong statistical correlations. They then hope to be able to explain the cause of these correlations. There may be many different possible causes, and researchers have to examine as many possible causes as they can, to give themselves a better chance of identifying the real cause correctly. As scientists say, "correlation is not causation" —— identifying a statistical relationship does not explain why that relationship exists —— so Mr. Eppig and his colleagues tried to eliminate other possible explanations.

Previous research teams have tried to suggest that income, education, low levels of agricultural labour (which is replaced by more mentally stimulating jobs), and climate (the challenge of surviving extreme weather might provoke the evolution of intelligence) could all be explanations for national differences in IQ scores. However, most of these possible causes are also likely to be linked to disease. By careful statistical analysis, Mr. Eppig and his colleagues show that all of these alternative possible causes of the correlation either disappear or are reduced to a small effect, when the consequences of disease are taken into account.

Importantly, there is also clear evidence that infections and parasites, such as malaria[6] and intestinal worms[7], have a negative effect on the development of the brain. A study of children in Kenya who survived the version of malaria that occurs in the brain suggests that one-eighth of them suffer long-term damage. In the view of Mr. Eppig and his colleagues, diarrhea[8] is the biggest threat. Diarrhea strikes children hard. It accounts for one-sixth of infant deaths, and even in those it does not kill, it prevents the absorption of food at a time when the brain is growing and developing rapidly.

The researchers predict that one type of health problem will increase with rising intelligence. Asthma[9] and other allergies are thought by many experts to be rising in frequency because the immune systems of young children, unchallenged by infection, are turning *against* the cells of the body that they are supposed to protect. Some studies already suggest a correlation between a country's allergy levels and its average IQ. Mr. Eppig and his colleagues predict that future work will confirm this relationship.

The other prediction, of course, is that as countries conquer disease, the intelligence of their citizens will rise. A rise in IQ scores over the decades has already been noticed in rich countries. It is called the "Flynn effect" after James Flynn, who discovered it. Its cause, however, has been mysterious —— until now. If Mr. Eppig is right, the almost complete absence of serious infections in rich countries, as a result of vaccination[10], clean water and the proper treatment of human waste, may explain much if not all of the Flynn effect.

When Dr. Lynn and Dr. Vanhanen originally published their IQ data, they used them to suggest that national differences in intelligence were the main reason for different levels of economic development. This new study reaches the opposite conclusion. It is actually lack of development, and the many health problems this brings, which explains the difference in IQ scores. No doubt, in a vicious circle, those differences help to keep poor countries poor. But the new theory offers a way to break the circle. If further work by researchers supports the ideas of Mr. Eppig and his colleagues, they will have done enormous good by providing policymakers with yet another reason why the elimination of disease should be one of the main aims of development.

注　infectious disease[1]：伝染病　　parasites[2]：寄生虫
　　pathogens[3]：病原菌　　　　　　metabolic[4]：（新陳）代謝の
　　immune system[5]：免疫システム　malaria[6]：マラリア
　　intestinal worms[7]：回虫　　　　diarrhea[8]：下痢
　　asthma[9]：ぜんそく　　　　　　vaccination[10]：予防接種

(1) **Choose the best way to answer each of the questions in accordance with the content of the passage.**

　1. Why are researchers especially concerned about the effects of parasites and pathogens on young children?
　　a. Their developing brains require more energy than those of adults.
　　b. Their immune systems are not yet as developed as those of adults.
　　c. They have a higher rate of infection than adults do.
　　d. They have a lower rate of recovery than adults do.
　　e. None of the above

2. What was the concept of the DALY (disability-adjusted life year) developed to measure?
   a. The adjusted average life expectancy
   b. The daily rate of parasite infections in developing countries
   c. The inverse correlation between disability and health
   d. The potential years of active life lost as a result of death or illness
   e. None of the above

3. How does Japan's DALY score compare to other countries' scores?
   a. As high as Singapore
   b. As low as Cameroon
   c. Equivalent to that of South Korea
   d. Higher than that of China
   e. None of the above

4. Which of the following was NOT used by previous researchers to explain national differences in IQ?
   a. Climate
   b. Education
   c. Ethnicity
   d. Income
   e. None of the above

5. What is true of diarrhea according to the passage?
   a. It causes brain damage in one-eighth of children in Kenya.
   b. It increases with intelligence.
   c. It kills 25% of all babies.
   d. It prevents the absorption of food among children.
   e. None of the above

   _____

6. According to the study by Mr. Eppig and his colleagues, what is the correct sequence of cause and effect?
   a. Lack of development together with health problems leads to low national IQ scores.
   b. Low levels of income and education lead to low national IQ scores.
   c. Low national intelligence leads to lack of development and health problems.
   d. The challenge of an extreme climate leads to high national IQ scores.
   e. None of the above

   _____

(2) Which of the following statements agree with what is written in the text? Mark your answers true (T) or false (F).

1. An inverse correlation means that as X increases, Y decreases, or vice versa.

   T ／ F

2. A number of studies suggest that there is a positive correlation between the frequency of asthma in a country and that country's average IQ scores.

<u>　T　／　F　</u>

3. The "disease burden" of a country refers to the cost of providing medical care to people who are ill.

<u>　T　／　F　</u>

4. The research of Eppig and his colleagues helps to explain why IQ has been rising in rich countries.

<u>　T　／　F　</u>

5. The research of Eppig and his colleagues largely supports the conclusions of earlier research by Lynn and Vanhanen.

<u>　T　／　F　</u>

6. The research of Eppig and his colleagues shows that lack of education is an important factor in explaining the national differences in IQ.

<u>　T　／　F　</u>

(Lesson5 問題解答は p.231, 232 にあります)

問題(1)

Choose the best way to answer each of the questions in accordance with the content of the passage.

1. Why are researchers especially concerned about the effects of parasites and pathogens on young children?
   a. Their developing brains require more energy than those of adults.
   b. Their immune systems are not yet as developed as those of adults.
   c. They have a higher rate of infection than adults do.
   d. They have a lower rate of recovery than adults do.
   e. None of the above

■指示文訳：本文の内容と一致するように，以下の質問に最も適するものを選べ。

二本柳のひとことコメント

英問英答問題については Lesson2 参照。

「なぜ研究者たちは，幼い子どもたちに対する寄生虫と病原菌の影響を特に気にするのか」
 a. 子供たちの発達中の脳は，大人の脳よりも多くのエネルギーを必要とする。
 b. 子供たちの免疫システムは，まだ大人ほど発達していない。
 c. 子供たちは，大人よりも感染率が高い。
 d. 子供たちは，大人よりも回復率が低い。
 e. 上記のいずれでもない

> **They note that the brains of newly-born children require 87% of those children's metabolic[4] energy.** In five-year-olds the figure is still **44%** and even in **adults** the brain —— a mere 2% of the body's weight —— uses **about a quarter** of the body's energy.

問題文訳［198ページ］ **1** 参照

2. What was the concept of the DALY (disability-adjusted life year) developed to measure?
   a. The adjusted average life expectancy
   b. The daily rate of parasite infections in developing countries
   c. The inverse correlation between disability and health
   d. The potential years of active life lost as a result of death or illness
   e. None of the above

二本柳のひとことコメント

疑問文と該当文に同じ単語があるので速やかに正解したい。

「DALY（障害調整生命年）という概念は，何を測定するために作り出されたのか」
 a. 調整された平均余命
 b. 発展途上国における１日あたりの寄生虫感染率
 c. 障害と健康との逆相関
 d. 死か病気の結果として失われる活動的な生活の潜在的年数
 e. 上記のいずれでもない

The WHO has developed the concept of a "disability-adjusted life year" (DALY), which is a measure of overall disease burden. **The DALY measures not only potential years of life lost due to early death, but also years of healthy life lost by a person as a result of their being in a condition of poor health or disability.**

問題文訳［198 ページ］ **2** 参照

3. How does Japan's DALY score compare to other countries' scores?
   a. As high as Singapore
   b. As low as Cameroon
   c. Equivalent to that of South Korea
   d. Higher than that of China
   e. None of the above

二本柳のひとことコメント

選択肢 **a** から **d** は，いずれも知能指数に関する記述であり，日本の **DALY** の数値は比較されていない。思い込みで読むと気づかない可能性がある。注意したい。

「日本の DALY の数値は，他の国々の数値と比べるとどうであるか」
 a. シンガポールと同じくらい高い　　b. カメルーンと同じくらい低い
 c. 韓国と等しい　　d. 中国より高い　　e. 上記のいずれでもない

> At the bottom of the list of average **IQ scores** is Equatorial Guinea, followed by St Lucia. Cameroon, Mozambique and Gabon tie at third from bottom. These countries are also among those that have the highest infectious disease burden. At the top of the list of countries with the highest average IQ score is Singapore, followed by South Korea. **China and Japan tie in third place.**

問題文訳［198 ページ］ 3 参照

Lesson5　超長文問題-1

4. Which of the following was NOT used by previous researchers to explain national differences in IQ?
   a. Climate
   b. Education
   c. Ethnicity
   d. Income
   e. None of the above

二本柳のひとことコメント

該当文が 1 つだけなので容易なはず。

「以前の研究者たちが，各国の知能指数の違いを説明するために用いなかったのは以下のうちのどれか」
a. 気候　　b. 教育　　c. 民族性　　d. 収入　　e. 上記のいずれでもない

> Previous research teams have tried to suggest that **income**, **education**, low levels of agricultural labour (which is replaced by more mentally stimulating jobs), and **climate** (the challenge of surviving extreme weather might provoke the evolution of intelligence) could all be explanations for national differences in IQ scores.

問題文訳［199 ページ］ 4 参照

5. What is true of diarrhea according to the passage?
   a. It causes brain damage in one-eighth of children in Kenya.
   b. It increases with intelligence.
   c. It kills 25% of all babies.
   d. It prevents the absorption of food among children.
   e. None of the above

二本柳のひとことコメント

正解の選択肢と同じ表記の語句が本文中にあるので手早く正解したいところ。

「本文によれば，下痢について当てはまるものはどれか」
a. 下痢は，ケニアの子供たちの8分の1において，脳の損傷を引き起こす。
b. 下痢は，知能とともに増加する。
c. 下痢は，すべての赤ん坊のうちの25%の命を奪っている。
d. 下痢は，子供たちの間の食物の吸収を妨げる。
e. 上記のいずれでもない

> It accounts for one-sixth of infant deaths, and even in those it does not kill, **it prevents the absorption of food** at a time when the brain is growing and developing rapidly.

問題文訳［199 ページ］ 5 参照

Lesson5 超長文問題-1

6. According to the study by Mr. Eppig and his colleagues, what is the correct sequence of cause and effect?

   a. Lack of development together with health problems leads to low national IQ scores.
   b. Low levels of income and education lead to low national IQ scores.
   c. Low national intelligence leads to lack of development and health problems.
   d. The challenge of an extreme climate leads to high national IQ scores.
   e. None of the above

二本柳のひとことコメント

正解以外の選択肢を検討する必要がないほど，明確に記載されている。

「エピグ氏と彼の同僚たちの研究によれば，正しい因果関係はどれか」
 a. 健康上の問題を伴った発展の欠如が，国の知能指数の低さにつながる。
 b. 収入と教育水準の低さが，国の知能指数の低さにつながる。
 c. 国の低い知能が，発展の欠如と健康上の問題につながる。
 d. 過酷な気候という難題が，国の知能指数の高さにつながる。
 e. 上記のいずれでもない

It is actually lack of development, and the many health problems this brings, which explains the difference in IQ scores.

問題文訳［200ページ］ 6 参照

問題(2)

Which of the following statements agree with what is written in the text? Mark your answers true (T) or false (F).

■指示文訳：次の記述のうち本文と一致するものはどれか。一致するものはT，一致しないものはFをマークせよ。

> 二本柳のひとことコメント

1. **vice versa**「その逆」は定番表現。

   An inverse correlation means that as *X* increases, *Y* decreases, or vice versa.
   「逆相関とは，Xが増加するにつれてYが減少する，あるいはその逆という意味である」

> The higher the country's **disease burden**, the lower the average **IQ scores** of its people. This is an example of an inverse correlation.

2. 連続する３文を総括している。

   A number of studies suggest that there is a positive correlation between the frequency of asthma in a country and that country's average IQ scores.
   「ある国のぜんそくの頻発度とその国の平均知能指数との間には，正の相関関係があることを示唆している研究は多い」

> The researchers predict that one type of health problem will increase with rising intelligence. Asthma[9] and other allergies are thought by many experts to be rising in frequency because the immune systems of young children, unchallenged by infection, are turning *against* the cells of the body that they are supposed to protect. **Some studies already suggest a correlation between a country's allergy levels and its average IQ.**

3. 第3パラグラフの内容に関する選択肢。「費用」に関する記述がない。

The "disease burden" of a country refers to the cost of providing medical care to people who are ill.
「ある国の『疾病負荷』とは，病気の人々に対して医療を提供する費用のことである」

　There is a clear relationship between a country's disease burden and the average IQ scores of its people. The higher the country's disease burden, the lower the average IQ scores of its people. This is an example of an inverse correlation. To calculate the disease burden, the researchers used data from the World Health Organization (WHO). The WHO has developed the concept of a "disability-adjusted life year" (DALY), which is a measure of overall disease burden. The DALY measures not only potential years of life lost due to early death, but also years of healthy life lost by a person as a result of their being in a condition of poor health or disability.

4. 主に第 10 パラグラフの内容に関する選択肢。

The research of Eppig and his colleagues helps to explain why IQ has been rising in rich countries.
「エピグ氏と彼の同僚たちの研究は，富裕国ではなぜ知能指数が上昇しているのかを説明するのに役立つ」

> The other prediction, of course, is that as countries conquer disease, the intelligence of their citizens will rise. **A rise in IQ scores over the decades has already been noticed in rich countries.** It is called the "Flynn effect" after James Flynn, who discovered it. Its cause, however, has been mysterious —— until now. If Mr. Eppig is right, the almost complete absence of serious infections in rich countries, as a result of vaccination[10], clean water and the proper treatment of human waste, may explain much if not all of the Flynn effect.
>
> When Dr. Lynn and Dr. Vanhanen originally published their IQ data, they used them to suggest that national differences in intelligence were the main reason for different levels of economic development.

5. 特に **This new study reaches the opposite conclusion.**「反対の結論に達している」に注目。

The research of Eppig and his colleagues largely supports the conclusions of earlier research by Lynn and Vanhanen.
「エピグ氏と彼の同僚たちの研究は，リンとヴァンハネンによるそれ以前の研究結果を大いに裏付けている」

When Dr. Lynn and Dr. Vanhanen originally published their IQ data, they used them to suggest that national differences in intelligence were the main reason for different levels of economic development. **This new study reaches the opposite conclusion.** It is actually lack of development, and the many health problems this brings, which explains the difference in IQ scores.

6. 主語のすり替え。総じて設問は平易。

The research of Eppig and his colleagues shows that lack of education is an important factor in explaining the national differences in IQ.
「エピグ氏と彼の同僚たちの研究は，教育の欠如が，国家間の知能指数の違いを説明する際の重要な要素であることを示している」

Previous research teams have tried to suggest that income, education, low levels of agricultural labour (which is replaced by more mentally stimulating jobs), and climate (the challenge of surviving extreme weather might provoke the evolution of intelligence) could all be explanations for national differences in IQ scores.

問題文訳

　人間の知能は謎である。知能の測定に知能指数（IQ）の得点を用いることには賛否両論あるが，ある地域では他の地域よりも平均して知能が高い，ということを立証するために，知能指数を使用できると考えている科学者もいる。それに，最近数十年で知能は高くなっているらしい。この２つのことが真実であることの理由についても議論が分かれる。しかし，最近ニューメキシコ大学の研究者グループが，そのどちらについても同じ理由説明を提示している。それは，伝染病の影響である。もし彼らが正しいなら，そういった病気を抑制することが，これまでには理解されていなかった意味において，国の発展にとってきわめて重要だということになる。寄生虫や病原菌が蔓延している国は，労働力だけでなく１人１人の個人的な発達までも弱体化させる病気の悪影響に悩まされている。

　クリストファー・エピグとその同僚たちは，『英国王立協会紀要』の中で彼らの提案をしている。 1 新生児の脳は，その子自身の代謝エネルギーの 87% を必要とすることに彼らは言及している。５歳児でもその数値は 44% であり，成人でさえ，脳は，体重のわずか２%の重さでしかないのに，身体のエネルギーのおよそ４分の１を使っている。このエネルギーを求めて競い合うことはなんであれ，脳の発達を損なうことになる可能性が高いのだが，寄生虫や病原菌は，様々な方法でこのエネルギーを求めて競い合うのである。宿主の体を直接の栄養源として繁殖するものもある。とりわけ腹部に生息するもののように，人間の食物吸収を妨げかねないものもいる。そして，寄生虫や病原菌はすべて，宿主の免疫システムを刺激して活性化させ，そのために貴重なエネルギーがより生産的な目的に用いられることが妨げられているのである。

　国の疾病負荷と，その国民の知能指数の平均値との間に，明確な関連がある。その国の疾病負荷が高ければ高いほど，国民の平均知能指数は低い。これは逆相関の一例である。疾病負荷を算出するために，研究者たちは世界保健機関（WHO）のデータを用いた。 2 WHO は，「障害調整生命年」（DALY）という概念を作り出したが，全般的な疾病負荷を測るものである。DALY は，早期死亡によって失われたかもしれない寿命だけでなく，病弱や障害を負っている状況にある結果として個人が失う健康な生活の年数も測定する。

　WHO では，28 種の伝染病の影響の結果として失われる DALY を算出することができる。192 カ国に関してこれらのデータが存在する。知能指数は，113 カ国の知能指数調査を分析した，イギリスの心理学者リチャード・リンとフィンランドの政治学者タトゥ・ヴァンハネンによってこの 10 年間のはじめに行われた調査と，オランダの心理学者イェルテ・ウィヘルツによるその後の研究によるものである。

　 3 平均知能指数リストの最下位は赤道ギニアで，その次がセントルシアである。カメルーン，モザンビーク，ガボンが下から３位で並んでいる。これらの国々は，伝染病の疾病負荷が最も高い国々にもなっている。平均知能指数リストの最上位はシンガポールで，韓国がそれに次ぐ。中国と日本が３位で並んでいる。これらの国々はどこも，疾病のレベルが比較的

低い。アメリカ，イギリス，多くのヨーロッパ諸国がトップレベルの国々の後に続く。
　疾病負荷と知能指数の低さとの相関関係は，およそ67％で，こうした統計上の強い関連が偶然生じる確率は，1万分の1未満である。研究者たちは常に，強力な統計上の相関関係を突き止めようと努力している。そして，こうした相関関係の原因を説明できることを願っている。多様な原因と考えられるものが数多く存在するかもしれず，研究者たちは，真の原因を正しく特定する可能性を高めるために，考えられる原因をできるだけ数多く検証しなければならない。科学者たちが言うように，「相関関係は因果関係ではない」，つまり，統計上の関係を特定したからといって，なぜその関係が存在するのかを説明したことにはならないのだ。そこで，エピグ氏と彼の同僚たちは，他の考えられる理由を除外しようと試みた。
　■4▶それ以前の研究チームは，収入，教育，農業労働の水準の低さ（精神的により刺激のある仕事に取って代わられる），気候（過酷な気候を生き抜くという難題が知能の発達を誘発するかもしれない）といったものすべてが，国ごとの知能指数が異なる理由を説明しうる，と示そうとしてきた。しかし，これらの考えられる原因のほとんどは，病気と関連する可能性の高いものでもある。統計を慎重に分析することによって，エピグ氏と彼の同僚たちは，病気がもたらす結果を考慮に入れると，このような相関関係について他に考えられる原因は，消滅するか，わずかな影響にとどまるということを示している。
　重要なことに，マラリアや回虫などのような伝染病や寄生虫は，脳の発達に悪影響を及ぼす，という明確な証拠もある。脳内に生じる種類のマラリアを生き延びたケニアの子供たちについての研究では，彼らの8分の1が長期にわたる損傷を被っていることが示されている。エピグ氏と彼の同僚たちの見解では，下痢が最大の脅威である。■5▶下痢は，子供たちを大変苦しめる。下痢は，乳幼児の死因の6分の1を占め，死に至らずにすんだ子供においても，脳が急速に成長し，発達している時期に，食べ物の吸収を妨げるのである。
　研究者たちは，知能の上昇とともに，ある種の健康問題が増加するだろうと予測している。ぜんそくやその他のアレルギーの頻度が増すのは，幼い子供たちの免疫システムが，伝染病感染の脅威にさらされていないがゆえに，本来守るべき体細胞を攻撃対象とするためだ，と多くの専門家が考えている。国のアレルギーの多さと，その国の平均知能指数との相関関係を示唆する研究もすでにある。エピグ氏と彼の同僚たちは，今後の研究でこの関係が裏付けられるだろう，と予測している。
　もちろん，もう1つの予測は，各国が病気を克服するにつれて，国民の知能も高まるだろう，というものである。富裕国では，この数十年間にわたって知能指数が上昇していることがすでに指摘されている。それは，発見者であるジェームズ・フリンにちなんで「フリン効果」と呼ばれている。しかしながら，その原因は，今に至るまでわかっていない。もしエピグ氏が正しければ，予防接種，清潔な水，排泄物の適切な処理などにより，富裕国では深刻な伝染病がほとんどなくなったことで，フリン効果のすべてではないとしても，その多くについて説明がつくかもしれない。
　そもそもリン博士とヴァンハネン博士が知能指数のデータを公表したとき，彼らは，各国

の知能の違いが経済発展の度合いが異なる主要な理由である，ということを示すために，それらのデータを用いた。この新しい研究では，それとは反対の結論に達している。 ▶6 実際には，発展の欠如と，そのことがもたらす数多くの健康上の問題こそ，知能指数の違いを説明するものなのだ。確かに，悪循環によって，そういった格差が貧困国を貧しいままにするのに寄与している。しかしながら，この新説は，その悪循環を断ち切る方法を提示している。研究者たちによるさらなる研究によって，エピグ氏と彼の同僚たちの考えが裏付けられれば，病気の根絶が発展の主な目的の1つであるべきさらにもう1つの理由を，政策立案者たちに提供することによって，大変な貢献をしたということになるだろう。

☑ word check !

- controversial　議論の余地のある
- suggestion　提案
- provoke ... into ～　…を刺激して～させる
- burden　負担・負荷
- overall　全体の
- subsequent　その後の
- causation　因果関係
- consequence　結果
- immune system　免疫システム
- colleague　同僚
- competition　競争，競い合うこと
- inverse correlation　逆相関
- impact　強い影響
- statistical　統計上の
- eliminate ～　～を除外する
- predict ～　～を予測する
- vicious circle　悪循環

Lesson5 超長文問題-2

2 Read the passage and answer the questions below.
（法学部出題）
TRACK 09〜17

① It might sound odd to say this about something people deal with at least three times a day, but food in America has been more or less invisible, politically speaking, until very recently. At least until the early 1970s, when a bout of food-price inflation and the appearance of books critical of industrial agriculture threatened to propel the subject to the top of the national agenda, Americans have not had to think very hard about where their food comes from, or what it is doing to the planet, their bodies, and their society.

② Most people count this as a blessing. Americans spend a smaller percentage of their income on food than any people in history —— slightly less than ten percent —— and a smaller amount of their time preparing it: a mere thirty-one minutes a day on average, including clean-up. The supermarkets brim with produce summoned from every corner of the globe, a steady stream of novel food products (17,000 new ones each year) crowds the middle aisles, and in the freezer case you can find "home meal replacements" in every conceivable ethnic stripe, demanding nothing more of the eater than opening the package and waiting for the microwave to chirp. Considered in the long sweep of human history, in which getting food dominated not just daily life but economic and political life as well, having to worry about food as little as we do, or did, seems almost a kind of dream.

③ The dream that the age-old "food problem" had been largely solved for most Americans was sustained by the tremendous postwar increases in the productivity of American farmers, made possible by cheap fossil fuel (the key ingredient in both chemical fertilizers and pesticides) and changes in agricultural policies. Asked by President Nixon to try to drive down the cost of food after it had spiked in the early 1970s, Agriculture Secretary Earl Butz shifted the historical focus of federal farm policy from supporting prices for farmers to boosting yields of a small handful of commodity crops (corn and soybeans especially) at any cost. The administration's cheap food policy worked almost too well: crop prices fell, forcing farmers to produce still more simply to break even. This led to a deep depression in the farm belt in the 1980s, followed by a brutal wave of consolidation resulting in the loss of smaller farms to larger businesses. Most importantly, the price of food came down, or at least the price of the kinds of foods that could be made from corn and soybeans: processed foods and sweetened beverages and feedlot meat. Prices for fresh produce have increased since the 1980s. Washington had succeeded in eliminating food as a political issue —— an objective dear to most governments at least since the time of the French Revolution.

④ But although cheap food is good politics, it turns out that there are significant costs —— to the environment, to public health, to the public purse, even to the culture —— and as these have become impossible to ignore in recent years, food has come back into view. Beginning in the late 1980s, a series of food safety scandals opened people's eyes to the way their food was being produced, each one drawing the curtain back a little further on a food system that had changed beyond recognition. When BSE, or mad cow disease, surfaced in England in 1986, Americans learned that cattle, which are herbivores, were routinely being fed the flesh of other cattle; the practice helped keep meat cheap but at the risk of a hideous brain-wasting disease. The 1993 deaths of four children in Washington State who had eaten hamburgers from the fast-food chain, Jack in the Box, were traced to meat contaminated with *E.coli* O157:H7, a mutant strain of the common intestinal bacteria first identified in feedlot cattle in 1982. Since then, repeated outbreaks of food-borne illness linked to new antibiotic-resistant strains of bacteria have turned a bright light on the shortsighted practice of routinely administering antibiotics to food animals, not to treat disease but simply to speed their growth and allow them to <u>withstand</u> the filthy and stressful conditions in which they live.

⑤ In the <u>wake</u> of these food safety scandals, the conversation about food politics that briefly flourished in the 1970s was picked up again in a series of books, articles, and movies about the consequences of industrial food production. Food journalism began in 2001 with the publication of Eric Schlosser's *Fast Food Nation* and Marion Nestle's *Food Politics* the following year. These and other books published in the last decade have succeeded in making clear connections between the methods of industrial food production, agricultural policy, food-borne illness, childhood obesity, the decline of the traditional family meal, and, notably, the decline of family income beginning in the 1970s.

⑥ Besides drawing women into the workforce, falling wages made fast food both cheap to produce and a welcome option for struggling families. The picture of the food economy Schlosser painted resembles an upside-down version of the social compact sometimes referred to as "Fordism." That is, instead of paying workers well enough to allow them to buy things like cars, as Henry Ford proposed to do, companies like Wal-Mart and

McDonald's pay their workers so poorly that they can afford only the cheap, low-quality food these companies sell, creating a kind of vicious cycle driving down both wages and the quality of food. The advent of fast food and cheap food in general has, in effect, subsidized the decline of family incomes in America.

⑦ The rise of fast food and the collapse of everyday cooking have also damaged family life and community by undermining the institution of the shared meal, eroding the civility on which our political culture depends. By continually snacking instead of sitting down for leisurely meals, and watching television during mealtimes instead of conversing —— forty percent of Americans watch television during meals —— we have unthinkingly wrecked one of the nurseries of democracy: the family meal. It is the temporary democracy of the table that teaches children the art of conversation and helps them to acquire the habits of civility —— sharing, listening, taking turns, negotiating differences, arguing without offending —— and it is these habits that are lost when we eat alone and on the run.

⑧ The invisibility of these issues until recently is due to the identification of food work with women and the related fact that eating, by its very nature, falls on the wrong side of the mind-body divide. Food is experienced through the senses of touch, smell, and taste, which rank lower on the hierarchy of senses than sight and hearing, which are typically thought to give rise to knowledge. In most philosophy, religion, and literature, food is associated with body, animal, female, and appetite —— things civilized men have sought to overcome with reason and knowledge.

(1) **Choose the best way to complete the following sentences about Paragraphs ① to ⑧.**

1. In Paragraph ① the writer mainly

   _____

2. In Paragraph ② the writer mainly

   _____

3. In Paragraph ③ the writer mainly

   _____

4. In Paragraph ④ the writer mainly

   _____

5. In Paragraph ⑤ the writer mainly

   _____

6. In Paragraph ⑥ the writer mainly

   _____

7. In Paragraph ⑦ the writer mainly

   _____

8. In Paragraph ⑧ the writer mainly

   _____

a. argues that the availability of cheap, poor-quality food has enabled big businesses to get away with paying their workers less.
b. criticizes American eating habits for their negative effects on both family life and the way people communicate with one another in society.
c. describes the absence of concern in America about where the next meal will come from as unprecedented.
d. explains how America was the first country to produce cheap food since the French Revolution.
e. notes the revival of food as a controversial issue at the beginning of the twenty-first century.
f. proposes that instead of eating while watching television, women should return to the kitchen and spend more time cooking.
g. provides several examples of the dangers to public health posed by modern agricultural practices.
h. states that children died because they ate hamburgers that contained meat contaminated with BSE.
i. suggests that because food has traditionally been associated with women, it was thought to be unworthy of serious consideration.
j. summarizes the policies that made food cheap and the effects of these policies on farmers.
k. worries that children are failing to learn how to speak because they seldom sit down to eat meals with their families.
l. writes that food was not an important political issue in America until about forty years ago.

(2) **Choose the ONE way to complete each of these sentences that is NOT correct according to the passage.**

1. Most Americans
    a. are able to buy a wide variety of easily-prepared food at supermarkets.
    b. have access to food made cheaper at the expense of farmers' incomes.
    c. have not had to pay much attention to the effect food has on their health until recently.
    d. mainly eat the kinds of food that can be made from corn and soybeans.
    e. spend less time and money on food than any other people in history.

    _____

2. The results of America's agricultural policies have included
    a. enabling women to enter the workforce.
    b. farmers losing money and selling their farms.
    c. lower wages, lower food prices, and lower quality food.
    d. the outbreak of diseases such as mad cow disease.
    e. the widespread use of antibiotics in the production of meat.

    _____

3. The social cost of modern American eating habits includes
   a. a decline in the interpersonal skills that are necessary for democracy to function.
   b. a decline in the number of families who sit down to eat dinner together.
   c. a relatively large number of people who watch television while they eat.
   d. children who do not learn how to take part in conversations.
   e. the increasing number of women who are required to prepare food for their families.

   _____

(3) **Choose the best way to complete each of these sentences, which relate to the underlined words in the passage.**

   1. Here "withstand" means
      a. to clean.   b. to oppose.   c. to protest.
      d. to remove.   e. to resist.

   _____

   2. Here "wake" means
      a. aftermath.   b. awakening.   c. funeral
      d. trace.   e. watch.

   _____

208

(4) Which ONE of the following sentences best sums up the author's argument in the passage?

　a. Although most foods are cheap in America, food safety scandals have shown that fast food and convenience foods are bad for human and animal health.
　b. Americans spend less time and money buying and preparing food than people in other countries, but they worry about food more.
　c. Government policy has helped not only to lower food prices in America, but also to reduce family incomes.
　d. In America, food has not been a political issue because food work is traditionally associated with women and their bodily appetites.
　e. Lower family incomes, food safety scandals, and a decline in civility have been the unintended consequences of America's cheap food policy.

（Lesson5 問題解答は p.231, 232 にあります）

問題(1)

Choose the best way to complete the following sentences about Paragraphs ① to ⑧.

■指示文訳：第1段落から第8段落について，以下の文を完成させるのに最も適するものを選べ。

> 二本柳のひとことコメント

1. 「重要な政治問題ではなかった」については第1文，「40年ほど前」については第2文参照。

   I. (In Paragraph ① the writer mainly) writes that food was not an important political issue in America until about forty years ago.
   「（第1段落で筆者は主に）食べ物は，40年ほど前までアメリカにおける重要な政治問題ではなかったと書いている」

> It might sound odd to say this about something people deal with at least three times a day, **but food in America has been more or less invisible, politically speaking, until very recently. At least until the early 1970s**, when a bout of food-price inflation and the appearance of books critical of industrial agriculture threatened to propel the subject to the top of the national agenda, Americans have not had to think very hard about where their food comes from, or what it is doing to the planet, their bodies, and their society.

問題文訳［227ページ］ **1** 参照

2. 特に,以下の文参照。本文中の **seems almost a kind of dream** が,**unprecedented** と言い換えられている。このような表現の言い換えを学習段階ではじっくりと味わって感覚を養ってもらいたい。

   c. (In Paragraph ② the writer mainly) describes the absence of concern in America about where the next meal will come from as unprecedented.
   「(第2段落で筆者は主に) 次の食事がどこからくるものなのかアメリカで関心がもたれていないことを先例のないことだと説明している」

> Considered in the long sweep of human history, in which getting food dominated **not just** daily life **but** economic and political life as well, having to worry about food as little as we do, or did, **seems almost a kind of dream**.

問題文訳［227ページ］ 2 参照

3. 特に以下参照。

   j. (In Paragraph ③ the writer mainly) summarizes the policies that made food cheap and the effects of these policies on farmers.
   「(第3段落で筆者は主に) 食品を安価にした政策と,こうした政策が農業従事者に及ぼす影響をまとめている」

> The administration's cheap food policy worked almost too well: crop prices fell, forcing farmers to produce still more simply to **break even**.

問題文訳［227ページ］ 3 参照

4. 以下に2種類の事例が挙げられている。具体例の総括。

g. (In Paragraph ④ the writer mainly) provides several examples of the dangers to public health posed by modern agricultural practices.

「(第4段落で筆者は主に)現代の農業の慣行によって公衆衛生がさらされている危険性の事例をいくつか提示している」

> When **BSE, or mad cow disease,** surfaced in England in 1986, Americans learned that cattle, which are herbivores, were routinely being fed the flesh of other cattle; the practice helped keep meat cheap but at the risk of a hideous brain-wasting disease. The 1993 deaths of four children in Washington State who had eaten hamburgers from the fast-food chain, Jack in the Box, were traced to meat contaminated with **E.coli O157:H7**, a mutant strain of the common intestinal bacteria first identified in feedlot cattle in 1982. Since then, repeated outbreaks of food-borne illness linked to new antibiotic-resistant strains of bacteria have turned a bright light on the shortsighted practice of routinely administering antibiotics to food animals, not to treat disease but simply to speed their growth and allow them to withstand the filthy and stressful conditions in which they live.

問題文訳［228ページ］ 4 参照

5. 特に以下参照。

e. (In Paragraph ⑤ the writer mainly) notes the revival of food as a controversial issue at the beginning of the twenty-first century.
「(第5段落で筆者は主に) 21世紀の初めに，食べ物が議論の余地がある問題として再び取り上げられるようになったことを述べている」

> **In the <u>wake</u> of these food safety scandals, the conversation about food politics that briefly flourished in the 1970s was picked up again in a series of books, articles, and movies about the consequences of industrial food production.** Food journalism began in **2001** with the publication of Eric Schlosser's *Fast Food Nation* and Marion Nestle's *Food Politics* the following year.

問題文訳［228ページ］ **5** 参照

6. 特に以下参照。

a. (In Paragraph ⑥ the writer mainly) argues that the availability of cheap, poor-quality food has enabled big businesses to get away with paying their workers less.
「(第6段落で筆者は主に) 安価で低品質の食品が手に入ることで，大企業は従業員への賃金の支払いを抑えることが可能になったと主張している」

> **That is, instead of paying workers well enough** to allow them to buy things like cars, as Henry Ford proposed to do, **companies** like Wal-Mart and McDonald's **pay** their **workers so poorly that they can afford only the cheap, low-quality food** these companies sell, creating a kind of vicious cycle driving down both wages and the quality of food.

問題文訳［228ページ］ **6** 参照

7. 「家庭生活」については前文,「社会における人々の意思疎通のあり方」については後文参照。

   b. (In Paragraph ⑦ the writer mainly) criticizes American eating habits for their negative effects on both family life and the way people communicate with one another in society.
「(第7段落で筆者は主に)アメリカ人の食習慣が,家庭生活にも,社会における人々の意思疎通のあり方にも悪影響を及ぼしていることを批判している」

> **By** continually **snacking** instead of sitting down for leisurely meals, and **watching television** during mealtimes **instead of conversing** —— forty percent of Americans watch television during meals —— we have unthinkingly wrecked one of the nurseries of democracy: the family meal. It is the temporary democracy of the table that teaches children the art of conversation and helps them to acquire the habits of civility —— sharing, listening, taking turns, negotiating differences, arguing without offending —— and it is these habits that are lost when we eat alone and on the run.

問題文訳［228ページ］ 7 参照

8. 特に以下参照。

   i. (In Paragraph ⑧ the writer mainly) suggests that because food has traditionally been associated with women, it was thought to be unworthy of serious consideration.
「(第8段落で筆者は主に)食べ物は伝統的に女性と結びつけて考えられてきたので,真剣に論じる価値がないと考えられていたことを示唆している」

> **The invisibility of these issues until recently is due to the identification of food work with women** and the related fact that eating, by its very nature, falls on the wrong side of the mind-body divide. Food is experienced through the senses of touch, smell, and taste, which rank lower on the hierarchy of senses than sight and hearing, which are typically thought to give rise to knowledge.

問題文訳［229ページ］ 8 参照

Lesson5　超長文問題-2

正解とはならないその他の選択肢

TRACK 10

二本柳のひとことコメント

d. 第3段落に関連する記述があるが，下線部の記述がない。

explains how America <u>was the first country</u> to produce cheap food since the French Revolution.
「フランス革命以降，アメリカが安価な食品を生産する最初の国となったいきさつを説明している」

f. 第2段落などに関連する記述があるが，女性だけがそうするべきだという記述がない。

<u>proposes</u> that instead of eating while watching television, <u>women should return to the kitchen and spend more time cooking.</u>
「テレビを見ながら食事をするのではなく，女性は台所に戻り，調理をすることにより多くの時間を費やすべきだと提案している」

h. 第4段落に関連する記述があるが，原因はBSEではなくO157である。情報のすり替え。

states that children died because they ate <u>hamburgers that contained meat contaminated with BSE.</u>
「子供たちが，BSEで汚染された肉を用いたハンバーガーを食べたために亡くなったことを述べている」

k. 第7段落に関連する記述があるが，結論部分がすり替わっている。ここで懸念されているのは，「話し方が身につけられなくなっていること」ではなく，「民主主義を育む条件の破壊」である。情報のすり替え。

worries that <u>children are failing to learn how to speak</u> because they seldom sit down to eat meals with their families.
「子供たちが腰かけて家族と共に食事をすることがほとんどないため，話し方が身につけられなくなっていることを心配している」

215

問題(2)

Choose the ONE way to complete each of these sentences that is NOT correct according to the passage.

1. Most Americans
    a. are able to buy a wide variety of easily-prepared food at supermarkets.
    b. have access to food made cheaper at the expense of farmers' incomes.
    c. have not had to pay much attention to the effect food has on their health until recently.
    d. mainly eat the kinds of food that can be made from corn and soybeans.
    e. spend less time and money on food than any other people in history.

■指示文訳：本文に従って，各英文を完成させる上で，正しくないものを1つ選べ。
「大部分のアメリカ人は…」

Lesson5 超長文問題-2

> 二本柳のひとことコメント

a. 第2段落第3文の内容と一致。

are able to buy a wide variety of easily-prepared food at supermarkets.
「スーパーマーケットで，非常に様々な簡単に調理できる食品を買うことができる」

> **The supermarkets brim with produce summoned from every corner of the globe**, a steady stream of novel food products (17,000 new ones each year) crowds the middle aisles, and in the freezer case you can find "home meal replacements" in every conceivable ethnic stripe, demanding nothing more of the eater than opening the package and waiting for the microwave to chirp.

b. 第3段落第3文の内容と一致。

have access to food made cheaper at the expense of farmers' incomes.
「農業従事者の収入を犠牲にして，より安く作られた食品を手に入れることができる」

> The administration's cheap food policy worked almost too well: crop prices fell, forcing farmers to produce still more simply to break even.

c. 第1段落第2文の内容と一致。

have not had to pay much attention to the effect food has on their health until recently.
「最近まで，食べ物が彼らの健康に及ぼす影響についてあまり関心を払う必要がなかった」

> At least until the early 1970s, when a bout of food-price inflation and the appearance of books critical of industrial agriculture threatened to propel the subject to the top of the national agenda, **Americans have not had to think very hard** about where their food comes from, or what it is doing to the planet, their bodies, and their society.

> 二本柳のひとことコメント

d. 第3段落第5文参照。価格が下がったとしか述べられていないので，不一致。

mainly eat the kinds of food that can be made from corn and soybeans.
「主としてトウモロコシや大豆から作られる食品を食べている」

> Most importantly, the price of food came down, or at least the price of the kinds of foods that could be made from corn and soybeans: processed foods and sweetened beverages and feedlot meat.

> 二本柳のひとことコメント

e. 第2段落第2文の内容と一致。

spend less time and money on food than any other people in history.
「歴史上他のどの国民と比べても，食べ物に費やす時間とお金が少ない」

> Americans spend a smaller percentage of their income on food than any people in history —— slightly less than ten percent —— and a smaller amount of their time preparing it: a mere thirty-one minutes a day on average, including clean-up.

Lesson5 超長文問題-2

2. The results of America's agricultural policies have included
   a. enabling women to enter the workforce.
   b. farmers losing money and selling their farms.
   c. lower wages, lower food prices, and lower quality food.
   d. the outbreak of diseases such as mad cow disease.
   e. the widespread use of antibiotics in the production of meat.

「アメリカの農業政策の様々な結果には…が含まれている」

> 二本柳のひとことコメント

a. 第6段落第1文に女性の労働力に関する記述があるが，農業政策の結果であるという記述がないので，不一致。

enabling women to enter the workforce.
「女性が労働力に参加可能なこと」

> Besides drawing women into the workforce, falling wages made fast food both cheap to produce and a welcome option for struggling families.

b. 第3段落第3・4文の内容と一致。「農場を売った」という表現はないが，下記の内容から類推できる。

farmers losing money and selling their farms.
「農業従事者がお金を失い，農場を売ること」

> The administration's cheap food policy worked almost too well: crop prices fell, forcing farmers to **produce still more** simply to break even. **This led to a deep depression in the farm belt in the 1980s**, followed by a **brutal wave** of **consolidation resulting in the loss of smaller farms to larger businesses.**

c. 低価格については第3段落第5文と一致。

lower wages, lower food prices, and lower quality food.
「より低い賃金，より安価な食品価格，より低品質の食品」

> Most importantly, the price of food came down, or at least the price of the kinds of foods that could be made from corn and soybeans: processed foods and sweetened beverages and feedlot meat.

低賃金と低品質の食品については第6段落第3文と一致。

> That is, instead of paying workers well enough to allow them to buy things like cars, as Henry Ford proposed to do, companies like Wal-Mart and McDonald's pay their workers so poorly that they can afford only the cheap, low-quality food these companies sell, creating a kind of vicious cycle driving down both wages and the quality of food.

d., e. 第4段落最終文の内容と一致。

d. the outbreak of diseases such as mad cow disease.
「狂牛病のような病気の発生」
e. the widespread use of antibiotics in the production of meat.
「食肉の生産において抗生物質が広く使用されていること」

> Since then, repeated outbreaks of food-borne illness linked to new antibiotic-resistant strains of bacteria have turned a bright light on the shortsighted practice of **routinely administering antibiotics** to food animals, not to treat disease but simply to speed their growth and allow them to <u>withstand</u> the filthy and stressful conditions in which they live.

3. The social cost of modern American eating habits includes

   a. a decline in the interpersonal skills that are necessary for democracy to function.
   b. a decline in the number of families who sit down to eat dinner together.
   c. a relatively large number of people who watch television while they eat.
   d. children who do not learn how to take part in conversations.
   e. the increasing number of women who are required to prepare food for their families.

「現代アメリカ人の食習慣が払っている社会的代償には…が含まれる」

二本柳のひとことコメント

a. 第 7 段落第 2・3 文の内容と一致。

a decline in the interpersonal skills that are necessary for democracy to function.
「民主主義が機能するために必要な対人関係の技能の低下」

> By continually snacking instead of sitting down for leisurely meals, and watching television during mealtimes instead of conversing —— forty percent of Americans watch television during meals —— we have unthinkingly wrecked one of the nurseries of democracy: the family meal. It is the temporary democracy of the table that teaches children the art of conversation and helps them to acquire the habits of civility —— sharing, listening, taking turns, negotiating differences, arguing without offending —— and it is these habits that are lost when we eat alone and on the run.

b. 第 7 段落第 1 文の内容と一致。

a decline in the number of families who sit down to eat dinner together.
「共に食事をとるために腰かける家族の数の減少」

> The rise of fast food and the collapse of everyday cooking have also damaged family life and community by undermining the institution of the shared meal, eroding the civility on which our political culture depends.

c. 第 7 段落第 2 文の内容と一致。

a relatively large number of people who watch television while they eat.
「食事をしながらテレビを見る人の数が比較的多いこと」

> By continually snacking instead of sitting down for leisurely meals, and watching television during mealtimes instead of conversing —— forty percent of Americans watch television during meals —— we have unthinkingly wrecked one of the nurseries of democracy: the family meal.

d. 第 7 段落第 3 文の内容と一致。

children who do not learn how to take part in conversations.
「会話への加わり方が身につかない子供たち」

> It is the temporary democracy of the table that teaches children the art of conversation and helps them to acquire the habits of civility —— sharing, listening, taking turns, negotiating differences, arguing without offending —— and it is these habits that are lost when we eat alone and on the run.

e. 本文中に記述がないので，不一致。

the increasing number of women who are required to prepare food for their families.
「家族のために食事の準備をする必要がある女性の数の増加」

Lesson5 超長文問題-2

問題(3)

Choose the best way to complete each of these sentences, which relate to the underlined words in the passage.

TRACK 14

1. Here "withstand" means
    a. to clean.   b. to oppose.   c. to protest.
    d. to remove. e. to resist.

■指示文訳：本文中の下線部に関して，各英文を完成させる上で，正しいものを1つ選べ。

二本柳のひとことコメント

以下の該当文参照。「抗生物質の投与は，ストレスのかかる住環境に…するためであった」を埋める。

「ここでは withstand は…という意味である」
a. …をきれいにすること。
b. …に反対すること。
c. …に抗議すること。
d. …を取り除くこと。
e. …に耐えること。

> Since then, repeated outbreaks of food-borne illness linked to new antibiotic-resistant strains of bacteria have turned a bright light on the shortsighted practice of routinely administering antibiotics to food animals, not to treat disease but simply to speed their growth and allow them to <u>withstand</u> the filthy and stressful conditions in which they live.

•223

2. Here "wake" means

    a. aftermath.   b. awakening.   c. funeral.
    d. trace.   e. watch.

二本柳のひとことコメント

以下の該当文参照。「食の安全にまつわるこうしたスキャンダル…，1970年代に短期間，盛んになった食糧政策に関する話題が，再び取り上げられるようになった」という内容から，因果関係をつかむ。正解の選択肢の語彙は難解だが，消去法を駆使して正解したい。

「ここでは wake は…という意味である」
a. 結果。
b. 目覚め。
c. 葬式。
d. 跡。
e. 見張り。

> **In the wake of these food safety scandals, the conversation about food politics** that briefly flourished in the 1970s was picked up again in a series of books, articles, and movies about the consequences of industrial food production.

Lesson5　超長文問題-2

問題(4)

Which ONE of the following sentences best sums up the author's argument in the passage?

a. Although most foods are cheap in America, food safety scandals have shown that fast food and convenience foods are bad for human and animal health.

b. Americans spend less time and money buying and preparing food than people in other countries, but they worry about food more.

c. Government policy has helped not only to lower food prices in America, but also to reduce family incomes.

d. In America, food has not been a political issue because food work is traditionally associated with women and their bodily appetites.

e. Lower family incomes, food safety scandals, and a decline in civility have been the unintended consequences of America's cheap food policy.

■指示文訳：本文中の筆者の主張を最もよく要約しているのは以下の文のうちのどれか。

> 二本柳のひとことコメント

a. 第4段落のみの内容。

Although most foods are cheap in America, food safety scandals <u>have shown</u> that fast food and convenience foods are <u>bad for human and animal health.</u>
「アメリカでは大部分の食品が安価だが，食品の安全に関するスキャンダルは，ファストフードやインスタント食品が人間や動物の健康にとってよくないことを示している」

b. 第 2 段落の内容から，むしろ逆。

Americans spend less time and money buying and preparing food than people in other countries, but <u>they worry about food more.</u>
「アメリカ人は他国の人々に比べると，食品を購入したり調理したりするのに費やす時間やお金は少ないが，食品について他国の人々よりも心配している」

c. 価格と収入だけでは，本文全体の要約とは言えない！

Government policy has helped not only to lower food prices in America, but also to reduce family incomes.
「政府の政策は，アメリカの食品価格を下げるだけでなく，家庭の収入を減らす原因にもなっている」

d. 第 8 段落に関連するが，このような因果関係について本文中に記述がない。

In America, food <u>has not been a political issue</u> because food work is traditionally associated with women and their bodily appetites.
「アメリカでは，食べ物に関する仕事は伝統的に女性や女性の身体的欲求と結びつけて考えられているので，政治的問題とはなっていない」

e.「<u>家庭の収入の減少</u>（第 5 段落・第 6 段落），<u>食品の安全に関するスキャンダル</u>（第 4 段落），<u>礼節の衰退</u>（第 7 段落）は，<u>アメリカの安価な食糧政策</u>（第 1 段落〜第 3 段落）の<u>意図せぬ結果</u>（第 8 段落）である」

Lower family incomes, food safety scandals, and a decline in civility have been the unintended consequences of America's cheap food policy.
「家庭の収入の減少，食品の安全に関するスキャンダル，礼節の衰退は，アメリカの安価な食糧政策の意図せぬ結果である」

問題文訳

① ▶1 人々が少なくとも1日に3回対処するものについてこんなことを言うのは奇妙に聞こえるかもしれないが，アメリカにおいて食べ物は，政治的に言えば，ごく最近まで多かれ少なかれ目につかないものだった。少なくとも1970年代初めに，一定期間の食品価格の暴騰と工業的な農業に批判的な書籍の登場が，この話題を国家の議題の最重要項目に押し上げそうな兆しのあった頃まで，アメリカ人は自分たちが食べるものがどこから来るのか，あるいはそれが地球や自分たちの身体や社会にどのような影響を与えているのかについて，それほど真剣に考える必要はなかった。

② ほとんどの人々はこのことをありがたいことだと考えている。アメリカ人は，歴史上どの国民よりも食べ物に費やす収入の割合が低く，10%をわずかに下回るほどであるし，それを調理するのに費やす時間も少なく，後片付けも含めて1日平均たったの31分だ。スーパーマーケットは，世界各地から集められた農産物であふれ，目新しい食品（毎年17,000点の新商品）が絶え間なく押し寄せて中央の陳列棚に流れ込み，冷凍ケースには，考えられる限りのありとあらゆる種類のエスニック料理の「家庭料理に代わるもの」があり，食べる人には，包みを開けて，電子レンジがチンと鳴るのを待つこと以外何も求めないのだ。▶2 人類の長い歴史の中では，食べ物を手に入れることが，日常生活だけではなく，経済的，政治的生活をも支配してきたことを考慮すると，食べ物について現在の私たちと同じくらいしか心配しなくてすむ，あるいはすんだことは，ほとんど夢のように思われる。

③ ほとんどのアメリカ人にとって長年の「食糧問題」がおおむね解決された，という夢は，安価な化石燃料（化学肥料と殺虫剤双方にとっての主要な成分）と農業政策の変更によって可能になった，アメリカの農業従事者による戦後の生産性の飛躍的向上によって維持された。1970年代初期に急騰した後，ニクソン大統領に食糧コストの引き下げを試みるよう求められて，アール・バッツ農務長官は，長年にわたって継続してきた連邦農業政策の重点を，農業従事者のための価格保護から，一握りの商品作物（特にトウモロコシと大豆）の生産高を是が非でも増加させることへと転換した。▶3 政府の食糧安価政策は，うまく行き過ぎと言ってよいほど機能し，穀物価格は下落し，農業従事者は収支を合わせるためだけにさらに多く生産せざるを得なかった。このことが1980年代の穀倉地帯での大不況につながり，その後に小規模農家がより大規模な事業に屈して消失する結果となる，情け容赦ない整理統合の波が起きた。最も重要なことは，食品価格が下がった，あるいは少なくともトウモロコシと大豆から作られる類いの食品，すなわち加工食品や甘味飲料や畜舎産の肉の価格は下がったということだ。新鮮な農作物の価格は1980年代以来上がっている。ワシントンは，食べ物を，少なくともフランス革命期以降，ほとんどの政府にとって重要な目標であった政治的課題としては除外することに成功した。

④ だが，安価な食品というのはよい政策ではあるものの，環境，公衆衛生，国庫，そして文化に対してさえも相当な代償を払っていることが判明し，近年こうしたことが無視できな

くなってきたため，食べ物は再び目につく問題となった。1980年代後期に起き始める食の安全に関する一連のスキャンダルが，自分たちの食べるものがどのように生産されているのかということに対して人々の目を開かせ，スキャンダルの度に，見る影もないほど変貌した食糧システムを隠していたカーテンがさらに少しずつ開かれていった。 4 1986年に，イギリスでBSE，すなわち狂牛病が表面化すると，草食動物であるはずの牛が，他の牛の肉を日常的にえさとして与えられていることをアメリカ人は知ったが，こういった慣行は，肉の価格を安く抑えるのには役立つが，重度の脳障害を起こす病気にかかるリスクを抱えていた。ファストフードチェーンのジャック・イン・ザ・ボックスのハンバーガーを食べたワシントン州の4人の子供たちが1993年に亡くなったのは，大腸菌O157-H7型という，1982年に畜舎の牛で初めて検出された一般的な腸内細菌の突然変異株に汚染された肉がそもそもの原因だった。それ以来，抗生物質耐性菌株に関連する食品感染の病気が頻発したことで，食用動物に抗生物質を繰り返し投与するという近視眼的な慣行が表面化したが，これは病気治療のためではなく，単に成長を早め，不衛生でストレスのかかる住環境に耐えられるようにするためだけだったのである。

⑤　 5 食の安全にまつわるこうしたスキャンダルの結果として，1970年代に短期間盛んになった食糧政策に関する話題は，工業的な食糧生産の影響を扱った一連の書籍，記事，映画の中で再び取り上げられるようになった。2001年のエリック・シュロッサーの『ファストフードが世界を食いつくす』と，その翌年のマリオン・ネスルの『フード・ポリティクス - 肥満社会と食品産業』の出版と共に，食品ジャーナリズムが始まった。これらの書籍や最近10年間に出版された他の書籍は，工業的食糧生産，農業政策，食品が媒介する病気，幼年期の肥満，伝統的な家族の食事の減少，そしてとりわけ，1970年代に始まる世帯所得の減少を明確に関連づけることに成功している。

⑥　女性を労働力に引き入れたことに加えて，賃金が下落したことで，ファストフードは安価で生産可能なものになり，生活苦と闘う家族にとって歓迎すべき選択肢となった。シュロッサーが描いた食品経済の実像は，時に「フォーディズム（フォード主義）」と呼ばれる社会契約の逆バージョンのようだ。 6 つまり，ウォルマートやマクドナルドのような会社は，ヘンリー・フォードが提案したように，労働者が自動車のようなものを買えるほど十分な賃金を支払うのではなく，労働者にわずかな賃金しか支払わないため，労働者は，こうした企業が販売する安価で低品質の食品しか購入する余裕がなく，そのことが，賃金も食品の質もどちらも低下させる一種の悪循環を生み出している。ファストフードや安価な食品全般の出現は，事実上，アメリカの世帯収入の低下を後押ししてきたのである。

⑦　ファストフードの隆盛と日々の調理の崩壊は，食卓を共にする慣行を衰退させ，我々の政治的文化が依存している礼節を蝕むことによって，家族生活や共同体をも損なっている。 7 腰かけてゆったりと食事をする代わりに絶えず簡単なものを口にしたり，会話する代わりに食事中にテレビを見たりする（アメリカ人の40%は，食事中にテレビを見ている）ことによって，我々は何も考えずに民主主義を育む条件の1つである家族での食事を台無しにし

てきた。子どもたちに会話の作法を教え，分かち合い，耳を傾け，交替で話し，意見の相違を話し合いでさばき，相手の感情を害することなく議論するといった礼儀に関する様々な習慣を彼らが身につけるのに役立つのは，食卓におけるひとときの民主主義であり，1人で食べたり，大急ぎで食べたりするときに失われるのは，こういった習慣なのである。

⑧　8　こういった問題が最近まで目につかなかったのは，食事に関する仕事を女性と結びつけてきたことと，それに関連して，食べるということが，まさにその性質上，心身の分割に関して間違った側におかれているという事実のためである。食べ物は，触覚，嗅覚，味覚を通じて経験されるが，これらの感覚は，一般的に知識のもとになると考えられている視覚や聴覚に比べると，五感の序列の中では下位に位置する。ほとんどの哲学，宗教，文学において，食べ物は，身体，動物，女性，そして食欲と結びつけて考えられているが，これらのことは，文明人が理性と知識で克服しようと努めてきた事柄なのだ。

✅ word check !

- propel 〜 〜を推進する
- blessing 祝福，ありがたいもの
- brim with 〜 〜でいっぱいになる
- replacement 替わりの物
- chirp 甲高い音を出す
- drive down 〜 〜を引き下げる
- soybean 大豆
- at any cost 費用がいくらかかっても，是が非でも
- break even 損益のない
- consolidation （会社などの）合併・統合
- sweetened beverage 甘味飲料
- issue 問題点，課題
- beyond recognition 見分けも付かないほど，跡形もなく
- herbivore 草食動物
- hideous 醜悪な
- trace ... to 〜 …を〜まで（原因を）調査する
- contaminate 〜 〜を汚染する
- outbreak 大発生，多発
- antibiotics 抗生物質
- obesity 肥満
- advent 出現，到来
- collapse 崩壊
- erode 〜 〜を阻む，衰退させる
- wreck 〜 〜を台無しにする
- associate ... with 〜 …を〜と関連させる
- agenda 議題
- clean-up 清掃，後片付け
- summon 〜 〜を呼び出す，招集する
- microwave 電子レンジ
- sustain 〜 〜を維持する，持続させる
- yield 収穫量，生産高
- depression 不況
- eliminate 〜 〜を除く，除去する
- turn out 〜 〜ということがわかる
- practice 慣習・慣例
- intestinal 腸の，腸管内の
- administer 〜 〜を投与する
- filthy 不衛生な
- social compact 社会契約
- subsidize 〜 〜に補助金を出す
- institution 慣例
- civility 礼儀正しさ
- on the run 急いで，あわてて

Lesson5-1　問題解答

(1) 1. a. Their developing brains require more energy than those of adults.
2. d. The potential years of active life lost as a result of death or illness
3. e. None of the above
4. c. Ethnicity
5. d. It prevents the absorption of food among children.
6. a. Lack of development together with health problems leads to low national IQ scores.

(2) 1. T　　2. T　　3. F　　4. T　　5. F　　6. F

Lesson5-2　問題解答

(1) 1. l. (In Paragraph ① the writer mainly) writes that food was not an important political issue in America until about forty years ago.
2. c. (In Paragraph ② the writer mainly) describes the absence of concern in America about where the next meal will come from as unprecedented.
3. j. (In Paragraph ③ the writer mainly) summarizes the policies that made food cheap and the effects of these policies on farmers.
4. g. (In Paragraph ④ the writer mainly) provides several examples of the dangers to public health posed by modern agricultural practices.
5. e. (In Paragraph ⑤ the writer mainly) notes the revival of food as a controversial issue at the beginning of the twenty-first century.
6. a. (In Paragraph ⑥ the writer mainly) argues that the availability of cheap, poor-quality food has enabled big businesses to get away with paying their workers less.
7. b. (In Paragraph ⑦ the writer mainly) criticizes American eating habits for their negative effects on both family life and the way people communicate with one another in society.

8. i. (In Paragraph ⑧ the writer mainly) suggests that because food has traditionally been associated with women, it was thought to be unworthy of serious consideration.

(2) 1. d. mainly eat the kinds of food that can be made from corn and soybeans.
2. a. enabling women to enter the workforce.
3. e. the increasing number of women who are required to prepare food for their families.

(3) 1. e. to resist.   2. a. aftermath.

(4) e. Lower family incomes, food safety scandals, and a decline in civility have been the unintended consequences of America's cheap food policy.

LESSON 6 ライティング問題・リスニング問題

1 一文要約型ライティング問題
10分で満点を狙え！

TRACK 01

使用学部：文学部，文化構想学部。

一文要約型のライティング問題

《おすすめアプローチ》
1. 英文全体の論理構造，必須のキーワード，要約に必ず盛り込まなければならない内容を一読してつかむ。
2. 用いるべき接続語句，言い換えるべき表現を速やかに決定して一気に書く。見直す時間がない前提で急ぎつつも慎重に書き上げること。
3. 書き上げた後に時間が余れば，正誤問題に取り組むつもりで間違い探しに徹する。
4. 英文を読んで要約6〜7分→英文記述2〜3分→見直し1分。答案用紙は **16cm×4行**。

《得点力アップの道筋》
1. 平素の読解の段階からパラグラフの内容を総括する意識を保つ。当初は復習段階でもよいので，日本語で極力要約を書いてみること。
2. 接続詞，関係詞，イディオム等の例文を英訳できるよう反復練習する。
3. 英語で要約を書いたら，必ず添削してもらい，自分のミスの癖，改善点などをアドバイスしてもらうこと。

（Lesson6 問題解答は p.265〜267 にあります）

問題 1 (文化構想学部出題)

Read the following passage and write an English summary in one sentence <u>in your own words.</u>

As media for conveying stories to readers, it might seem that comics and novels are very different: the former 'shows' the story through giving visual images like films do, while the latter cannot provide such images except when books are illustrated. However, readers of comics and novels are allowed at least one kind of liberty in the way they enjoy them that viewers of film do not have. In the case of comics and novels, you can read them as quickly, or as slowly, as you like. You also can stop and resume reading at any time or you can interrupt reading with thoughts relevant or irrelevant to the story. No author could seriously make a complaint that some readers hurry through a long work in only a few hours, or that other readers start recollecting the good old days with the book on their laps. Viewers of films can perhaps have the same kind of liberty, especially when watching a DVD, but such ways of reception would be far beyond the expectations of filmmakers as time is one of the most crucial components in the presentation of stories in that genre.

Lesson6　ライティング問題・リスニング問題 -1

_____

_____

_____

_____

_____

_____

_____

■指示文訳：次の英文を読み，その内容を<u>自分の言葉を用いて</u> 1 文の英語に要約して書け。

二本柳のひとことコメント

「漫画と小説」の相違点と類似点，できれば「映画」との比較にも触れたい。対比中心の流れをつかむこと。

:: 問題文訳

　読者に物語を伝える媒体として，漫画と小説とではかなり異なるように思われるかもしれない。前者は映画のように視覚的なイメージを通して物語を「見せる」が，一方後者は本にイラストが載せられている場合を除いて，そのようなイメージを提供できないからだ。しかしながら，漫画や小説の読者は，少なくとも同種の，映画鑑賞者にはない楽しみ方の自由を，与えられている。漫画や小説の場合，自分の好きなように早くも遅くも読むことができる。また，いつでも読むのをやめたり再び始めたりすることができるし，物語に関係あることや無関係なことを考えて読書を中断することもできる。長編作品をほんの数時間で読破してしまったり，本を膝の上に載せたまま懐かしい昔の良き日のことを回想したりする読者がいることについて，真面目に文句を言う作家はいないだろう。映画鑑賞者もおそらく，とりわけDVDを見るときには，同種の自由を持ち得ているが，この分野で物語を表現する際には，時間が最も重要な構成要素の1つであるので，そのような受容方法は映画製作者の予想をはるかに超えたものと言えるだろう。

問題 2 (文学部出題)

Read the following passage and write an English summary in one sentence in your own words.

In 1529, the Bishop of London, the person responsible for religious and public order in the city, became very concerned about the circulation of certain religious books. He decided that it would be necessary to buy all of the copies of these books, and then burn them, thus solving the problem. What he had not anticipated was that, although all of the copies had been burned, it was now a simple matter for the printers of the books, with the money he had so generously provided, to print yet more books, and so it turned out within a few months even more of the offending texts were circulating in London and elsewhere. The bishop had fallen into the false belief, which has continued to be held by governors and rulers to the present era, that suppression of disagreeable ideas can be implemented by the blocking or removal of the media of those ideas. It is clear, however, that in an age of rapid, mechanical production of texts such suppression is pointless; a fact which is, of course, even more the case in the present day with the immediate, electronic transfer of information.

Lesson6 ライティング問題・リスニング問題-1

■指示文訳：次の英文を読み，その内容を<u>自分の言葉を用いて</u> 1 文の英語に要約して書け。

> 二本柳のひとことコメント

具体例が一般化され，現代ではそのことがなおいっそう当てはまる，という流れをつかみたい。

問題文訳

　1529 年，ロンドンの司教は，町の宗教的，公共的秩序に対する責任者だったが，ある宗教書が発行されることに大きな懸念を抱いた。彼は，これらの本をすべて買い上げ，焼却してしまう必要があると判断し，そのようにして問題を解決した。彼が予期していなかったことは，本はすべて焼却されたが，彼が非常に気前よくお金を支給してしまったために，今度は単に，そのお金で本の印刷業者がいっそう多くの本を印刷するだけのことになってしまい，結果的に数か月のうちにその問題の本がロンドンやその他の地域でいっそう多く出回ることになってしまった。気に入らない考えを弾圧することは，その考えを伝える媒体を妨害したり除去することで実行できる，という誤った信念に司教は陥ってしまったのだが，その信念は統治者や指導者が現在まで抱き続けている。しかし，書物が迅速に機械生産される時代に，そのような弾圧が無意味であることは明らかであるし，実際，情報を即時かつ電子機器を通して伝達できる現代においては，もちろんなおさらのことである。

237

LESSON 6 ライティング問題・リスニング問題

2 意見論述型ライティング問題
意見の内容が重要な訳ではない。

使用学部：国際教養学部，法学部，政治経済学部。

TRACK 04

意見論述型のライティング問題

《おすすめアプローチ》
1. 書き出しで自らの立場を明確にし，次にその理由を明確にし，さらにその理由の根拠もしくは具体例を付加する。
2. 自分の信念に基づいて書くのではなく，書きやすい立場を選んで書く。ミスしないことを最優先に考える。
3. 構想2〜3分→英文記述6〜7分（政治経済学部は8〜10分）→見直し1分。

《得点力アップの道筋》
1. 一文要約型と同様，接続詞，関係詞，イディオム等の例文を英訳できるよう反復練習する。
2. 国際教養学部，法学部，政治経済学部の過去問を受験の有無にかかわらず書いてみる。国公立大学の二次試験にもたくさん素材がある。
3. 答案を作成したら，必ず添削してもらうこと。自分のミスの癖，改善点などをアドバイスしてもらうこと。

（Lesson6 問題解答は p.265〜267 にあります）

問題 1 （法学部出題）

Your answer must be written in English in the space provided on this page.

In Japan, some high schools prohibit students from having part-time jobs, even though they are legally allowed to work. Do you agree with such a school policy or not?

Write a paragraph explaining your opinion. Give one or more convincing reasons to support your answer.

_____

_____

_____

_____

_____

_____

（「ひとことコメント」は p.241 にあります）

問題 2（政治経済学部出題）

Read the statement below and write a paragraph giving at least two reasons why you agree or disagree with it. Write your answer in English.

(*It is suggested that you spend no more than 15 minutes on this section.*)

"The Olympic Games should be abolished."

Lesson6　ライティング問題・リスニング問題-2

■問題(1) 指示文訳：解答はこのページの空欄に英語で書け。
　日本では，高校生が仕事をすることは法的に許されているのに，生徒がアルバイトをすることを禁止している高等学校もある。このような学校の方針に賛成か反対か。
　「自分の意見を説明するパラグラフを 1 つ書け。その答えを裏付ける説得力のある理由を少なくとも 1 つ示すこと」

二本柳のひとことコメント

理由を 2 つ以上挙げる場合には，2 つ目以降の理由が舌足らずにならないように気をつけること。

■問題(2) 指示文訳：以下の記述を読み，それに賛成または反対する理由を少なくとも 2 つ挙げてパラグラフを 1 つ書け。解答は英語で書くこと（この問題には 15 分以上かけないことを提案する）。
　『オリンピックは廃止すべきである』

二本柳のひとことコメント

理由付けを明確にしてから一気に書き上げるのがよい。途中で止まってしまうと書くべき内容が思うように浮かばないことが多い。

LESSON 6 ライティング問題・リスニング問題

3 講義型リスニング問題
設問からアプローチ！

TRACK 07

使用学部：国際教養学部で出題。

講義型のリスニング問題

《おすすめアプローチ》
1. 極力，設問に目を通しておきたい。選択肢まで目を通せなくても，リード部の疑問文だけでもよい。聞き取るべき情報を明確にしておく。
2. 放送は2回行われるので，1回目で答えが決められなくてもあわてず，選択肢に目を通す。
3. 必要に応じてメモを取る。

《得点力アップの道筋》
1. 英検準1級，もしくはTOFELテストの同形式のリスニング問題を，スクリプトに頼らず聞き取れるようにするのが目標。
2. メモをどの程度とるか，自分なりに決定すること。
3. 1回目で極力解答し，2回目は確認することを目標にしたい。

（Lesson6 問題解答は p.265〜267 にあります）

Lesson6 ライティング問題・リスニング問題-3

Listening Test
(国際教養学部出題)

TRACK 08

First listen to the lecture, which you will hear TWICE. Choose the correct answer for each question based on the lecture, by indicating A, B, C, or D.

1. This lecture mentions two reports. When and by whom were these two reports published?

    A. In 2005 by a United Nations panel and in 2007 by Dutch journalists.
    B. In 2007 by Dutch journalists and in 2010 by a United Nations panel.
    C. In 2010 by Dutch scientists and in 2005 by a United Nations panel.
    D. In 2010 by Dutch scientists and in 2007 by a United Nations panel.

2. What is one difference between the two reports?

   A. Only the most recent report considers river basins in Bangladesh and Bhutan.
   B. The most recent report predicts that the impact of melting glaciers will be much worse than predicted in the earlier report.
   C. Unlike the earlier report, the most recent report considers the atmospheric concentration of greenhouse gases.
   D. Unlike the earlier report, the most recent report considers the impact of change in rainfall patterns.

   _____

3. On what point do scientists disagree?

   A. Whether glaciers around the world are melting at an increasing rate.
   B. Whether global warming is related to higher concentrations of carbon dioxide in the atmosphere.
   C. Whether the areas around the Himalayan mountains will suffer food shortages.
   D. Whether the Himalayan glaciers could remain for hundreds of years in a warmer world.

   _____

4. Why has the 2010 study been criticized?

    A. For including only Dutch researchers on the team.
    B. For not considering the impact of the melting glaciers on poverty and pollution.
    C. For not dealing with river basins in central Asia and northwest China.
    D. For not giving possible solutions.

    _____

5. According to scientists, how should governments in the region adapt to the predicted water shortages?

    A. By growing crops that use less water.
    B. By improving irrigation practices.
    C. By storing more water for longer.
    D. All of the above.

    _____

講義型リスニング問題 （国際教養学部出題）

TRACK 09

First listen to the lecture, which you will hear TWICE. Choose the correct answer for each question based on the lecture, by indicating A, B, C, or D.

1. This lecture mentions two reports. When and by whom were these two reports published?
    A. In 2005 by a United Nations panel and in 2007 by Dutch journalists.
    B. In 2007 by Dutch journalists and in 2010 by a United Nations panel.
    C. In 2010 by Dutch scientists and in 2005 by a United Nations panel.
    D. In 2010 by Dutch scientists and in 2007 by a United Nations panel.

■指示文訳：最初に講義を聞くこと。講義は2回放送される。講義に基づいて各質問に対する正しい答えを選び，A,B,C,Dのいずれかを書け。
「この講義は2つの報告に言及している。いつ誰によってこれら2つの報告は発表されたか」

二本柳のひとことコメント

数字と名詞の聞き取り。予め疑問文に目を通しておけば容易なはず。

《放送された英文》

> This is according to a study published in June 2010 by Dutch scientists writing in the journal *Science*. However, the same study also concludes that the impact would be much less than previously estimated in 2007 by the United Nations Intergovernmental Panel on Climate Change.

A. 2005年の国連のパネルと2007年のオランダのジャーナリストらによるもの。
B. 2007年のオランダのジャーナリストらによるものと2010年の国連のパネルによるもの。
C. 2010年のオランダの科学者らによるものと2005年の国連のパネルによるもの。
D. 2010年のオランダの科学者らによるものと2007年の国連のパネルによるもの。

2. What is one difference between the two reports?
   A. Only the most recent report considers river basins in Bangladesh and Bhutan.
   B. The most recent report predicts that the impact of melting glaciers will be much worse than predicted in the earlier report.
   C. Unlike the earlier report, the most recent report considers the atmospheric concentration of greenhouse gases.
   D. Unlike the earlier report, the most recent report considers the impact of change in rainfall patterns.

 二本柳のひとことコメント

以下参照。この聞き取りができなければ他の選択肢と迷うところ。

《放送された英文》

> The reason for **the difference** in the conclusions of the two reports, the Dutch scientists say, is that some river basins surrounding the Himalayas depend more heavily on rainfall than on melting glaciers for their water sources.

「2つの報告の違いの1つは何か」
A. 最近の報告だけがバングラデシュとブータンの河川流域のことを考慮している。
B. 最近の報告は，氷河が融けることによる影響は以前の報告で予想されたよりもひどいと予測している。
C. 以前の報告とは異なり，最近の報告は温室効果ガスの大気中の濃度を考慮している。
D. 以前の報告とは異なり，最近の報告は降雨パターンの変化が及ぼす影響を考慮している。

3. On what point do scientists disagree?

   A. Whether glaciers around the world are melting at an increasing rate.
   B. Whether global warming is related to higher concentrations of carbon dioxide in the atmosphere.
   C. Whether the areas around the Himalayan mountains will suffer food shortages.
   D. Whether the Himalayan glaciers could remain for hundreds of years in a warmer world.

二本柳のひとことコメント

文頭の **But** が目印となりうる。

《放送された英文》

> **But** some scientists say that the glaciers in the Himalayas could still exist for centuries in a warmer world, and the 2007 U.N. report has been criticized for several errors, including the claim that the glaciers in the Himalayas could disappear by 2035.

「科学者たちの意見が一致しないのはどの点か」
A. 世界中の氷河が急速に融けているのかどうか。
B. 地球温暖化は大気中の二酸化炭素の濃度が高まっていることと関係しているのかどうか。
C. ヒマラヤ山脈周辺の地域は食糧不足に見舞われるのかどうか。
D. ヒマラヤ山脈の氷河はより気温の高い世界でも数百年間残りうるかどうか。

4. Why has the 2010 study been criticized?
   A. For including only Dutch researchers on the team.
   B. For not considering the impact of the melting glaciers on poverty and pollution.
   C. For not dealing with river basins in central Asia and northwest China.
   D. For not giving possible solutions.

> 二本柳のひとことコメント

criticize が聞き取れれば，地名が含まれているので，正解は容易。

《放送された英文》

> Other scientists **criticize** the study for neglecting to consider several other important river basins in central Asia and northwest China, which could be hit hard by the loss of water from melting glaciers.

「2010年の研究が批判されているのはなぜか」
A. 研究チームにオランダの研究者しか入っていないため。
B. 氷河が融けることで貧困や汚染にどのような影響があるか考慮していないため。
C. 中央アジアや中国北西部の河川流域を扱っていないため。
D. 考えられる解決策を提示していないため。

5. According to scientists, how should governments in the region adapt to the predicted water shortages?
   A. By growing crops that use less water.
   B. By improving irrigation practices.
   C. By storing more water for longer.
   D. All of the above.

 二本柳のひとことコメント

以下参照。疑問文とまったく同じ表現が含まれているので，これまた正解は容易。

《放送された英文》

> They say that governments in the region should adapt to the predicted water shortages **by changing** to crops that use less water, by adopting better irrigation practices, and by building more and larger facilities to store water for long periods of time.

「科学者たちによれば，この地域の政府は予測される水不足にどのように対応すべきか」
A．水をさほど使用しなくてすむ作物を栽培することによって。
B．灌漑事業を改善することによって。
C．より多くの水をより長期にわたって備蓄することによって。
D．上記のすべて。

音声スクリプト

Nearly 60 million people living in the areas surrounding the Himalaya mountains will suffer food shortages in the coming decades as glaciers shrink and the water sources for rivers dry up. This is according to a study published in June 2010 by Dutch scientists writing in the journal *Science*. However, the same study also concludes that the impact would be much less than previously estimated in 2007 by the United Nations Intergovernmental Panel on Climate Change. The 2007 U.N. report warned that hundreds of millions of people were at risk from disappearing glaciers.

The reason for the difference in the conclusions of the two reports, the Dutch scientists say, is that some river basins surrounding the Himalayas depend more heavily on rainfall than on melting glaciers for their water sources. Those that do depend heavily on glaciers, such as the Indus River basin and the Ganges River basin in South Asia, could see their water supplies decline by as much as 19.6 percent by 2050. In contrast, China's Yellow River basin would see a 9.5 percent increase in rain as monsoon patterns change due to the changing climate.

This study is one of the first to examine the impact of shrinking glaciers on the Himalayan river basins. It is likely to fuel the debate over the degree to which climate change will affect the river basins in India, Pakistan, Nepal, Bangladesh, Bhutan and China. Scientists for the most part agree that glaciers around the world are melting at an increasing rate as temperatures rise. And most relate that warming directly to the higher concentrations of carbon dioxide in the atmosphere. But some scientists say that the glaciers in the Himalayas could still exist for centuries in a warmer world, and the 2007 U.N. report has been criticized for several errors, including the claim that the glaciers in the Himalayas could disappear by 2035. This date was apparently an error in which *the actual date* —— 2350 —— was mistakenly printed as 2035.

The findings by the Dutch team in the journal *Science* were greeted with caution by glacier experts who had not taken part in the research. They said that the uncertainties and lack of data for the region make it difficult to say exactly what will happen to water supply in the next few decades. Other scientists criticize the study for neglecting to consider several other important river basins in central Asia and northwest China, which could be hit hard by the loss of water from melting glaciers. But still, several of these outside researchers argue that the region will suffer food shortages due to climate change. This would add to already existing problems such as overpopulation, poverty, pollution, and weakening monsoon rains in parts of South Asia. They say that governments in the region should adapt to the predicted water shortages by changing to crops that use less water, by adopting better irrigation practices, and by building more and larger facilities to store water for long periods of time.

Lesson6 ライティング問題・リスニング問題-3

音声スクリプト訳

　ヒマラヤ山脈を囲む地域で暮らしている6000万人近い人々は，氷河が縮小し，川に流れ込む水源が干上がるにつれて，今後数十年のうちに食糧不足に見舞われることになるだろう。これは，『サイエンス』誌に書かれている，オランダの科学者たちによって2010年6月に発表された研究による。しかし，この同じ研究はまた，その影響が2007年に国連の気候変動に関する政府間パネルによって以前に推定されていたよりもはるかに小さいものである，と結論づけている。2007年の国連の報告は，氷河の消滅で何億人もの人たちが危険にさらされる，と警告していた。

　2つの報告の結論が異なっている理由は，オランダの科学者たちによれば，ヒマラヤ山脈周辺の河川流域は，その水源として，解ける氷河よりも降雨の方に大いに依存している点にある。南アジアのインダス川流域やガンジス川流域のように，実際のところ氷河に大いに依存しているところでは，流れ込む水の量が2050年までに19.6%も減少することになるだろう。対照的に，中国の黄河流域は，気候変動が原因となってモンスーンのパターンが変わることで，雨量が9.5%増加することになる。

　この研究は，縮小する氷河がヒマラヤ山系流域に与える影響を初めて検証したものの一つである。これは，インド，パキスタン，ネパール，バングラデシュ，ブータン，中国の河川流域に，気候変動がどの程度影響を及ぼすかに関して，議論を巻き起こす可能性が高い。気温が上昇するにつれて，世界中の氷河が急速に融けるだろう，ということについて，科学者たちは大部分同意している。そしてほとんどの科学者たちが，そういった温暖化と大気中の二酸化炭素濃度の高まりを直接関連づけている。しかし，世界の気温がより高くなってもヒマラヤ山脈の氷河はなお何世紀も存在しうる，と語る科学者もおり，国連の2007年の報告は，誤りがいくつかあるとして批判されており，その中には，ヒマラヤの氷河が2035年には消滅してしまう可能性があるという主張も含まれている。この年代は，明らかに2350年という本当の年代が間違って2035年と印刷されたミスである。

　『サイエンス』誌のオランダの科学者たちによる発見は，その研究に加わらなかった氷河専門家たちからは，慎重な態度でもって迎えられた。その地域に関するデータの不確実さと欠如のせいで，今後数十年で水の供給がどうなるか正確に言うのは困難になっている，と彼らは言う。別の科学者たちは，その研究は，中央アジアや中国北西部における，融ける氷河からの水が失われると甚大な被害を受ける可能性ある，その他のいくつかの重要な河川流域を考慮していない，として批判している。しかしそれでも，こうした外部の科学者たちのうちの数名は，その地域が気候変動のために食糧不足に見舞われることになる，と主張している。これによって，人口過剰，貧困，汚染，モンスーンがもたらす雨の量の減少といったような，南アジアの各地にすでに存在している問題がさらに厄介なものになるだろう。水をさほど使用しなくてすむ作物に変えたり，よりよい灌漑事業を取り入れたり，長期にわたって水を備蓄しておけるより多くのより大きな設備を建設したりすることで，その地域の政府は予想される水不足に対応すべきである，と彼らは語っている。

LESSON 6 ライティング問題・リスニング問題

4 会話型リスニング問題
一回勝負！

TRACK 10

使用学部：国際教養学部で出題。

会話型のリスニング問題

《おすすめアプローチ》
1. 会話→設問の順でそれぞれ1度しか読まれない。メモが決め手。
2. ただし，内容重視なので流れをつかむことに徹したい。
3. それでも固有名詞は内容把握の手がかりにもなるので注意したい。

《得点力アップの道筋》
1. **TOEIC** テストのリスニング問題などは，日常的にどん欲に取り組みたい。
2. キーワードの頭文字だけメモする，などというような自分なりのメモの取り方の工夫も必要。
3. **L6-3** の「講義型リスニング問題」に慣れるのが先決。その後はスクリプトに頼らず多聴していくこと。

（Lesson6 問題解答は p.265〜267 にあります）

Lesson6 ライティング問題・リスニング問題-4

Listening Test
(国際教養学部出題)

TRACK 11

Now listen to a news report, which you will hear ONCE. After hearing the interview once, you will hear five questions. For each question, choose the correct answer according to the news report, by indicating A, B or C. The questions will be read only ONCE.

1. _____

2. _____

3. _____

4. _____

5. _____

会話型リスニング問題（国際教養学部出題）

Now listen to a news report, which you will hear ONCE. After hearing the interview once, you will hear five questions. For each question, choose the correct answer according to the news report, by indicating A, B or C. The questions will be read only ONCE.

■指示文訳：次にニュース・レポートを聞きなさい。放送は1回行われる。インタビューを1度聞いた後，質問が5問放送される。ニュース・レポートに基づいて各質問に対する正しい答えを選び，A,B,C,Dのいずれかを書くこと。質問は1度しか読まれない。

《放送された質問》

> 1. What is unusual about the postal system on Floreana Island?
>
>   A. Mail delivery takes more time than regular international mail.
>   B. The mail is carried in barrels by travelers.
>   C. The mail is delivered by travelers all over the world.

《放送された英文》

> Instead of stamps and postal workers, this island relies on a barrel and the kindness of travelers to move its mail ……
> 　　　　　　　　　　（中略）
> …… The guests, mainly eco-tourists, sort through the piles, looking for addresses within delivery distance of their homes.
>
> 1.「フロレアーナ島の郵便制度について普通ではない点は何か」

A. 郵便物の配達は，通常の国際郵便よりも時間がかかる。
B. 郵便物は，樽に入れて旅行者によって運ばれる。
C. 郵便物は，世界中の旅行者によって運ばれる。

《放送された質問》

2. Who first started this unusual system?

A. Eco-tourists from England.
B. Local people of the Galapagos.
C. Sailors from England.

《放送された英文》

This all started in the late 1700s, as a way for English whalers to communicate with friends and family back home.

2.「この風変わりな仕組みを最初に始めたのは誰か」
　A. イギリスから来たエコツーリストたち。
　B. ガラパゴス諸島の地元の人たち。
　C. イギリスから来た船乗りたち。

《放送された質問》

3. Who built the island post office box?

A. Descendants of Robinson Crusoe.
B. Hollywood poster decorators.
C. People working with driftwood and organic material.

《放送された英文》

> Stickers, graffiti, and a Hollywood poster decorate the postbox which is made of driftwood and organic material.

3.「島の郵便ポストを作ったのは誰か」
 A. ロビンソン・クルーソーの子孫たち。
 B. ハリウッドのポスターの飾りつけをする人たち。
 C. 流木や自然の素材を用いて作業する人たち。

《放送された質問》

> **4. Why couldn't the female tourist deliver the card to Los Angeles?**
>
> A. Because she is from Florida.
> B. Because she isn't stopping in Los Angeles.
> C. Because she won't have time when she stops in Los Angeles.

《放送された英文》

> Someone approached me with mail to be delivered to Los Angeles.

4.「女性旅行者がロサンゼルス行きのハガキを配達できないのはなぜか」
 A. 彼女がフロリダ出身だから。
 B. 彼女がロサンゼルスに立ち寄る予定がないから。
 C. 彼女がロサンゼルスに立ち寄る際に時間がないから。

《放送された質問》

> 5. According to local custom, what is "against the rules" in mail delivery?
>
>   A. Buying a stamp.
>   B. Taking more than one piece of mail at a time.
>   C. Using an airplane to reach your destination.

《放送された英文》

> Buying a stamp and posting it are considered cheating, the locals warned us.

5.「地元の習慣によると,郵便物の配達で『規則に反している』のはどれか」
　A. 切手を買うこと。
　B. 1度に2通以上の郵便物を持ち帰ること。
　C. 目的地に行くのに飛行機を使うこと。

音声スクリプト

EBC: We are reporting live from Floreana Island in the Galapagos. Astonishingly, this island has a postal service that has not evolved from its origins hundreds of years ago. Unlike Darwin's birds, this postal service does not need to adapt to survive. Instead of stamps and postal workers, this island relies on a barrel and the kindness of travelers to move its mail. Twice a day, boatloads of unofficial mail carriers land in Post Office Bay and walk a few sandy meters to a wooden barrel filled with postcards and notes left by past visitors. The guests, mainly eco-tourists, sort through the piles, looking for addresses within delivery distance of their homes. They also drop their own messages into the barrel, adding another link to the chain of mail. Let's ask one of the locals to explain. Excuse me Sir, are you involved in the distribution of mail?

Local Man: Yes, I am. Sometimes it's faster than the regular mail. This all started in the late 1700s, as a way for English whalers to communicate with friends and family back home. Sailors continuing on their journeys from the Galapagos would drop off their mail, while other sailors returning home to England would collect and deliver it.

EBC: As you can see, the local "post office" looks like it could have been put together by Robinson Crusoe himself. Stickers, graffiti, and a Hollywood poster decorate the postbox which is made of driftwood and organic material. We are here with a group of 16 people. Everyone knows everyone else's hometown and calls out city names, hoping to find a match between the various mail destinations and individual travelers. So where are you from, Ma'am?

Eco-tourist Woman: I'm from the United States. But I can't take some of the cards offered to me. Someone approached me with mail to be delivered to Los Angeles. If I could make a stopover in Los Angeles on the way back home to New York, I would deliver it, but I can't do that this time. But I will take the ones for Florida, because

I'm planning a trip there next month.

EBC: And what about you, Sir?

Eco-tourist Man: I'm taking back some cards addressed to various places in Japan. However there are some others I can't take —— there is a strange colored envelope that needs to go to Spain! But I can't possibly take care of that one. It *is* exciting to see an address you recognize. But then you realize that you actually have to deliver the mail. Buying a stamp and posting it are considered cheating, the locals warned us. But I think that arriving at a stranger's house with a "surprise" for someone you've never met could be a little scary for them. Don't you think? So when I get back to Tokyo, I will have to give some serious thought to the question of how to actually get these cards to their final destinations.

EBC: And so we see on this island that cooperation really does make the world go round! This is Carlos Gonzales, EBC News, Floreana, the Galapagos.

1. What is unusual about the postal system on Floreana Island?
   A. Mail delivery takes more time than regular international mail.
   B. The mail is carried in barrels by travelers.
   C. The mail is delivered by travelers all over the world.

2. Who first started this unusual system?
   A. Eco-tourists from England.
   B. Local people of the Galapagos.
   C. Sailors from England.

3. Who built the island post office box?
   A. Descendants of Robinson Crusoe.
   B. Hollywood poster decorators.
   C. People working with driftwood and organic material.

4. **Why couldn't the female tourist deliver the card to Los Angeles?**
   A. Because she is from Florida.
   B. Because she isn't stopping in Los Angeles.
   C. Because she won't have time when she stops in Los Angeles.

5. **According to local custom, what is "against the rules" in mail delivery?**
   A. Buying a stamp.
   B. Taking more than one piece of mail at a time.
   C. Using an airplane to reach your destination.

Lesson6　ライティング問題・リスニング問題-4

音声スクリプト訳

EBC: ガラパゴス諸島のフロレアーナ島から生中継でお伝えしています。びっくりしてしまうんですが，この島には数百年前の人が初めて暮らすようになって以来，進化していない郵便業務があるんです。ダーウィンの鳥たちとは異なり，この郵便業務は生き残るために順応する必要がないというわけです。切手や郵便屋さんの代わりに，この島では，樽と，郵便物を運んでくれる旅行者の親切心に頼っているのです。1日に2回，船に乗った非公式の郵便配達員たちがポスト・オフィス湾に上陸し，以前にやって来た人たちが残したハガキやメモが詰まった木の樽のところまで，砂地を何メートルか歩きます。やって来る人たちは主にエコツーリストで，郵便の山を分類して，自分の家から配達できる距離にある住所がないか探します。彼らもまた，自分のメッセージを樽に入れ，郵便の連鎖にもう1つのつながりを加えるのです。お1人地元の方に説明していただきましょう。すみません，あなたは郵便の配達に関わっていますか？

地元の男性：ええ，関わっています。普通の郵便よりも速いことだってありますよ。この方法全体は，イギリスの捕鯨船員が母国の友人や家族に連絡をする方法として，1700年代の終わり頃に始まりました。ガラパゴス諸島から航海を続ける船員たちが，自分の手紙を入れ，そして，イギリスに帰る別の船員たちがそれを集荷して配達していたんです。

EBC: ご覧のように，当地の「郵便局」は，見た目にはロビンソン・クルーソー本人が組み立てたと言ってもよいくらいですね。ステッカーや落書き，ハリウッドのポスターが，流木と自然の素材で作られた郵便ポストを飾っています。こちらに16人グループの方々がいらっしゃいます。どの方も他の皆さんの出身地をご存知で，郵便物のいろいろな宛先と個々の旅行者がうまく合うように願いながら，都市の名前を読み上げています。さて，あなたはどちらからいらしたのですか？

エコツーリストの女性：アメリカです。でも，私に手渡されたハガキの中には持って帰れないものもあります。どなたかが私のところに，ロサンゼルスに配達されるはずの郵便物を持ってきたんです。ニューヨークの家に帰る途中でロサンゼルスに立ち寄って配達できるといいのですが，今回はできないんです。でもフロリダ宛のハガキは持って帰りますよ。来月フロリダに行く予定がありますから。

EBC: あなたはいかがですか？

エコツーリストの男性：日本の各地が宛先になっているハガキを何枚か持って帰るつもりです。けれど，持って帰れないものもあります。変わった色の封筒のものがあるんですが，これはスペインへ持って行く必要があります！でもそこまではとても面倒見切れません。わかる住所が書いてあるのを見つけるとほんとうにわくわくしますよ。でもその次に，本当に配達しなくちゃいけないということを自覚します。切手を買って投函するのはズルだと思われると，地元の人たちに注意されました。ですが，会ったこともない人への「思いがけないもの」を持って，見知らぬ人の家に行くっていうのは，相手にはちょっと怖いこ

とかもしれません。そう思いませんか？ですから，東京に戻ったら，実際にどうやってこれらのハガキを最終的な宛先に届ければいいかという問題を，ちょっと真剣に考えなくてはいけませんね。

EBC：このように，この島では，協力し合うことで本当に世界をぐるりと1回りしてしまうようなことが見られるのです。以上，ガラパゴス諸島，フロレアーナ島から，EBCニュースのカルロス・ゴンザレスがお伝えしました。

Lesson6 ライティング問題・リスニング問題-4

Lesson6-1　問題解答

(1)

解答例1： Comics use pictures to tell stories while novels usually do not, but these media are much alike in that people can read them at their own pace, and can stop reading and start again whenever they want to. （38 words）

解答例2： Comics and novels greatly differ in the way they convey stories, but are similar because their readers can enjoy them at the pace they like, while people watching films normally cannot. （31 words）

(2)

解答例1： History shows us that it is a mistake for rulers to believe that they can easily prevent disagreeable ideas from spreading in an age when texts can quickly be produced by machines. （32 words）

解答例2： Those with power have always believed that they can suppress texts they find offensive, but they haven't been successful because information can be easily transferred due to electronic forms of media. （31 words）

Lesson6-2　問題解答

(1)

解答例1： I agree with such a school policy. Needless to say, schools want students to focus on their studies and most of their parents do so. After school, they spend their time devoting themselves to club activities and reviewing or preparing a lot of subjects. It is true that working part-time jobs helps young people learn a variety of things about the society, but if it prevents students from studying hard at school, they should not have part-time jobs. （78 words）

解答例2： I disagree with this school policy. It is true that high school students should study hard. But having part-time jobs teaches them a lot of things, such as responsibility and cooperation, which they cannot acquire only at school. And it is important that they may face various problems to solve which they can never experience in their classrooms. These are other important lessons than what teachers never teach them. （69 words）

(2)

解答例1： I agree. One of the biggest problems the Olympic Games face is that they require too much money. A few years ago, Tokyo had to pump a lot of money into the invitation of the Olympic Games to Tokyo in 2016, At last, Tokyo failed to invite them. We should spend the same amount of money on developing alternative energy or helping the people in disaster areas. Another problem is that the Olympic Games are not the festival of sports. It is said that the Olympics have been commercialized, and recently, they were rocked by the big drug-abuse scandal. That's why they should be abolished or reduced. （107 words）

解答例2： I don't think the Olympic Games should be abolished for two reasons. First, the Olympics can bring the world closer. During them the people all over the world cheer not only athletes from their own countries but also athletes from other countries. This is a happy period. Second, I love the concept that in the Olympic Games, participation is more significant than winning. If this concept is kept and various peoples around the world are able to take part in them, the Olympics can contribute to world peace in the future. （91 words）

Lesson6-3　問題解答

1. D. In 2010 by Dutch scientists and in 2007 by a United Nations panel.
2. D. Unlike the earlier report, the most recent report considers the impact of change in rainfall patterns.
3. D. Whether the Himalayan glaciers could remain for hundreds of years in a warmer world.
4. C. For not dealing with river basins in central Asia and northwest China.
5. D. All of the above.

Lesson6-4　問題解答

1. C. The mail is delivered by travelers all over the world.
2. C. Sailors from England.
3. C. People working with driftwood and organic material.
4. B. Because she isn't stopping in Los Angeles.
5. A. Buying a stamp.

二本柳啓文
Hirofumi NIHONYANAGI

　河合塾講師。対面授業では，高3生および浪人生の講義を1週間に10校舎以上こなし，映像授業では高校1年生からセンター試験対策や早慶大入試対策まで数多くの講座を担当。高校の先生方からの信頼も厚い。また，保護者会のシーズンともなれば，いくつもの河合塾校舎をかけ持ちし，最近では保護者向けの英語の授業も行ない始めている。驚異のスタミナから繰り出される力強い言葉の速射砲と，説得力のあるフレーズの数々が聞く人を心底納得させる。カリスマ講師の活躍の場は，ますます拡がっている。

　　　主な著作：『英会話スクールへ行く，その前に　10時間授業で中学英語を卒業する』(語学春秋社)

《英文ナレーター》

　　Bianca Allen……アメリカ出身。ロンドン大学，オックスフォード大学卒業。女優として多数のドラマ・映画に出演。ボイスアーティストとしても大活躍の毎日で，ナレーター暦は20年以上。NHK基礎英語をはじめ，大企業のCMナレーション，教材出版会社のプロジェクトに多く参加。

　　Dominic Allen …アメリカ国籍。NHK新基礎英語，教育関連，多数の企業VP，文部省(現文部科学省)VP，機内ラジオ番組DJ。キャラクターボイスもこなす声優・ナレーター。日本育ちのバイリンガル。

教科書をよむ前によむ 実況中継シリーズ

「3日で読める!!」と評判の「実況中継」は，高校生の定番参考書です。

「読むだけで，スルスル頭に入ってくるから不思議です!!」「もっと早めに読むんだった!!」などなど，人気の「実況中継」シリーズは，1,000万部を超えるベストセラーです。

実況中継シリーズ

山口英文法（上）	1050円
同　　（下）	1050円
同　　問題演習	1050円
本英語長文（初級）（上）	1050円
同　（初級）（下）	1260円
同　（中級）（上）	1050円
同　（中級）（下）	1260円
同　（上級）（上）	1155円
同　（上級）（下）	1260円
横山ロジカル・リーディング	1260円
横山メタロジック会話英語	1260円
大矢英作文	998円
大矢英語読み方	1155円
西英文読解	1155円
石井看護医療技術系英語	1470円
NEW出口現代文①	1155円
同　　②	1155円
同　　③	1260円
出口小論文①	1365円
同　　②	1155円
NEW望月古典文法（上）	1260円
同　　　　　　（下）	1470円
飯塚漢文入門（上）	1050円
同　　　　　（下）	1260円
野竿数と式ほか	1155円
野竿確率ほか	1155円
朝田指数・対数ほか	1155円
朝田図形と方程式ほか	1155円
朝田数列／ベクトル	1155円
権田地理B（上）	1029円
同　　（下）	1050円
NEW石川日本史B①	1050円
同　　　　　②	1155円
同　　　　　③	1260円
同　　　　　④	1260円
同　　文化史⑤	1260円
石川日本史B　CD解説問題集①1029円
同　　　　　　　　　　　②1029円
同　　　　　　　　　　　③1029円
同　　　　　　　　　　　④1029円
同　　　　　　　　　　　⑤1155円
NEW青木世界史B①	1155円
同　　　　　②	1260円
同　　　　　③	1260円
同　　　　　④	1365円
同　　文化史⑤	1365円
青木世界史B　CD解説問題集①1029円
同　　　　　　　　　　　②1029円
同　　　　　　　　　　　③1029円
同　　　　　　　　　　　④1029円
NEW浜島物理Ⅰ・Ⅱ（上）	1050円
同　　　　　　　　（下）	1260円
NEW斉藤化学Ⅰ・Ⅱ①	1155円
同　　　　　②	1155円
同　　　　　③	1260円
同　　　　　④	1260円
NEW鞠子医歯薬獣生物①	1995円
同　　　　　　　　②	1995円
同　　　　　　　　③	1995円

センター実況中継シリーズ

中川センター英語	1260円
石井センターリスニング	1575円
出口センター現代文	1470円
望月センター古文	1470円
飯塚センター漢文	1260円
野竿センター数学Ⅰ・A	1365円
朝田センター数学Ⅱ・B	1365円
小川センター化学Ⅰ	1260円
宇城センター生物Ⅰ	1260円
安藤センター地学Ⅰ	1365円
樋口センター日本史B	1575円
植村センター世界史B	1575円
瀬川センター地理B①	1470円
同　　　　　　②	1470円
川本センター倫理	1260円
川本センター政治・経済	1470円
川本センター現代社会	1260円

2011年10月 現在

只今，全国書店で発売中です。

＊インターネットからでもご注文いただけます＊

語学春秋　　検索　　http://www.goshun.com

聞けば「わかる!」「おぼえる!」「力になる!」

スーパー指導でスピード学習!!
実況中継CD-ROMブックス

📗 山口俊治のトークで攻略 英文法
- **Vol.1** 動詞・文型〜名詞・代名詞・冠詞
- **Vol.2** 形容詞・副詞・疑問詞〜出題形式別実戦問題演習

練習問題(大学入試過去問)&CD-ROM(音声収録 各600分)

📗 出口汪のトークで攻略 現代文
- **Vol.1** 論理とはなにか〜記述式問題の解き方
- **Vol.2** 評論の構成〜総整理・総完成

練習問題(大学入試過去問)&CD-ROM(音声収録 各500分)

📗 望月光のトークで攻略 古典文法
- **Vol.1** 用言のポイント〜推量の助動詞
- **Vol.2** 格助詞・接続助詞〜識別

練習問題(基本問題+入試実戦問題)
&CD-ROM(音声収録 各600分)

📗 石川晶康のトークで攻略 日本史B
- **Vol.1** 古代〜近世日本史
- **Vol.2** 近現代日本史

空欄補充型サブノート &CD-ROM(音声収録 各800分)

📗 青木裕司のトークで攻略 世界史B
- **Vol.1** 古代〜近代世界史
- **Vol.2** 近現代世界史

空欄補充型サブノート &CD-ROM(音声収録 各720分)

📗 浜島清利のトークで攻略 物理 Ⅰ・Ⅱ

練習問題(入試実戦問題)&CD-ROM(音声収録600分)

●定価/各冊　**1,575円**(税込)

実況中継CD-ROMブックス

小川裕司のトークで攻略 センター化学I塾
練習問題（センター試験過去問）＆CD-ROM（音声収録300分）
● 定価／**1,260**円（税込）

宇城正和のトークで攻略 センター生物I塾
練習問題（センター試験過去問）＆CD-ROM（音声収録300分）
● 定価／**1,260**円（税込）

安藤雅彦のトークで攻略 センター地学I塾
練習問題（センター試験過去問）＆CD-ROM（音声収録300分）
● 定価／**1,575**円（税込）

近刊 瀬川聡のトークで攻略 センター地理B塾
Vol.①系統地理編　Vol.②地誌編

西きょうじのトークで攻略 東大への英語塾
練習問題（東大入試過去問）＆CD-ROM（音声収録550分）
● 定価／**1,890**円（税込）

竹岡広信のトークで攻略 京大への英語塾
練習問題（京大入試過去問）＆CD-ROM（音声収録600分）
● 定価／**1,890**円（税込）

二本柳啓文のトークで攻略 早大への英語塾
練習問題（早大入試過去問）＆CD-ROM（音声収録600分）
● 定価／**1,680**円（税込）

2011年10月現在

CD-ROMのご利用にはMP3データが再生できるパソコン環境が必要です。

実況中継CD-ROMブックスは順次刊行いたします。

http://goshun.com　　語学春秋　　検索

〒101-0061 東京都千代田区三崎町 2-9-10　TEL. 03-3263-2894

既刊各冊の音声を聞くことができます。

実況中継 CD-ROMブックス

私たちが応援します!!

"実況中継CD-ROMブックス"は，自宅での学習を手助けする"実況中継セミナー"として，CD版・WEB版の形で販売されてきたものを書籍化した教材です。"実況中継セミナー"を受講し，志望校に見事合格した先輩たちから寄せられたメッセージより，いくつかを拾って，ここにご紹介いたします。皆さんのこれからの学習にお役立てください。

❀ 慶応義塾大学理工学部・合格　　K・Nさん

僕は現役時代，理科が大の苦手でした。受験生ともなると，何から勉強すればよいのか見当もつかず，焦るばかりでした。ある日，友だちから『実況中継』を薦められ，書店で手に取ってみると「これなら自分にもできそうだ！」と直感しました。浪人生活を迎え，偶然予備校で『実況中継』や「実況中継セミナー」（"実況中継CD-ROMブックス"を指します。以下略）にも登場されている浜島先生の物理の授業を受けました。『実況中継』を読み終え，次は何を……？と思っていたとき，信頼している浜島先生の推薦もあり，「実況中継セミナー」に入会することを決めました。

集中して勉強するために1日1単元，2〜3時間ほどを「実況中継セミナー」に費やしました。僕の場合，基礎知識がほとんどなかったため，ゼロからのスタートでした。『実況中継』を読み，「実況中継セミナー」の問題を解きます。納得できない箇所は繰り返しCD講義を聴きます。

CD講義の良い点は，参考書と違って字面を目で追う面倒臭さがなく，耳からスッと入ってくるところです。部屋でくつろぎながらCD講義を聴いたことも少なくありません。

「実況中継セミナー」を始める前と後では，勉強の進め方に大きな違いが表れました。以前からの悪い癖で，難関大学対策用問題集を次々と買いあさっては，少し解くだけで別のに目移りしてしまうといった具合でしたが，「実況中継セミナー」で自分なりのペースをつかんでくると，多くのことに手をつけず，ひとつひとつ学習したものを忘れないよう努力することが大切だということに気づくようになりました。成績も徐々に上がり，40台だった偏差値が，夏の終わりには67にまでなっていて，信じられない思いでした。

❀ 筑波大学人間学群・現役合格　　K・Uさん（宮城県立第一女子）

私が大学受験に本格的に取り組み始めたのは，受験まであと1年という時期になってからでした。そんな時，学校中でみんなが愛用していた『実況中継』シリーズに挟まっていた広告で「実況中継セミナー」の存在を知り，特に成績の波が激しく，苦手だった古文の望月先生の講座を受講してみることにしました。

「実況中継セミナー」を選んだ決め手は，なんと言っても自分の都合のいい時間に講義が受けられる，という点でした。予備校などでは，こちらの都合や決められた時間に決められた分量ずつ進んでいってしまいますが，「実況中継セミナー」ならそんな心配はいりません。いつでもどんなときでもこちらの都合に合わせて取り組めるので，自分が一番集中できるときに利用して，効率よく学習を進められました。

私の活用法は，問題集をコピーしてから解いて，間違えたところや関連事項をそのコピーに赤ペンで書き込み，自分だけのオリジナルガイドを作って，復習などに役立てる，というものでした。

「実況中継セミナー」の教材は問題量がちょうどよく，1題1題きちんとポイントが設定されていて，「ここがわかっていなかった！」というところをするどく突いてきます。自分がどこを理解していてどこを理解していなかったのかがわかり，勉強を進めていく上で課題が明確になって，大変助かりました。始めてから3ヶ月ほどで成績に波がなくなり，それに伴って自信もついていきました。

集中力が落ちてきたときには，CDから聞こえてくる先生の熱意あふれる声に「がんばるぞ」と自分を奮い立たせました。そんな経験が何度もあります。

たとえ現在の自分の偏差値が志望校に届いていなくても、「合格するぞ」という気持ちで取り組めば必ず合格できるはずです。これから受験に立ち向かわれる皆さん、「実況中継セミナー」を信じて決して諦めることなくがんばってください!

❁ 東京大学理科一類・現役合格　　Y・Fさん

私は昔から**現代文**が苦手で、受験生になったのを機に、本格的に現代文の勉強に取り組み始めました。まずは**出口先生**の『実況中継』から始め、併用する形で「実況中継セミナー」に入会しました。活用法は、本をしっかり読み込んでから、「実況中継セミナー」の問題に取り組み、その後で肉声の講義を聞く。この繰り返しです。こうすることで、現代文の読み方をしっかり身につけられます。私の場合、入会後2ヶ月の模試でいきなり偏差値が50から70に跳ね上がりました。東大の入試を突破できたのは、本当に「実況中継セミナー」のおかげです。

❁ 立教大学文学部・現役合格
　　　　　　　　N・Kさん（神奈川県立大原）

大学受験を意識しはじめた高校2年の終わりのころ、何をすればいいかもわからずに、ただただあせるばかりだったので、とりあえず受験生ならだれもが知っている『実況中継』シリーズを読むことにしてみました。
いろいろな科目を読んだのですが、中でも**山口先生**の『**英文法**講義の実況中継』には、それまでの自分の英語の世界観が一変させられるほど感動しました。そして山口先生の肉声の講義も聴きたいと思い、迷わず「実況中継セミナー」の「英文法講座」を申し込みました。
CDから聞こえてくる山口先生の語り口は丁寧でやさしく、大変リラックスして講義を受けられました。もちろんテキストの内容も充実していて、志望大学にも十分対応しうるものでした。
私は、「予習してわからなかったところをノートにまとめ、その後CDを聴いて復習する」という学習スタイルを決め、それを1日に2回分ずつ、全部で20回の講座を10日で終わらせるというサイクルで3回繰り返しました。一見つらいように思えますが、それよりも理解できたことの「充足感」が先に立ったので、全く苦痛に感じませんでした。
「充足感」を味わえることが嬉しくて、何度も何度もCDを聴き、それに伴って偏差値も上昇していきました。
志望校に合格し大学生になった今、早い時期から「実況中継セミナー」を信じて頑張ってきて本当に良かったと思っています。

❁ 慶応義塾大学文学部・現役合格　　M・Sさん

学校の授業は遅い……あの膨大な知識と範囲を覚えなければいけない。受験科目で**世界史**をとった私は、限られた時間で効率良く覚えたい一心で音声教材を探していました。「実況中継セミナー」のすばらしい点は、十分な量の講義に加え、歴史の流れがすんなり理解できることです。苦手な人には教科書の橋渡しとなり、得意な人もおさらいすることで記憶の定着を助けてくれます。聞くだけでよいので、気分転換になり、通学時間などにも利用できました。高校3年の1学期の偏差値は48。「実況中継セミナー」を繰り返し聞き、問題も解くことで秋には72にまで上がり、それを維持して入試を迎えられました。**青木先生**のわかりやすく、無駄のない講義は必聴です。ぜひ体感してみてください。

❁ 同志社大学法学部・現役合格
　　　　　　　　N・Yさん（兵庫県立北須磨）

石川先生の『**日本史B**講義の実況中継』はとてもおもしろく、CD講義はもっとおもしろいのではないか? というのが「実況中継セミナー」入会のきっかけでした。質・量ともに予備校の授業には劣らないのに、受講料が安い。『実況中継』には書かれていないことも講義されていて、「実況中継セミナー」を聞くと歴史の流れがスムーズに理解できます。学校の授業だけでは足りないことを「実況中継セミナー」で補いました。10月までには全範囲を終え、その後は苦手な分野に力を入れました。志望大学に合格できる程の力がついたことは言うまでもありません。

❁ 大阪大学経済学部・現役合格
　　　　　　　　K・Aさん（岡山県立岡山朝日）

現代文の解き方がわからず、適当に解いているような状態で、良いときは良い、悪いときは悪いと点数にばらつきがあり困っていました。姉からの薦めで『実況中継』を読み始め、全てを読み終えた後、**出口先生**の講義が聴けるんだという魅力に惹かれ、入会を決めました。現代文は論理的に文章

を読めば必ず正解にたどり着くことができるということを学び、どんな問題でも精一杯取り組みました。解答を重視するのではなく、解答を導くまでの過程を重視できるようになりました。思うとおり解けなくて嫌気がさしても、CDから流れてくる出口先生の声を聴くと、先生が自分を応援してくれているかのような気がして、また頑張ろう!と思えました。そして、センター試験ではこれまでにない高得点を獲得できました。現代文の読み方をマスターしておけば、受験だけでなくこれから先もずっと役に立ちます。後輩のみなさんにも「実況中継セミナー」や『実況中継』の存在を教えてあげたいです。絶対オススメです!

津田塾大学学芸学部・現役合格
K・Tさん（千葉県立佐倉）

山口先生の『実況中継』に出会い、それまで得意だとばかり思っていた英文法がしっかり理解できていなかったことを実感しました。文法は英語すべての基礎なので、もっと勉強したいと考え、「実況中継セミナー」に入会しました。実際取り組んでみると、わかりやすい解説を何度でも聴けて、予備校よりオトクだと思いました。全20回を3回聞きましたが、その結果偏差値は70近くに達し、予想以上の成果に大満足です。これは確実な基礎力がついたからだと思います。

横浜国立大学教育人間科学部・現役合格
K・Tさん（神奈川県立緑ヶ丘）

「実況中継セミナー」は値段が高そう…、でも塾に行くことを考えると安い。というわけで入会を決めました。石川先生の講座を受講し、最低でも1日に1枚は聴くこと。とにかく覚えなければいけないことが多く、大変でした。ところが「実況中継セミナー」で講義してくれるように歴史を流れで理解していれば、正誤問題でもセンター試験でも、どんな形式の問題にも惑わされなくなるということがわかってきました。何と言ってもCD教材であることが一番のお気に入りです。先生が言ったことを自分で口ずさむとより効果的に覚えられます。iPodに落として通学途中はもちろん暇さえあれば聴いていました。覚えることが多かったのですぐに結果が出たわけではありませんが、繰り返し聴いて一度学んだことを忘れないようにしたので確実に成績が伸びました。写真や史料が豊富な『実況中継』と併用することでさらに実力UPしました。もう怖いものナシ!というくらい実力がつきますよ。

早稲田大学教育学部・合格
S・Nさん（千葉市立千葉）

私は浪人が決まってからも、趣味のバンド活動を続けたかったので、予備校のように決められた時間を拘束されるのは、避けたいと思っていました。そこで、現役の頃から愛用していた『実況中継』シリーズが、大変分かりやすく楽しく学習できたので、「実況中継セミナー」なら、自宅浪人でも十分学習できると思い入会しました。

実際に入会してみると、「実況中継セミナー」はとても素晴らしい教材でした。その利用法ですが、まずは何と言っても、『実況中継』の本をじっくり読みこんで知識の基礎固めからはじめます。その後でいよいよ解説のCDの講義を聴きます。すると、先生の肉声は、まるで自分に語りかけてくるようにすんなりと耳に入り、記憶に残っていきました。とくに最も活用した『近現代世界史』に関しては、ほとんど毎晩欠かさずに寝る時に聞いていたので、先生の声がそのまま記憶に残ってしまうほどでした。また、この方法を繰り返し、「実況中継セミナー」だけを集中して学習していくことで、解き方に一貫性がもてるようになり、さまざまな形式の問題にも迷いなく対応できる応用力もついていきました。

首都大学東京都市教養学部・現役合格
M・Fさん（群馬県立前橋女子）

私は高校2年になった頃から、現代文の成績が伸びずに悩んでいました。特に記述問題が大の苦手で、模試でも成績はイマイチ、場合によっては何を書いていいのかわからないときもありました。3年になり、友人の勧めで『実況中継』を購入し、その中のチラシで「実況中継セミナー」を知りました。さっそく案内書を取り寄せて、「これなら本で得た知識を発展させることができる」と思い、入会しました。入会してみると、自分の都合のいい時間に、外に出向くことなく勉強が進められるので、「なんて便利なんだろう」と思いました。先生の肉声を耳で聴いて学習していくので、なかなか緊張感があり、記憶にも残りやすく、まるでマンツーマンで講義を受けているようでした。

出口先生は問題文を解説するだけでなく、現代文を解く上で必要とされる知識・概念も解説してくだ

さったので，よりいっそう論理的・客観的に文章が読めるようになりました。現代文にも数学のような明確な答えがあることがわかり，いままで漠然としていた解き方が形になって，すらすら解答できるようになったのです。調子がいいときには，問題文を読んだだけで答えが見えてくるようなこともあったほどです。

こうして「実況中継セミナー」の問題演習を繰り返すごとに苦手意識も徐々に解消され，良くても50台後半だった偏差値はぐんぐん上昇していき，難関大学を狙うのにも自信が持てるようになりました。

これは，一緒に「実況中継セミナー」を始めた友人の言葉ですが，「受験では常に上を目指す気持ちが大切」です。上には上があることを忘れずに限界まで挑戦する覚悟で取り組んでみてください。きっと最初に思っていたレベルよりずっと上にいけるはずです。

❀ 青山学院大学文学部・現役合格　　S・Kさん

「実況中継セミナー」を知ったのは友人からの紹介でした。時すでに遅く，3年の夏休みを過ぎていました。当時，持病が悪化し，一応，予備校に通っていましたが，ついに通えなくなってしまいました。ちょうど，自宅で学習できる教材がないか……と探していたので，「実況中継セミナー」に入会することを決めました。私大の文学部を志望していたため，必修教科は3教科です。

スタートが遅かった私は，10月頃，「実況中継セミナー」が届くとともに開始し，体調に合わせて学習しました。まず，不得意分野の克服と，得意教科のさらなる成績UPを目標に「実況中継セミナー」に取り組んでみました。受講科目は「**世界史**」と「**古典文法**」です。世界史は得意教科でしたが，中国史は苦手。**青木先生**は，重要事項をわかりやすく簡潔にまとめていて，専用テキストでも十分なほどでしたが，先生の落ち着いた声での説明はとても記憶に残りました。苦手な中国史もきちんと克服できたと思います。古典文法の**望月先生**も，基礎から丁寧に講義してくださって，苦手意識をなくすことができました。先生の穏やかな口調でリラックスしながら勉強できましたし，わからないところは何度でも聞きなおせるのが「実況中継セミナー」の最大の魅力でした。「もうダメかも……」と思っても先生方の声を聞くと，不思議とやる気が湧いてくるのです。

朝の支度のとき，CDをかけていると，集中していないのに，無意識のうちに覚えていて，模試のとき役立ちました。センター前には世界史の偏差値が55→64に，国語は63→70になりました。無事に第一志望合格です。

❀ 日本大学芸術学部・現役合格　　S・Jさん

「実況中継セミナー」に入会したのは夏休み前です。塾に通うことを考えると，それよりもはるかに安いという理由から入会を決めました。

私は当時，進路を迷っていて，**日本史**で受験するかどうか決めかねたまま，とうとう12月までできてしまいました。結局，日本史で受験しようと決めた私は，12月から**石川先生**の「実況中継セミナー」と『実況中継』を使って猛勉強を始めました。今までは，何かと理由をつけては勉強に集中できなかった自分ですが，好きなときに石川先生の講義が聞けると思うと気楽で，落ち着いて勉強ができました。電車の中でもiPodで聞いていたので，自宅では他の教科に時間を割くことができました。試験までの貴重な時間を有意義に過ごせたと思っています。

「実況中継セミナー」のおかげで試験までになんとか日本史を終わらせることができました。当日，試験会場に行く途中も「実況中継セミナー」を聞いていたのですが，ラッキーなことに，その箇所がそのまま試験に出たんです。

試験直前になると緊張が強くなりますが，「実況中継セミナー」なら先生の声が聞こえるので安心します。どたんばで日本史受験を決めた私でも合格できたのは，学習効率のよい「実況中継セミナー」のおかげです。時間を上手に使えたのが勝因だと思っています。

❀ 慶応義塾大学法学部・現役合格
S・Yさん（神奈川県立川和）

「実況中継セミナー」には受験のプロの英知がぎっしりつまっていて，予備校に行っていない僕にはとてもありがたい存在でした。僕はCDを何度も聴き直すと同時に，「実況中継セミナー」のテキストに他の問題集や参考書から語句などを書き足し，自分だけの「実況中継セミナー参考書」を作りました。この過程で早慶を含めどの私大にも対応できる力がついていったと思います。受験前の不安な時にもCDで先生の声を聞くととても自信がわくという，副次的な効果もありました。

英熟語イディオマスター

山口俊治 著

新書判（3色刷）　定価／**1,050円**（税込）

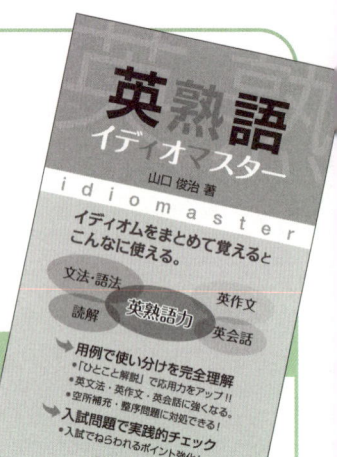

ベストセラー『NEW 山口英文法講義の実況中継』の山口俊治先生が贈る、「最小の努力で最大の成果」を生む、熟語集イディオマスター!!

■ 必要十分な量を最長 10 週間でマスター。
本書では標準的な「10 週プラン」を提案していますが、重要語句だけに絞って「4 週」でこなすなど、あなたの学習プランをつくることができます。

■ どのレベルからでも開始できる、5 段階構成。
英熟語を重要度に応じて 5 つのステージに分類してあります。どのステージからでも学習が可能です。

■ 英作文、穴埋め、読解問題から英会話表現まで応用範囲の広い熟語を、セットで覚える 800 項目。
まとめて覚えられるように、大学入試に必要なすべての熟語を 800 項目にまとめました。

■ 例文はすべて入試出題例から。合否を決定づけるレベルには実戦問題を掲載。
もちろんすべての熟語に、入試英文に出た例文付き。さらに最重要ステージの「合否を左右する熟語」については、実戦例題も併記してあります。

＊ インターネットからでもご注文いただけます ＊

http://goshun.com　　語学春秋　　検索